Kings, Nobles and Commoners

Kings, Nobles and Commoners

States and societies in early modern Europe,
a revisionist history

JEREMY BLACK

I.B. TAURIS

LONDON · NEW YORK

Published in 2004 by I.B.Tauris & Co. Ltd
6 Salem Road, London W2 4BU
175 Fifth Avenue, New York NY 10010
Website: http://www.ibtauris.com

In the United States of America and in Canada distributed by Palgrave
Macmillan, a division of St Martin's Press, 175 Fifth Avenue, New York
NY 10010

ISBN 1 86064 985 8 hbk ISBN 1 86064 986 6 pbk

A full CIP record for this book is available from the British Library
A full CIP record for this book is available from the Library of Congress
Library of Congress catalog card: available

Set in Monotype Dante by Ewan Smith, London
Printed and bound in Great Britain by MPG Books, Bodmin

Contents

Preface

Sometimes it is best to pause and to sacrifice continuity for further reflection. The synopsis for this book was written in the late 1980s at a time when the criticism of conventional views of absolutism was cutting edge.[1] Indeed, in 1992 Nicholas Henshall published a rejection of the entire concept with his *The Myth of Absolutism: Change and Continuity in Early Modern European Monarchy* (Harlow).[2] Absolutism was dismissed as an anachronistic historical construct, imposed on the sixteenth, seventeenth and eighteenth centuries by later generations seeking false patterns in the past.

An awareness of the pendulum of historical research suggested that this approach would, in time, be countered and, indeed, a decade later, John Hurt published *Louis XIV and the Parlements. The Assertion of Royal Authority* (Manchester, 2002), a work that deliberately and explicitly contested the revisionist interpretation and, instead, sought to demonstrate a harsh reality of expropriation and lack of consultation at the core of absolute government.

This riposte served the purpose of encouraging another look at the whole question. The conceptual points that encouraged early revisionism can now be clarified by a mass of important new research that can help both in addressing the entire period and in considering those elements that were genuinely different about later-seventeenth and eighteenth-century European monarchy. In particular, studies of court culture have mushroomed, while there has been a welcome 'thickening' of the geographical network of our detailed knowledge of the period. It is also easier now to try to bring the overseas activities of the European states of the period into the analysis. This is far less true, however, of the necessary comparative dimension with non-European powers, much of which still requires probing. This serves as a reminder of the tentative nature of many of the evaluations offered in this book.

After an introduction that identifies and questions key elements of the orthodox interpretation of this period of European history and offers a brief survey of the major European polities, Chapter 2 concentrates on the internal structure of European states from the sixteenth to eighteenth centuries, emphasising long-term structural continuities and the primarily consensual nature of ruler–élite relations. The international dimension is covered in Chapter 3, which offers a critique of those interpretations of European relations that stress the historical necessity of the centralised nation state. Chapter 4 explores the wider social, economic and intellectual context, providing a balance to the issues of high politics covered by the preceding two chapters. Chapters 5 and 6 consider these developments over time, questioning the extent to which chronological patterns can be detected. Chapter 7 locates (Christian) European development in its global context through comparisons with other states. Greater attention is paid here to the unique elements of European development, notably the growth of maritime power and the ability to profit from the gradual globalisation of human development, which accelerated from the sixteenth century. The global perspective is retained in the conclusion as a means of drawing the threads together and speculating how future research might revise the 'revisionism'. The book ends by making a case for the contemporary relevance of the early modern European experience.

The book's central argument is a rejection of schematic models for European political development, particularly those stressing either conscious 'state-building', or change driven by a Darwinian selection through warfare of the 'fittest' form of government. Instead, change is described as incremental, and determined largely by circumstance and contingency. In particular, states emerged through a process of constantly renegotiated compromises between rulers and ruled. Political systems founded on consent have proved more flexible and durable than centralised, authoritarian ones.

It is a great pleasure to mark nearly a quarter-century of teaching early modern European history by writing this study. The difficulties of summarising views for generations of students is in part a testimony to the stimulus offered by the latter. I have benefited from the comments of Nigel Aston, Jan Glete and David Sturdy on an earlier draft and of Rafe Blaufarb, Marc Forster, Greg Hanlon, Nicholas Henshall, Munro Price and Chris Storrs on sections of the book. It is a particular pleasure in dedicating this book to note a friendship that has lasted for over thirty-five years. Harry Hyman is a shrewd observer and a good friend.

Notes

1. For a summary of my views at the time, 'Absolutism', in J. W. Yolton et al. (eds), *The Blackwell Companion to the Enlightenment* (Oxford, 1991), pp. 11–12, and *A Military Revolution? Military Change and European Society 1550–1800* (Basingstoke, 1991).

2. For the debate this gave rise to, R. G. Asch and H. Duchhardt (eds), *Der Absolutismus – ein Mythos? Strukturwandel monarchischer Herrschaft in West- und Mitteleuropa, ca. 1550–1700* (Cologne, 1996).

Abbreviations

BL.   London, British Library, Additional Manuscripts.
Unless otherwise stated, all books are published in London.

For Harry Hyman

CHAPTER I

Introduction

§ MUCH of the work on the period, especially that available to those who read only English, is based on a number of questionable assumptions that, together, constitute what could fairly be described as the established interpretation of the period. Crucial to this are the following notions:

- Protestantism was 'better' than Catholicism, not least because it was more likely to produce an expanding and well-organised society, especially because of its supposed favour towards economic enterprise. Thus the new religion was, apparently, as much a solvent of economic arrangements, and therefore traditional social assumptions and practices, as it was of the old religious order. This was particularly important for commentators who stressed socio-economic causes for structures and developments. The rise of science and technology is also particularly attributed to two Protestant societies, the Dutch Republic and Britain.
- Linked to this is the notion that, because of Catholic conservatism, Austria and Spain were somehow 'reactionary' states and societies, the two being closely linked. Conversely, the future is held to have lain with progressive, bourgeois societies, a process exemplified in the success of the Dutch Revolt in the sixteenth century, the decline of Spain in the following century, and the Austrian failure to regain control of the Holy Roman Empire in the Thirty Years' War (1618–48). The rise of French power in the seventeenth century is a development that does not fit easily into this pattern, although France is seen as a rationally governed and successful state, in contrast to Austria and Spain. France is succeeded in the eighteenth century by Britain, which appears to exemplify the process. Catholic conservatism is also implicitly seen as responsible for the relative decline of the Mediterranean, with the centre of gravity of European progress moving to the Atlantic periphery.
- That the early modern period saw both the development of the state, understood in modern terms as a rational entity governed by bureaucratic means and ethos, and that the polities of the period were nascent *nation* states.
- Different national histories have been overlaid by the East–West dichotomy in European history, a long-established approach that was entrenched

during the Cold War. This is generally characterised by a series of binary comparisons in favour of the West, for example Western 'free' peasants against Eastern serfs.

• Eurocentrism, if not triumphalism, characterises the discussion of Europe's impact on the rest of the world.

Stated baldly, these ideas are clearly weak, but they underlie a tremendous amount of work both in domestic history and in international relations. In the latter, Spain is generally presented as bound to fail and a north-western European perspective is adopted. The agenda is set out clearly in the titles of the relevant volumes of the *New Cambridge Modern History*, an apparently authoritative compendium of established interpretations. Volume 4, *The Decline of Spain*, is followed by Volume 5, *The Ascendancy of France*, and Volume 6, *The Rise of Great Britain and Russia*. Inconvenient facts, such as the mid-seventeenth-century resilience of Spain, or apparently superfluous areas, such as Italy and Portugal, are omitted or sidelined.[1]

Furthermore, the rise of the state is a major topic in the modern domestic history of the period. It embodies an attempt to date the onset and early development of the modern age to the 'early modern' period (*c.* 1450/1500–*c.* 1750), with a stress on sophistication (new government agencies) and on state power (military revolution; the extension of government power into the localities). In short, the picture is of the state working on society, in order to modernise it; and the concept of the state is very much a nineteenth-century one.

In contrast, a revisionist approach emphasises the extent to which the state is not outside society. The more subtle view of the early modern state draws on a greater interest in social and, more recently, cultural history, plus a better understanding of the earlier 'medieval' situation. While they do not completely dispense with the dichotomy of 'state' and 'society', the weakness of the early modern state, as a dedicated governmental agency, is emphasised by revisionist scholars. Contributing to this approach, historians from a variety of specialisations, not least, recently and fruitfully, the royal courts, have stressed the personal bond between monarchs and traditional élites, rather than royal reliance on bureaucrats; and have also emphasised negotiation, rather than coercion, as the favoured tactic by which rulers sought to win and retain the support of the élites.

Scholars have also queried state formation as the agenda that 'early modernists' should address. In addition, thinking on the composite state (a state composed of a number of separate territories with distinctive senses of identity) has huge implications, not least since, despite the attentions of 'absolutist' monarchs and their ministers, it survived until the twentieth century. Rulers had to tread carefully in devising strategies that enabled them to meet the challenge of ruling such states without risking the confrontation provoked by attacks on 'provincial' (that is, territorial) liberties. In particular, it is argued that all 'states' were dependent on the support of the socially influential, or élite, whose co-operation was sought actively. Consensus and co-operation were crucial, both as goals of politics and as means of government.

This consensus and co-operation are approached not in the crude Marxist sense of shared exploitation (best presented by Perry Anderson,[2] and with an interesting, and better-grounded, subsequent variation offered by William Beik)[3], but via an approach that considers ideological factors. If the weakness of government, as an external force on local society, is appreciated, then the value of what it could offer in a shared exploitation of the lower orders can be seen to be minimal. Instead, the cohesive forces in society have to be considered. The essentially contractual nature of government inherited from the Middle Ages prevailed, whatever its constitutional or political form; and the conviction that rulers were answerable to God did not absolve them from the need to govern legally and to avoid arbitrary rule.

Nevertheless, the Protestant Reformation of the early sixteenth century enabled some rulers to gain greater control over the Church, while there was, also, a process of reformulation of government by intellectuals in the early modern period. In part, this was a necessary response to the Reformation, not least to the subsequent spread of Protestant and Catholic resistance theories and practice;[4] but it is important to note continuities with the Middle Ages, not least the vitality of corporate institutions, particularly the Estates (representative bodies), and their ability to co-operate with rulers.[5]

Outside the important sphere of Church government, there is little sign that the process of reformulation caused the establishment of a new governmental agenda or a novel political practice, with the important exception of Petrine (Peter the Great's) policy in Russia. The attempt during his reign (1689–1725) to break with the past and with privilege conflicted with general European patterns, although it exemplified certain tendencies in other militaristic states, especially Sweden and Prussia.[6]

To adopt the revisionist approach, it is necessary to reconsider the strength of *ancien régime* society and government. Particular attention has to be devoted to changes that are commonly held to have led to an increase in state power: military revolution; the extension of governmental power into the localities; increased governmental sophistication; mercantilism and economic regulation in general; control over the Church.

Having queried classic views of absolutism, we can also reinterpret the eighteenth century. The importance of Eastern European developments is apparent, as the major states there (Austria, Prussia, Russia) were those whose power increased most significantly. They lacked a 'national' focus / identity comparable to that of France, and Austria was very much a composite state, but these powers were, nevertheless, successful. In addition, the argument that the internal contradictions of the old order made revolution inevitable has to be scrutinised critically, and the flexibility of the late-eighteenth-century *ancien régime* discussed in order to indicate its strength and vitality. The absence of a general crisis within the states of Europe at the end of the eighteenth century comparable in extent to that of the 1640s and 1650s[7] serves to underline these points, as does the widespread resistance to the French Revolution.

Such a bold prospectus neglects the problems presented by the sources. These include the geographical concentration in printed material and secondary work on Western Europe. For example, the nature of local political culture, practice and authority across most of Russia is obscure, while there is still need to ground debate on the character and impact of Polish and Prussian developments on work yet to be done on the situation in the localities. In Austria, the reign of Charles VI (1711–40) is still obscure.

The problems of ranging widely encourages too often a focus on a familiar group of examples that, in turn, apparently define the subject. This misleading process of selection discourages the integration of other areas and examples, both those that have received attention and others. There are also serious methodological problems, not least the difficulties of re-creating the character, nuances and impact of political culture. Furthermore, there is a need to move away from the dominance in general accounts of sources that stress governmental pretensions and purposeful governmental activities. Instead, there is a need to devote more attention to the response to government initiatives.

There are also issues of conceptualisation and appropriate language. This can be seen clearly with the term absolutism (or *absolutismus* or *absolutisme*) which was not used until after the French Revolution. '*Monarchie absolue*' was employed, but as an apparent goal, not as a description of circumstances. A modern definition of absolutism has to combine two elements. First, it is used to describe a form of government in which sovereignty was vested in one person (the opposite being 'mixed' or 'shared' sovereignty). Sovereignty brought responsibilities and obligations (typically, to defend the Church and to defend the rights of subjects). Thus absolutism was different from despotism, in which the ruler had no responsibilities or obligations to subjects.

Second, however, absolutism was a historical phenomenon, with disputes arising over the nature and extent of the rights of subjects, and at what point a ruler's actions ceased to be absolutist and became despotic. There were few objective measures by which the boundaries between a ruler's legitimate actions over the defence of 'rights' and his or her invasion of those rights could be identified, and this led to disputes over taxation and other matters. Thus the powers attaching to sovereignty were not universally agreed and easily led to conflict.

Absolutism should not be employed to imply a royal monopoly of power underpinned by a military and bureaucratic apparatus and unrestricted by institutional or ideological limits. If, instead, the term is to be employed to define rulers who respected traditional liberties and conventions, then the authoritarian connotations must be discarded. A system of rule within legal limits involved circumscribing the monarch's prerogatives, the right of the monarch and his ministers to act alone in certain policy areas. For example, these limits did not usually require consultation with Estates on issues of foreign policy (which was very much royal), but might demand it if alteration of subjects' property rights was on the agenda. A re-conceptualisation of absolutism has to embrace practical limits, such as royal reliance on landed élites for implementation of policy; rather than on the standing armies and bureaucrats that have attracted attention.

On the other hand, there were also times, especially during prolonged war, when the term 'absolutism' in its original nineteenth-century sense, seems appropriate; namely for what contemporaries saw as despotic or arbitrary monarchy. The policies of Olivares, Richelieu and Strafford were seen in this light by contemporaries; as were some theoretical justifications for greater state power. But these initiatives were frequently counter-productive, and, for most rulers and ministers, in theory and in practice, absolutism, in its despotic sense, was not a goal.

For this book, absolutism, however anachronistic the term, is employed in order to describe the governmental system of the century from 1650 to 1750 in those states where royal authority was considerable, but was nevertheless based on a sense of respect for other rights that contributed to an image of government as far from tyrannical:[8] Western commentators maintained that the rulers of Russia and the Ottoman Empire were different kinds of rulers;[9] and there was an established vocabulary to employ to describe them: tyranny being the usual term until the close of the seventeenth century, and despotism thereafter.[10]

The potent impression of Russian tyranny rested, in part, on an informed assessment of Russian developments. Visitors did their best to amass information, and envoys and merchants argued that monarchical power was much stronger in Russia than in their homelands. Foreigners resident in Russia had a similar view and marked out a real diference between the basic patterns of Russian and non-Russian European government. Preconceptions played a role in shaping the Western experience of Russia.[11] The most important was tyranny, but several commentators noted that Russian tyranny was at odds with the Aristotelian ideal type. Tyrannies were supposed to be short-lived momentary phenomena created by rogue princes, but Russian tyranny seemed structural. This was seen to stem from the nature of Russian society rather than the character of its rulers. There were, indeed, important differences with the situation further west. Russian rulers wielded considerable power, in part because of the nature of Russian political practice and thought, specifically the absence of other institutions (bar the Church) with independent authority.

However, there were important checks, mostly informal it is true, which limited the freedom of action of Russian and Ottoman rulers.[12]

The definition of absolutism offered above is capable of further refinement, or, looked at differently, could, like most analytical concepts, be debated out of existence. It is valid to recall the origins of the term absolutism in the propagandist purposes of nineteenth-century historiography as the history of the states and government powers of the age was scrutinised,[13] but the term has value if seen as a tool of modern discussion, rather than as a template of past government. For these and other reasons, what follows is suggestive in intention, but designed to encourage new work and fresh speculation.

Personal temperament also plays a role, and it is important to engage with this directly. Assessments of the prospect of rulers and ministers in the past achieving their goals will reflect this, as will those of the possibility of modern scholars achieving an overall assessment. It is amusing to note the confidence with which, on 28 July 1753, the *Protestor*, a London newspaper, expressed its view that 'when these fluctuating objects shall be ascertained, methodised and reposed in history, the reader, having none of the difficulties or diversions, which misled or confounded the spectator, will have the full and free use of his judgement, and will pronounce accordingly'.

It is difficult to share this confidence in pronouncing judgement, and dangerous to praise and condemn with hindsight. Instead, it is worth noting the scepticism of another London newspaper, *Read's Weekly Journal*, on 10 October 1730, about the likely success of 'state chymists' because policies faced

> the shortness and inconsistency of man's life and temper for the bringing any great project or design about, the emergency of undiscernible accidents that will be sure to interpose, the miscarriage of instruments that must be employed, [and] the competition and recounter of adverse parties ... Who can so play his game as to prevent all the blots that the dice of time and change may put the best gamester upon? ... upon which miscarriages the historian concludes that men do not so much counsel things, as things do counsel men.

Before reading further, it is worth looking at a map of Europe in this period. Whether the date depicted is 1550 or 1800 (a year, it is all too easy to forget, closer to us than the outset of the period and one in which state boundaries in Western Europe in part reflected the success of the Revolutionary French), it is possible to note sufficient differences from a modern map to understand the need for caution in responding to names for countries or states. As far as European possessions were concerned, Portugal has remained largely unchanged (an area east of the Guadiana river was gained by Spain in 1801), and the same is true of Spain, although, as an acknowledgement of French military successes, Roussillon was ceded to France in 1659.

However, Spain is also used as a short term for the territories of the King of Spain. War and the division of the inheritance of Charles I of Spain (the Emperor Charles V) ensured that, by 1560, these dominions included half of Italy (Sicily, Sardinia, the Milanese, and the Tuscan coastal *presidios* – garrisons), as well as the Burgundian inheritance as enlarged by Charles: Franche-Comté (the region round Besançon) and the Low Countries (essentially modern Belgium, Netherlands and Luxembourg, but also including parts of modern France, especially Artois, while excluding the prince-bishopric of Liège). The last was one of the many prince-bishoprics that proved a major prize in dynastic diplomacy (as they could not be inherited), but also showed that the idea of rule by an ecclesiastic continued to seem a viable option to Catholics.

Spain's great rival in the late sixteenth and the seventeenth century, the kingdom of France, had not, by 1550, made the major advances to the Rhine and the Alps and in the Low Countries that were considerably to change its eastern frontier, although Henry II gained the prince-bishoprics of Metz, Toul and Verdun in 1552. The independent duchy of Savoy (a composite state with Piedmont and Nice) still reached to the Saône until 1601, Lorraine was an independent duchy, the English were, until 1558, in Calais (and in 1544–50 in Boulogne), and the Habsburgs in Artois, Franche-Comté and Alsace, until 1659, 1678 and 1648 respectively. It is all too easy to assume that expansion to France's subsequent frontiers was inevitable, not least because we tend to associate states with the modern shapes of countries, but this is misleading. In the case of France, its expansion was to take it into regions that had never hitherto been ruled as part of France. In particular, much of the expansion was into what had been part of the middle kingdom created in the ninth century from the Frankish inheritance. In the fifteenth century, much of this had been given international vitality as an expanding state by the Dukes of Burgundy. A large part of the Burgundian inheritance had been acquired first by Charles V and, subsequently, by his son Philip II of Spain. As a result, the struggle between Habsburg and Valois, Spain and France was, in part, a conflict between Burgundy and France that continued a long-established struggle.

In northern Europe, the collapse of the Union of Calmar, which had joined Denmark, Sweden, Norway, Finland and their ancillary territories, had left two competing states at the outset of our period. The King of Denmark also ruled Norway, Schleswig and Holstein, as well as parts of modern Sweden, particularly Gotland and Scania, while Finland was part of the kingdom of Sweden. Poland was a large composite state that included Ukraine, much of White Russia (Belarus), and Lithuania, as well as suzerainty over the duchy of Prussia (East Prussia), which was ruled by a branch of the house of Hohenzollern.

Russia provides another instance of a state whose modern name carries misleading geographical connotations. Based on Muscovy, in 1550 Russia, under Ivan IV (the Terrible, r. 1533–84), had not yet conquered the Tatar

Khanates of Kazan and Astrakhan (they fell in 1552 and 1556), and its frontier was nowhere near the Black Sea to the south nor across the Urals to the east. Since at least the Mongol attacks in the early thirteenth century, after which Muscovy became a tribute-paying vassal of the Khanate of the Golden Horde, there were important elements similar to those of other Asian monarchies of the steppe zone,[14] but Christianity represented an important difference. The fall of Constantinople to the Ottomans in 1453 ensured that Russia had become the major independent centre of Orthodox Christendom, and this was developed to give the ruler a more pronounced sacral quality that very much differentiated him from the greater aristocrats.

Germany, Italy and south-eastern Europe in 1550 were also very different to the situation today. The Balkans were ruled by the Ottoman (Turkish) Empire, an Islamic monarchy based, from 1453, at Constantinople (modern Istanbul) that also ruled Egypt (from 1517), much of South-West Asia, and the northern shores of the Black Sea, where the Khanate of the Crimea was a dependent state. The Ottoman conquest of much of Hungary after Suleiman the Magnificent's victory at Mohacs in 1526 had brought them into direct contact with Habsburg power, dramatically so when the Ottomans unsuccessfully besieged Vienna in 1529.

In addition, the Habsburgs benefited from Mohacs: the kingdoms of Bohemia and Hungary had been united under the same crown from 1490 and the Habsburgs were able to acquire what the Ottomans did not conquer. As a result, the Habsburg position in most of what is now Austria and Slovenia was enhanced by the acquisition not only of what became Habsburg Hungary (much of modern Slovakia, and parts of modern Croatia and Hungary) but also of Bohemia and Moravia (the modern Czech Republic), as well as Silesia (south-west modern Poland) and Lusatia (to the south east of Berlin).

Since 1438, the Austrian Habsburg ruler had been elected Holy Roman Emperor, which provided him with a measure of authority, although less power, in the Empire, an area roughly coterminous with modern Germany, Austria, the Netherlands, Belgium, Switzerland, the Czech Republic and much of northern Italy. In these areas, sovereignty was divided, and a large number of territorial princes, mostly lay but some ecclesiastical, as well as imperial free cities, exercised effective power, within the loose bounds of an imperial constitution. It was not only in the Empire that forms of political organisation other than monarchy remained important, especially those at the local and communal level. This both qualifies the traditional focus on the Europe of the monarchs, and also explains the later stress in this book on the interaction between localities and central government as crucial to political stability and development.

Most of Europe was ruled by hereditary monarchs, and its politics was therefore affected by what has been termed proprietary dynasticism.[15] The most important Christian dynasty, in their own eyes and those of most other commentators, was the Habsburgs. In 1550, the Valois ruled France, the Tudors England, the Vasas Sweden, the Stuarts Scotland, the Hohenzollerns Brandenburg, the Wettins Saxony, the Wittelsbachs Bavaria, and so on, down to small principalities in Germany and Italy. These principalities might not confer much power, but the families that ruled them, for example the Gonzaga of Mantua, followed dynastic goals of their own with the same ambition as their more prominent counterparts.

The Swiss Confederation, Venice and Genoa were the leading republics, while the Empire and the papacy were the most prominent of the elective monarchies, a group that included Bohemia, Hungary and, from the 1570s, Poland.[16] The attraction of the monarchical idea led the Medici to take the title of Grand Dukes of Tuscany, and ensured that the republican government in England became a Protectorate in the 1650s. Although neither Oliver Cromwell nor his son Richard took the title of king, a dynastic monarchy had been created.[17]

Monarchs helped provide unity and direction to policy, but royal and other courts and ministries were factious, and this challenges, even undermines, attempts to reify (make a coherent, active entity out of) the state and, even, to give policies consistency. Christer Bonde, a Swedish ambassador to England in the mid-1650s, who spoke good English and was friendly with Oliver Cromwell, reported, 'this régime is riddled with intrigues, and with such jealousies that I have some reason to doubt whether there may not be those who deliberately confuse sensible policies so that matters may go ill'.[18] Similar remarks could be made about other courts. They faced particular difficulties because the issue of the succession served as a question mark against the consistency of policies and the stability of ministries. Dynastic monarchy was also confronted by the problems of inadequate monarchs: infirmity was a major difficulty, but so also in some cases, such as Charles II of Spain (r. 1665–1700), were mental limitations, if not incapacity.

Other than in the cities, wealth and prestige across Europe were based on the ownership of land, most of which was owned by a hereditary nobility, whose most powerful members constituted an aristocracy. The legal status of the nobility and the extent to which there was a clearly differentiated aristocracy varied greatly by country.

The political role of the peasantry, the bulk of the population, was limited. It was most important in the Swiss Confederation (Switzerland), although there were examples of peasant autonomy elsewhere. Concerns about peasant independence rose after the Peasants' War of 1524–25 in the Empire. Dithmarschen, a small peasant republic within the Empire, was conquered in 1559. Peasant communities themselves reflected wider socio-political norms. Women were excluded from power and the communities were socially stratified. Dithmarschen had already become a patrician republic.[19]

Mention of Charles V, Holy Roman Emperor 1519–56, and ruler of Spain

1516–56,[20] serves as a reminder that, by beginning in 1550, we are starting at a moment of imperial apogee. The grandiloquent Latin inscription above the entrance to the royal mausoleum in the Escorial was to refer to him as 'the most exalted of all Caesars'. The Habsburg victory (under Charles in person) over John Frederick, Elector of Saxony, the leading German Protestant prince, at the battle of Mühlberg in 1547 had been followed by a series of reversals for the Protestant cause in the Empire, while a truce of 1547 had stabilised the frontier with the Ottomans in Hungary, bringing to a close a period of Ottoman conquest that had begun in 1521 and had helped shape the politics of the early Reformation period.

The Ottomans were the other great imperial power in Europe, but the attraction of such aspirations had also led other rulers to entertain imperial claims and to sponsor artistic and other comparisons with great emperors of the past. Henry VIII had claimed that England was a sovereign empire and also asserted his kingship over Ireland, as well as his claim to the throne of France; while in Russia the theme of the Third Rome was increasingly deployed.

The individual background to such claims varied, but they shared a sense that authority and power were hierarchical, with the hierarchy presided over by emperors, not kings. There was no sense of the equivalent rights of all states and rulers. The latter was to become an important concept, as new concepts of international law and diplomacy developed after the Peace of Westphalia in 1648, but it was one that had far less purchase earlier. Instead, in 1550, Christian Europe was dominated by the Habsburgs, in the person of Charles V and his brother Ferdinand, who had been elected king of Bohemia in 1526, and who was to inherit the dominions of the Austrian Habsburgs and to succeed Charles as emperor, thus ensuring that the Empire was linked, through the person of the emperor, to Bohemian and Hungarian crown lands and the anti-Ottoman cause. Had Charles's son, Philip II, who succeeded him as king of Spain, with his prominent possessions within the Empire in Lombardy and the Low Countries, become emperor then, even if only until his death in 1598, there would have been a different relationship between emperor and Empire. The family dynamics and dynastic politics of the Habsburgs ensured that this was not to be the case, but it serves as a reminder of the extent to which international alignments were dependent on dynastic issues. Furthermore, these alignments were to be important not only to the political culture of individual polities but also to the process of state development.

It is easy to point to the limited and precarious nature of Charles's position in 1550. The Augsburg Interim of 1548, a measure proposed to the Imperial Diet by Charles for a temporary settlement of religious differences in the Empire that would safeguard the Catholic position, was widely ignored. The previous year, the princes of the Empire, led by the Catholic dukes of Bavaria, had thrown out Charles's proposal for a league of all the states within the Empire, a measure that would have underlined the imperial position and provided support against foreign opponents. In 1552, Charles was successfully challenged by a new rebellion by Protestant princes supported by a French invasion, which left Henry II of France with the gain of the prince bishoprics of Metz, Toul and Verdun. This was to have a long-term impact in increasing French power in the region of Lorraine, and, more specifically, the vulnerability of its duke, while also giving the French crown a greater interest in Alsace. The ability of the French to intervene in the Empire was a challenge to the Habsburgs. The crisis of 1552 was eventually surmounted, but the tone set for Charles's last years, particularly, but not only, in the Empire, was that of compromise.

More generally, there was a contrast between the caution and respect for traditions and established political structures displayed by the Habsburgs as they rose, and the processes of expansion characteristic of the other great expanding Eurasian empires of the period: the Ottomans and the Mughals. Both the latter, in practice, co-operated with some existing interests, the Mughals, for example, with the Rajputs, and the Ottomans with native dynasties in Wallachia, Moldavia and Transylvania, but they were more able to push through change in their core areas of control, not least through the seizure of land.

In contrast, the rulers of Christian Europe compromised far more with existing interests and ruled by virtue of, and through, systems of privilege, rights and law that protected others as well as themselves. This contrast can be explained in a number of ways. Political culture was clearly important, but so also were the circumstances of power, and the legacy of war. Where authority in part rested on a process of conquest, then it was possible to sweep away the existing order, as with the Spaniards after they conquered Granada from the Moors in 1492, and in Ulster after the Irish Catholics had been defeated in the 1600s. Such cases need to be borne in mind when the revisionist argument for rule by consensus is considered, although the dominant political culture recognised rebellion and, to a lesser extent, conquest as exceptions to the rule that provincial liberties had to be respected. The newly established élite might benefit from such a system, as in Bohemia following the expropriation of the Protestants in the 1620s, when Catholic families were granted vast estates,[21] but this position rested on force and conquest.

This aspect of authority and power could be accentuated by external challenges, as with the threat, in the sixteenth and early seventeenth century, from the Ottoman Empire to the kingdom of Naples, which was ruled by the king of Spain after its conquest at the start of the sixteenth century. The pressure, in the same period, to contribute to Spanish commitments elsewhere was also significant. The impact of fiscal demands came to serve as a powerful destabilising force in the kingdom of Naples, undermining the achievements of the fifteenth-century monarchs: the imperatives of empire obliged the monarchs to extract substantial sums, with, as far as the locals were concerned, pernicious social, economic and political consequences.[22]

Mention of other Eurasian empires (or at least the empires of their monarchs) directs attention to an important aspect of the period 1550–1800, Christian Europe's changing position in the world. Here, it is possible to redress the customary stress on European expansion and, instead, to argue that it was more conditional than is generally appreciated. The major expansion of the period 1490–1550, in both the 'New World' and the Indian Ocean, was followed by two centuries of more modest expansion, particularly in Africa and South and East Asia. There were also major gains in North Asia (particularly Siberia) and North America, but these were both areas of low population density. Furthermore, in North America in the seventeenth century European settlers met strong resistance and some of their success stemmed from winning native allies.[23]

The limited success enjoyed by the Europeans in many parts of the world suggests that it is mistaken to imagine some necessary superiority in European war-making or state organisation. Instead, a more complex situation is indicated. This poses problems for the issue of governmental effectiveness, which is one of the major topics of the book. In particular, the more European military success is qualified, the less appropriate it becomes to stress the distinctiveness of European government, or, at least, factors likely to lead to its comparative advantage.

As with the discussion about relations between states and societies within Europe (see Chapter 2), so it becomes pertinent to link the two when considering Europe's external presence. However effective a given state might be in raising resources, that does not explain the degree to which its people are willing to accept deprivation and risk death for its ends, whether defence or expansion. This directs attention to the role of cultural and ideological factors in helping to explain success. Other cultural and ideological factors were important to domestic stability in Europe, and also played a role in affecting the ability of Europeans elsewhere to win local allies. For example, the syncretic quality of Christianity in what became Latin America helped in securing the establishment of Spanish and Portuguese power there.

European ideas were in part shaped by the experience of bitter and sustained conflict with non-Christians. The importance of Christianity as the prism through which non-Christians were viewed owed much to the significance and fervour of religious conflict. The ferocity of the fighting on Malta when the Ottomans invaded in 1565 indicated the intensity of religious conflict between Christians and Muslims. The few wounded captured Christian defendants of St Elmo fort were nailed to crosses and floated back across the harbour with their bowels hanging out to discourage the dispatch of additional reinforcements. The two wounded commanders were torn limb from limb as both, too seriously wounded to remain on their feet, directed the final defence from chairs. Six years later, the Venetian commander of Famagusta, the last position to hold out against the Ottomans on Cyprus, was flayed alive after he surrendered. This atrocity, which was also a breach of the surrender agreement, contributed to the rich diet of Christian literature about Muslim cruelty.

The Chinggisid Mongol Empire of the thirteenth century has been claimed as the starting point for *continuous* global history, since it led to the beginning of interlinking exchange circuits of technologies, ideas and even diseases. More generally, Eurasian nomads played a continuing and vital role in East Asian, Middle Eastern and European history, either directly or as catalysts for developments in these regions. Thanks, however, to European exploration of and beyond the Atlantic, and to the growing effectiveness of long-distance maritime links, by the start of our period the states with the most effective global range were Western European. This ensured that their societies were best informed about the world, a process that helped encourage further expansion and also provided the necessary information to assist it. The Europeans were able to produce the best maps and had the most far-flung understanding of ocean currents. While mapping in East and South Asia focused on cosmological understanding, in Europe this was complemented by global mapping. Furthermore, an understanding of the degree to which this was incomplete encouraged the development of cartography as part of a continuous process of the acquisition, integration and resolution of information. The willingness and ability of these societies to organise their resources for maritime enterprise were combined with a degree of curiosity about the – to them – unknown world, and a readiness to question received knowledge.

The global links that individuals established could become a sustainable economic, political and military reality only with resources and institutional support, whether governmental or corporate (trading companies). Similarly, information was ordered and sustained within the world of print. Institutional support was important to the financing and organising of activity, in particular to the utilisation of resources. European states were able to utilise the varied and rich resource base of Europe; one that was enhanced by trans-oceanic expansion to bring direct access to South Asian trade and New World bullion. Within Europe, there was heavy forest cover and abundant mineral resources, both essential for naval construction and metallurgy. Europeans probably had access to larger quantities of cheaper metal than was available elsewhere. Some of this metal, in the form of nails, was used to hold European ships together. Naval stores in the shape of hemp and pitch were also plentiful. The Europeans were able to build and maintain durable ocean-going ships that could cope with the tides and rough seas of the Atlantic and even sail round the world.

By the sixteenth century, Europe contained some of the most advanced industrial technology and organisation in the world, with water mills, windmills, heavy forge work, and mechanical clocks,[24] although, until the development and application of steam-engine technology in the eighteenth century, the 'bottleneck' to growth posed by the limitation in the volume and concentration of energy available for mechanical work remained important.[25] At the very least, however, in the sixteenth century (Christian) Europe already had one of the most advanced industrial systems of the time, and European primacy increasingly became the case. Along with a relative openness to new ideas, this economic strength helped Europeans in their adaptation and improvement of technology developed elsewhere, such as gunpowder or ship design. Africa, Australasia, Oceania and the native societies of the Americas definitely did not match these industrial systems, and this hindered their ability to benefit from new technologies. Thus, although the use of firearms spread from European traders to native societies in North America and Africa, in neither case did it prove easy to repair guns or cast shot.

Recent work on developments, not least trade,[26] elsewhere, particularly in China and the Indian Ocean, nevertheless makes it unclear how far a theme of European advantage can be pushed for the sixteenth and seventeenth centuries, at least with respect to these areas. Furthermore, it has been argued that the Ottoman Empire was more open to commercial interests and readier to develop maritime power and concerns than has been generally appreciated.[27] This questioning of the established view of the Ottoman Empire as fundamentally territorial, military and agrarian is one that requires fleshing out, and many Ottomanists continue to emphasise the established view. Nevertheless, in this respect, there appears to be scant contrast between the Ottoman Empire and the majority of European states in the sixteenth century, as most of the latter were not oceanic powers.

It has been claimed that 'European armed forces were not yet backed by an overwhelmingly more productive industrial system',[28] but, at least by the eighteenth century, European forces do appear to have been supported by effective financial systems, while the industrial system in Western Europe seems to have been well adapted to producing and supporting a large number of warships. The possibility of using colonial resources as collateral for loans, and thus of tapping far-flung credit networks, had been important from the early sixteenth century. Thus the Welsers of Augsburg made important loans to Charles V secured by territorial concessions in what is now Venezuela. The military–financial combinations of the early modern period, particularly the eighteenth century, preceded the military–industrial complexes of the nineteenth and twentieth centuries in raising and supporting effective military forces for European powers, and this challenges the claim that 'analysing the role of the state in the rise of the West in the end has to boil down to analysing the role of the state in industrialisation'.[29] However, as the military needs of particular states varied in accordance with their force structures and strategic cultures, while, in addition, no global indices exist for potential military expenditure, it is difficult to assess the effectiveness of particular states in raising resources for warfare. Furthermore, this effectiveness was a matter not only of governmental efficiency, but also of socio-cultural attitudes to the state.

Work on other societies has indicated that institutional reform was not restricted to Europe. This was true, for example, of eighteenth-century China,[30] and the Chinese ability to dominate Mongolia from the 1690s and conquer Zungharia in the 1750s has been seen as the product of a formidable administrative and financial achievement.[31] The end result was that, by 1760, the Manchu dynasty in China ruled

> the largest empire in the world in both size and population ... Whatever its inadequacies in the nineteenth and twentieth centuries, the Qing empire during the Golden Age met the challenges it faced with greater success than any of its predecessors. From the Chinese imperial point of view, population growth, territorial expansion, and commercial development were all indicators of the emperor's virtue and the grace of Heaven.[32]

There has also been a questioning of the tendency to stress differences between the organisation and functioning of the Chinese and Atlantic European economies.[33]

On a smaller scale, it is also possible to point to developments in military and government effectiveness elsewhere in Eurasia, including among a number of Indian states. Mughal India under Akbar (r. 1556–1605), Burma under Bayinnaung (r. 1551–81), Mataram under Agung (r. 1613–45), Persia under Abbas I (r. 1587–1629), and the Ottoman Empire under the first two Köprülü Grand Viziers, Mehmed (1656–61) and Fazil Ahmed (1661–76) were all examples of states that demonstrated the interaction between international ambitions, enhanced military capability and administrative reform. In the last case, the Ottomans revealed an impressive ability to recover from a period of grave difficulties in the mid-seventeenth century, including the deposition of the Sultan in 1648 and Venetian ships blockading the Dardanelles in the 1650s, and to take an assertive role in international relations in the 1660s, 1670s and early 1680s, until the last with considerable success.

Furthermore, consideration of these and other states and societies indicates that, throughout the period, change was far from a monopoly of European societies. Indeed, the dialectic of challenge and response extended to include the nomads of Inner Asia,[34] hitherto frequently primitivised and simplified in scholarly discussion.

If change is to be seen as widespread, that is not the same as indicating that all societies had an equal capacity to analyse problems, define solutions and implement policies accordingly. An absence of institutional continuity, by modern standards, can be seen as limiting these abilities, although, looked at differently, it was an aspect of the fitness for purpose that encouraged ruling groups to define goals, determine government systems and respond to circumstances and concepts in particular ways. Fitness for purpose helped create and contain organisational goals.

The degree of organisation required to create or support a large, permanent, long-range navy, or large, permanent armies, such as those of France and, even more, China, was not required to maintain military forces across most of the world. These contrasts reflected taskings that were set, within particular political cultures, by international systems and domestic circumstances. Only (some) European states had to decide how best to organise, control and support trans-oceanic land and sea operations. These goals and roles became more important from the mid-eighteenth century, but, until then, their role should not be exaggerated.

Notes

1. For important work on the concept of decline, H. G. Koenigsberger, 'The idea of decadence in early modern history, or the apples of Freia', *European History Quarterly*, 22 (1992), pp. 163–85, and M. C. Jacob and W. W. Mijnhardt (eds), *The Dutch Republic in the Eighteenth Century: Decline, Enlightenment, and Revolution* (Ithaca, NY, 1992).

2. P. Anderson, *Lineages of the Absolutist State* (1974).

3. W. Beik, *Absolutism and Society in Seventeenth-Century France: State Power and Provincial Aristocracy in Languedoc* (Cambridge, 1985).

4. V. Press, 'The system of the Estates in the Austrian hereditary lands and in the Holy Roman Empire: a comparison', in R. J. W. Evans and T. V. Thomas (eds), *Crown, Church and Estates: Central European Politics in the Sixteenth and Seventeenth Centuries* (1991), pp. 1–23.

5. G. Burgess, *Absolute Monarchy and the Stuart Constitution* (New Haven, CT, 1996).

6. C. Peterson, *Peter the Great's Administrative and Judicial Reforms* (1979); M. Raeff, *The Well-Ordered Police State. Social and Institutional Change through Law in the Germanies and Russia, 1660–1800* (1983).

7. This can be approached through T. Aston (ed.), *Crisis in Europe, 1560–1660* (1965); G. Parker and L. M. Smith (eds), *The General Crisis of the Seventeenth Century* (1978).

8. See, for example, R. Hatton (ed.), *Louis XIV and Absolutism* (1976); G. Symcox, *Victor Amadeus II. Absolutism in the Savoyard State 1675–1730* (1983); R. Vierhaus, *Germany in the Age of Absolutism* (1988). See, more recently, C. W. Ingrao, 'The Problem of Enlightened absolutism and the German States', *Journal of Modern History*, 58 (1986), supplement, pp. 173–8; C. Mueller, 'Enlightened Absolutism', *Austrian History Yearbook*, 25 (1994), pp. 159–83; H. Duchhardt, *Das Zeitalter der Absolutismus* (3rd edn, Munich, 1998); W. Schmale, 'The future of "absolutism" in historiography: recent tendencies', *Journal of Early Modern History*, 2 (1998), pp. 190–202; P. H. Wilson, *Absolutism in Central Europe* (2000), pp. 38–61. I have benefited from the advice of Nicholas Henshall and David Sturdy on this section.

9. T. Kaiser, 'The evil empire? The debate on Turkish despotism in eighteenth-century French political culture', *Journal of Modern History*, 72 (2000), pp. 8–14.

10. R. Koebner, 'Despot and despotism: vicissitudes of a political term', *Journal of the Warburg and Courtauld Institutes*, 15 (1951), pp. 275–302.

11. M. T. Poe, *'A People Born to Slavery'. Russia in Early Modern European Ethnography, 1475–1748* (Ithaca, NY, 2001), p. 195.

12. C. Imber, *The Ottoman Empire, 1300–1650. The Structure of Power* (Basingstoke, 2002), p. 320.

13. N. Henshall, 'Early modern absolutism 1550–1700: political reality or propaganda?' in R. G. Asch and H. Duchhardt (eds), *Der Absolutismus – ein Mythos? Strukturwandel monarchischer Herrschaft in West- und Mitteleuropa, ca. 1550–1700* (Cologne, 1996), pp. 48–51.

14. D. Ostrowsky, *Muscovy and the Mongols: Cross-Cultural Influences on the Steppe Frontier, 1304–1589* (Cambridge, 1998).

15. H. H. Rowen, *The King's State. Proprietary Dynasticism in Early Modern France* (New Brunswick, NJ, 1980); P. Fichtner, *Protestantism and Primogeniture in Early Modern Germany* (New Haven, CT, 1989).

16. For a recent introduction, R. Butterwick (ed.), *The Polish-Lithuanian Monarchy in European Context, c. 1500–1795* (Basingstoke, 2001).

17. R. Sherwood, *Oliver Cromwell. King in All but Name, 1653–1658* (Stroud, 1997).

18. M. Roberts (ed.), *Swedish Diplomats at Cromwell's Court, 1655–1656* (1988), p. 301.

19. W. L. Urban, *Dithmarschen. A Medieval Peasant Republic* (Lewiston, NY, 1991).

20. The best recent treatment is W. Maltby, *The Reign of Charles V* (Basingstoke, 2002).

21. R. J. W. Evans, *The Making of the Habsburg Monarchy 1550–1700* (Oxford, 1979).

22. A. Calabria, *The Cost of Empire. The Finances of the Kingdom of Naples in the Time of Spanish Rule* (Cambridge, 1991); J. Tracy, *Emperor Charles V, Impresario of War. Campaign Strategy, International Finance, and Domestic Politics* (Cambridge, 2002), pp. 274–88.

23. J. Black, *Europe and the World, 1650–1830* (2002).

24. D. Landes, 'The foundations of European expansion and domination: an equilibrium model', *Itinerario*, 5 (1981), pp. 52–3; W. H. McNeill, 'European expansion, power and warfare since 1500', in J. A. deMoor and H. L. Wesseling (eds), *Imperialism and War. Essays on Colonial Wars in Asia and Africa* (Leiden, 1989), pp. 17–18.

25. J. A. Goldstone, 'Efflorescences and economic growth in world history: rethinking the "rise of the West" and the Industrial Revolution', *Journal of World History*, 13 (2002), p. 379.

26. J. Tracy (ed.), *The Rise of Merchant Empires. Long-Distance Trade in the Early Modern World 1350–1750* (Cambridge, 1990), and *The Political Economy of Merchant Empires. State Power and World Trade 1350–1750* (Cambridge, 1992).

27. P. Brummett, *Ottoman Seapower and Levantine Diplomacy in the Age of Discovery* (Albany, NY, 1994).

28. P. J. Marshall, 'Western arms in maritime Asia in the early phases of expansion', *Modern Asian Studies*, 14 (1980), p. 13.

29. P. H. H. Vries, 'Governing growth: a comparative analysis of the role of the state in the rise of the West', *Journal of World History*, 13 (2002), p. 126.

30. M. Zelin, *The Magistrate's Tael: Rationalizing Fiscal Reform in Eighteenth-Century Ch'ing China* (Berkeley, CA, 1984); B. S. Bartlett, *Monarchs and Ministers: The Grand Council in Mid-Ch'ing China, 1723–1820* (Berkeley, CA, 1991).

31. P. C. Perdue, 'Military mobilization in seventeenth and eighteenth-century China, Russia, and Mongolia', *Modern Asian Studies*, 30 (1996), pp. 757–93.

32. P. C. Perdue, 'Fate and fortune in Central Eurasian warfare: three Qing emperors and their Mongol rivals', in N. Di Cosmo (ed.), *Warfare in Inner Asian History, 500–1800* (Leiden, 2002), pp. 390, 394.

33. P. H. H. Vries, 'Are coal and colonies really crucial? Kenneth Pomeranz and the great divergence', *Journal of World History*, 12 (2001), p. 417.

34. N. Di Cosmo, 'State formation and periodization in Inner Asian history', *Journal of World History*, 10 (1999), pp. 1–40.

CHAPTER 2

The Ancien Régime State: A Growing Power?

§ THE conventional view that states became considerably stronger in the early modern period rests essentially on an assessment of governmental changes combined with a consideration of their political culture. The former tends to focus on changes in relations between centre and localities, as well as a series of developments: those referred to as the Military Revolution and, in addition, the state role in the economy referred to as mercantilism, and developments in state influence over Churches and religious life. These developments can be separated out, but, common to all, there is the question of the extent to which changes arose as an intended result of planned policies and, alternatively, the degree to which the situation was less clear-cut.

An emphasis on the latter can also draw on the contrary assumption that 'states' were not only weak but also subject to outside pressures which they had only a limited ability to mould, let alone determine. In other words, a stress on weakness leads to a focus on attitudes, as well as on policies understood as reactive. This reactive character leads readily to an interpretation centred on crown–élite consensus, in which the crucial political question becomes that of the crown issuing orders that it knows will meet with a ready response, in large part because it is reacting to élite views. This may seem a glib formulation, but it captures much about the practice of power not only in the early modern period, but also more generally. The formulation may also seem over-optimistic, as co-operation was often limited, and that from both directions. Nevertheless, this formulation was not only true of 'state' authority, but also of aspects of social control and religious authority.

In part, however, the notion of sides is misplaced. A culture that stressed the ideal of a Christian community, and the model of good kingship and willing obedience, was matched by the reality of the politics of patronage, a social and political relationship that placed obligations on both parties and, thus, cut across any notion of government and subjects. This was particularly true at the level of the aristocracy, but was not only the case at that level.

Similarly, the nature of aristocratic society ensured that the social gap between monarch and subjects should not be exaggerated: rulers and greater aristocrats shared glorious lineages and a similar lifestyle. This encouraged the aristocrats to expect that they would not be dealt with like other subjects. Many of the leading aristocratic families were cadet branches of royal houses. This could act as a bridge between crown and nobility, but it could also serve to provide leadership and legitimation for aristocratic opposition to royal policies. This tension could focus, as in England, France and Spain in the early seventeenth century, on royal favour for ministers who lacked support from other aristocrats, and breached the conventions of aristocratic political society. The continued importance of informal channels of authority in political and governmental systems in which bureaucracy played only a limited role focused attention on such ministers, and also ensured that the role and skill of monarchs were important.

These points are important when considering the relationship between centre and localities. This relationship was of greater importance in the early modern period than subsequently because, prior to the urbanisation of the nineteenth and twentieth centuries, when a large percentage of the rural population of Europe moved to the major urban areas, the bulk of the population lived outside these areas (as well as outside the centre of government), and were, as a result, less subject to surveillance or ready influence by the agencies of central government. The geographical character of European societies has to be borne in mind, because power and authority had spatial dimensions that it is all too easy to forget or neglect.

Indeed, one of the narratives of political history that is underrated is that of the changing relationships of power and authority to space. These have to be variously understood because, for example, the spatial dimension to gathering information had a different impact to that of confronting and over-coming rebellion. Nevertheless, there is the common problem that modern readers fail to understand the central issue of distance when considering and assessing both strategies of rule and governance, and political capability, not only in early modern Europe but also further afield. It not only took longer to travel and to pass messages, but, in addition, journey times were more unpredictable, particularly as a consequence of the greater impact of both climate and weather, on land and sea.

To a small degree, problems of uncertainty about journeys stemmed directly from the deficiencies of government, particularly in road repair. This was frequently the responsibility of local agencies, but, whether it was their responsibility or that of central government, road repair generally proved beyond the capacity of government. Looked at differently, roads were fit for purpose as defined in terms of the combined capacity and interest of the varied levels of government, and the rapid and predictable dispatch of messages was not of sufficient concern to ensure that rulers leant hard on local élites to improve roads.

It is also necessary to consider the different cultures of authority. There has been an emphasis in the scholarly literature on agents sent from the centre to enforce the will of government, but, in many respects, the governments of early modern Europe were not only less able to do this than the Roman Empire, but also less ready to seek to do so. In addition, in so far as there were attempts to increase governmental capability, they were not new, a point that requires underlining. In order to redress the habit of ascribing excessive novelty to early modern government, it is worth pointing out that there were important medieval anticipations. One such was the emergence of coherent groups of professional administrators. In England, this was true from the reign of Henry I (1100–35). In England, as elsewhere, these *curiales* were mostly 'new men', who were resented by better-born nobles. Thanks to such officials, the enforcement of royal justice and the collection of royal revenues improved and the processes of government became more effective and regular. Similarly, the spread of the market economy, which encouraged a monetarisation of other aspects of life, and, through taxation, lent added flexibility to government, was long-established, as can be seen by the frequency with which markets were established in the Middle Ages.

In early modern Europe, the dispatch of new types of agents by central governments was generally regarded not as a desirable step, but, at least initially, as an extraordinary step, seen as the product of particular failures and as the result of a serious crisis. Thus, in England, the very use, in 1655–57, of major-generals as agents of local control and godly purpose by Oliver Cromwell's Protectorate helped to undermine the fragile legitimacy of the latter; in addition, the religious novelty and unprecedented taxation of the regime did not help.[1]

Across Europe, the habit of obedience towards authority was matched by a stubborn, and largely successful, determination to preserve local privileges. This helped to ensure that the focus of authority was often a local institution or a sense of locality, rather than a distant ruler. This determination was exacerbated by the failure of dynasticism to provide the ideological context for unity, and rationale for unification, that nationalism was to offer in some states in the nineteenth century. As a result, provincial Estates (representative bodies) played a potent political role as a signifier of identity, irrespective of their constitutional powers; and, whether or not such Estates existed, rulers had to take note of the strength of regional and local feelings. These owed something to the role of distance in defining senses of identity.

There were serious political costs to any attempt to extend central governmental control into the localities. There were also important practical issues about the value of such an attempt. Aside from the cost of the agents, there was the question of their oversight. Central government agencies, whether or not defined as ministries, lacked the facilities, techniques and understanding to oversee officials in an effective fashion. Disobedience, disaffection and corruption characterised much government. Office was widely seen as a source of personal and family profit, and financial irregularities flourished, all too often spilling over into corrupt practices.

This was abundantly shown in the independent Italian Grand Duchy of Tuscany in the seventeenth and eighteenth centuries, and there is every sign that this was also true of other states. The duty of integrity was a potent notion in the administrative systems of the *ancien régime* and corruption was denounced. Nevertheless, it was rampant throughout society. The highest-ranking officials were sometimes found guilty of corruption. In 1721, Prince Gagarin, the former Governor of Siberia, was executed in front of the Senate House in St Petersburg. He had run his province as a private fiefdom, acquiring great wealth. Gagarin's fate was exceptional. Executions of such prominent figures tended to follow the end of former regimes when their successors sought legitimacy by targeting a scapegoat for past 'crimes' or failures.

Siberia was far distant from the centre of Russian government. Medici Tuscany (1537–1737) provides an instructive contrast, as it was relatively small, prosperous, had a high level of urbanisation, and, at least for the late sixteenth century, has been regarded as a successful state. Corruption was frequently practised there by those who were well remunerated and at the summit of society; the same was true elsewhere. Therefore, corruption cannot be seen as a mechanism designed to compensate for low salaries or to aid social mobility, although aristocratic and other debt was a factor in some cases. The money gained was spent on gambling, women, comfort, display, in short ostentation, in order to demonstrate, and thus maintain, social prestige, as well as to enjoy life. The use of public funds for private business was also important. Both this, and corruption in general, reflected the openness of government to social pressures; or, rather, the capacity of the social system to respond to, enfold and integrate theoretically external constraints and pressures; and, as the distinction between corruption and gift-giving was often unclear, these processes were facilitated by contemporary assumptions.

Corruption helped officials from the élite to increase power and wealth, and enabled them to exploit the institutions they administered. This has been termed a means of staging a 'permanent *coup d'état*';[2] although, looked at differently, the situation was an aspect of crown–élite collaboration, and shared profits were not extraneous to the creation of absolutism. They were also aspects of the ministerial clientage that helped make government work.[3]

'Shared profits' can also be seen in the established Churches, with the socially prominent given the choice bishoprics, livings and other positions, and using these to further family strategies. This was particularly done by placing family members in ecclesiastical positions, but also, for example, by awarding leases on Church lands at favourable rents to relatives. In return, the prestige of the prominent was brought to the Church, as well as their influence on tenants and other dependants. The power of the prominent could also be directed towards the protection of Church interests, for example in litigation, and against the heterodox. Aside from this functional aspect, the choice of the socially prominent for Church positions also reflected the cultural norms of the period. This appointment pattern did not change throughout the period and, if anything, became stronger in Catholic states as the increased ability of local rulers to appoint to senior positions limited the earlier papal habit of appointing talented outsiders, especially Italians.

Clientage helped government, public, seigneurial and ecclesiastical, work throughout Europe. One related aspect was the widespread 'privatisation' of government functions, although that term can be misleading as it implies that these functions should obviously have been under the control of government. This is an approach that frequently involves an anachronistic working back from modern ideas.

Tax-farming was an important aspect of this process. It involved the granting out, for payment, of the right to collect taxes, and ensured that the resulting officials were employees not of the 'state' but of private bodies. Although tax-farming became less prominent in some states with time, with the Castilian Royal Treasury beginning to administer directly all its tax revenues in 1749 and the Milanese tax farm being abolished in 1770, it would be misleading to see it as an anachronism increasingly made redundant by greater governmental sophistication. Indeed, tax-farming spread in some states. In 1715, in wartime, the Swedish customs duties were farmed for the sake of the advance payment. Tuscan revenues were farmed in 1740–68, Austrian tobacco revenues from the 1730s, Bohemian and Austrian stamp duties, transit dues and tobacco revenues, and Austrian customs duties from 1765 until the mid-1770s, and the Moravian drink excise from 1771 to 1786. Frederick the Great of Prussia (r. 1740–86) farmed out payments in kind in East Friesland, and in 1766 farmed the excise duties, hitherto levied by local authorities, employing officials from the French tax farm, though on terms less favourable than they received in France.

Tax-farming was an effective way to raise revenue, and one made more necessary by the ability of the tax-farmers to provide credit, both from their own resources and by drawing on domestic and international credit networks. Thus the system short-circuited the administrative deficiencies of government, not least the difficulty of creating a system to collect taxes that would be able to raise taxes from those eligible to pay and, yet, would not take a major portion of the yield itself. Furthermore, tax-farming helped cope with the serious problems of government with cash flow, and, in particular, with the difficulties in ensuring long-term borrowing in the absence of a developed revenue system. Tax-farming was made more important by the spread of excises from the mid-seventeenth century in order to pay for permanent armies. Thus there were more taxes that it was viable to raise through tax-farming.

Tax-farming was symbolic of much of European government. The potential created by notions of sovereign authority, and arising from what was (by the global standards of the age) a relatively plentiful resource base, could not be realised by government, and, instead, it was necessary to turn to the compromises and exigencies of partnerships.

In Tuscany, the contrast between a secret world of corruption and a very different public discourse was resolved by restricting the application of strict, judicial and moral principles. This was a more general process, such that 'it is within the framework of a dialectic between the sovereign and the officials that the balance of corruption was established in the monarchies of the *ancien régime*'.[4] Despite the criminalisation of corruption, the Medici Grand Dukes (r. 1537–1737) generally exercised clemency when they were able to identify the corrupt, because of aristocratic pressures that arose, in part, from the extent to which a family suffered the shame visited on any culprit. Corruption was not extraneous to government or a costly irrelevance, but, instead, a major qualification of the effectiveness of administration.

The treatment of corruption was not the sole form of compromise in Tuscany. Work on criminal justice there in 1537–1609 has thrown light on the operation of social control and, again, the limited validity of the terms absolutist and absolutism. Unwilling to meet the high costs of rigid enforcement, and unable to control the poor, the Grand Dukes found that compromise secured acknowledgement of their power to administer justice and thus determine punishments.

In Tuscany, as elsewhere, financial restrictions played a major role in frustrating the hopes and plans of sixteenth-century reformers. Acquittals cut costs and kept magistrates within their budgetary limits. Local officials played a crucial role in the capture of fugitives and the reporting of crime, but police forces were small, poorly paid and generally enmeshed in local networks of family alliances.

This was not only true of Tuscany. Police forces were generally inadequate. Most watchmen or guards were employed by towns or rural parishes, and were usually unable to deal with major outbreaks of crime. In autocratic Russia, there was no national police force. Rural areas were left essentially to their own devices, and Catherine II's remodelling of local administration in 1775 allocated rural police responsibilities to a land commissar, generally a noble elected by his peers. In the major towns, the situation was frequently unsatisfactory. Jakob Sievers, governor of the province of Novgorod from 1764 to 1781, blamed corruption among the police there on the lack of an effective organisation and the absence of salaries.

In Tuscany, the stated aims of the penal system were relaxed to allow many offenders to redeem themselves through the performance of work in the service of the prince, with financial contributions in the case of the wealthy. This flexibility and moderation reflected the practical limits placed on courts, prisons and criminals. There were also issues of obedience. The

Medici sought to create loyalty among local élites by upholding their interests against those of their competitors; and they met a positive response from élites seeking to consolidate their position. This helped ensure a cartography of central government authority, and one that was indicated by the scale and organisation of both policing and violence: authority was more effective in the city of Florence. There, violent acts were mainly committed by individuals and small groups of close kin, rather than by the locally potent families and factions who feuded with less interference in the smaller cities and the countryside.[5]

Obedience was also an issue in another area which has been studied, Picardy, into which French power spread in the late fifteenth and early sixteenth century. Alongside the role of force, the winning over of a wide range of local notables was also crucial to this power. Their continued local power was complemented by the extension of the royal affinity into the region.[6] More generally, patronage structures, like intermediate institutions, such as town councils, could mediate between, and reconcile, the interests of rulers and localities in a way that could not be done by centralised bureaucracies and their local agents. This was particularly important in composite monarchies: in these, local élites were successfully integrated by the ability of rulers to work with these patronage systems.

At a very different level, a reminder of the ability to reconcile what might otherwise appear mutually inimical was provided by the relationship between towns and rural society. Although often presented as alien to, and in tension with, rural society, towns had a close symbiotic relationship with their hinterlands. Again, patronage was important in helping to create links between rural and urban society, as well as to lessen the tensions that could arise from economic links that were, at once, mutually beneficial and yet, also, subject to a frequent process of negotiation in order to resolve differences.[7]

Whatever the context, patronage entailed the granting of privileges. By subsequent bureaucratic standards, these were unnecessary and disruptive. However, privilege was not simply an obstacle to government, but often essential to its operation and effectiveness. In addition, a habit of regarding society in terms of distinct groups with different rights and functions, rather than the modern concept of a uniform citizenry, led to a corporate approach to privilege, as with aristocratic tax exemption and legal rights. More generally, justice, tax and other attributes of power, whether sovereign or not, were, in large part, understood in terms of their varied operation in response to such distinctions. To return to corruption, ministers at the summit of the governmental system, such as Sully, Richelieu, Mazarin and Fouquet in seventeenth-century France and Walpole in Britain, made vast fortunes, while, more generally, financial irregularities shaded into fiscal privilege, an inherent characteristic of the governmental systems and social structures of the age.

In addition, the entire governmental system was affected by the issues of communications and information. In a largely pre-statistical age, it was difficult to obtain the information necessary to make what would now be seen as informed choices, or to evaluate the success of policies; and these problems extend to modern scholarly evaluation. Most central governments had only a limited awareness of the size or resources of their population. This affected their ability to set realistic goals for recruitment and taxation, and to monitor these goals,[8] and also limit the scholarly value of considering policies in such terms.

Efforts to obtain information were not always successful. In the sixteenth century, the Spanish government sought maps to reveal, understand and display what overseas territories had been seized, and to help support further expansion. Philip II sought to have Spain mapped in a way that focused on the role of the government, but 'New Spain' proved less easy to map. Philip entrusted the task to two prominent cartographers, Alonso de Santa Cruz and Juan López de Velasco. Neither visited the New World, but, instead, they sent questionnaires to local officials. The replies were far fewer than had been anticipated, and this helped cause the abandonment of the mapping.[9]

A more widespread self-conscious search for information and interest in knowledge-based policies can be seen from the late seventeenth century. Cadastral mapping was employed extensively by the Swedes, both in Sweden and in their German conquests in the seventeenth century. Such mapping was seen as a necessary complement to land registers, and thus as the basis of reformed taxes. The Swedish Pomeranian Survey Commission of 1692–1709 was designed to provide the basis for a new tax system. Detailed land surveys of Piedmont and Savoy, establishing the ownership and value of land, were completed in 1711 and 1738 respectively, while the cadastral mapping of Lombardy was carried out in the late 1710s with the backing of Emperor Charles VI. In Castile in 1750–54, royal officials carried out a detailed survey of property and income which was seen as the basis for the *catastro*, a tax on income, that was related to wealth, and was to be paid by all. Citing such examples creates an impression of progress, but it is equally pertinent to emphasise how late such developments occurred. In the case of the *catastro*, opposition by the nobility killed the introduction of the tax. More generally, élite exemptions from taxation and the socially regressive character of many taxes that were levied were important aspects of the powerful character of socio-political constraints on governmental ability to raise revenue.

In part as a result of the limitations in the information at the disposal of government, the most effective way to govern was in co-operation with those who wielded social power and with the institutions of local authority. Far from seeking to foster a new ruling group to serve political, administrative and social needs, most rulers sought to employ the traditional élite, a means best served by maintaining existing governmental practices. This established a powerful continuity with past practices, which was appropriate in an age in which legitimacy and legality were derived from them. Much of the traditional élite was indeed keen to serve, both in the localities and at the centre, and this was, at once, a product of their views about their position and an important aspect of their ability to respond to circumstances and change.[10] Rulers might seek to define the process of service, not least by instituting formal tables of ranks linked to service, such as that introduced in Russia by Peter the Great in 1722, which was intended to encourage both government and nobility to emphasise merit as well as birth;[11] as well as by rewarding favoured servants with land, titles and other privileges. However, those who were thus ranked and paid were often from the social élite, and the others, who were not, readily adapted to the existing norms and interests of the élite.

An emphasis on local institutions, and on their ability to serve as links, is another important qualification to any notion that there was a simple contrast between central government and aristocracy-dominated localities. While the character, composition and objectives of local institutions, both urban and rural, were heavily influenced by the local élite, central governments were also influenced by these élites through their patrons at court.

It is possible to see early modern government as a continuation of the medieval practice of tension between different agencies and also between worlds of authority (crudely, central and local government). As earlier, there was a frequent jostling for control, but no 'big bang' of new forms of government, either in the age of the so-called new monarchies in the late fifteenth and early sixteenth centuries, or during the highpoint of what was subsequently termed absolutism in the late seventeenth century, or under the Enlightened Despots a century later. The most important changes that occurred were the need to address the issue of governing trans-oceanic territories, and also the widespread victory of lay over ecclesiastical interests, influence and government. Even so, Churches continued to play a major role in the widespread devolution of authority, power and responsibility that characterised early modern government, and also helped provide a co-herence and strength that the paucity of the central bureaucracy otherwise threatened.

The appearance of royal power contributed crucially to the reality of power; but, behind the façade, such as imposing palaces, and even behind larger armies, rulers were dependent on local institutions and also sought the co-operation of the locally influential, both in accordance with general political assumptions, and for reasons of distance and scale, and the related problems of surveillance. This was particularly the case in the larger states. Thus, the stress usually placed on the use by Louis XIV of France (r. 1643–1715) of *intendants* – powerful officials sent to exercise governmental functions in the provinces – can hide the fact that they had to co-operate with local institutions, such as provincial *Parlements*, and that much power remained with the *gouverneurs* of provinces, who were major aristocrats; although that did not preclude the conservatively minded Louis from being responsible for change, not least through increasing the size of the army and raising peace-time taxation to pay for it.[12]

Furthermore, administrative development in France was not a unilinear process towards stronger state agencies. For example, the Company of General Farmers, the consortium of financiers who leased the collection of French indirect taxes, was, in the 1780s, solely responsible for the salt and tobacco taxes, and was employing or organising over 30,000 agents. The company served increasingly after 1749 as a source of credit and capital for the government, and as a mechanism for making payments. It also illustrated the potential for administrative efficiency in the period. Although the system of taxes the company collected was very confused, it proved very efficient in collecting them, in part because it was unhampered by venal offices.[13]

The reality of power was not only complex in France. The impact of central and local government in Brandenburg-Prussia was limited on the estates of the nobility. Frederick William, the Great Elector (r. 1640–88), is now seen not, as he was until recently presented, as a conscious pursuer of a powerful state directed by a central government closely co-operating with the nobility, but rather as a more cautious ruler primarily concerned by dynastic interests and international strength, and keen to work with established institutions. As with other rulers, his attitudes, actions and interventions were crucial in what was very much a personal monarchy.[14]

Limitations could also be seen in what, from a different direction, have been regarded as progressive regimes. In the United Provinces (modern Netherlands), the weakness of central sources of revenue led to a dependence upon the individual provinces, which increased the emphasis on that level of government. Combined with the extensive role of credit, supporting a large public debt, this ensured that the central government lacked a large, permanent administrative apparatus. The élites in the most prosperous and heavily taxed province, Holland, accepted the situation because it helped them influence policy; but Holland's ability to become the dominant and directing force in the state was lessened by inter-city rivalries within it, particularly rivalry between the most prosperous city, Amsterdam, and the others, as well as by provincial particularism and outside Holland the role of the house of Orange.[15]

Across Europe, new governmental agencies frequently supplemented, rather than replaced, existing administrative systems, and, necessarily so, as the number of their officials was limited and as they operated in a world that was resistant to new pretensions on the part of government. The psychological reluctance to accept the new as valid was encoded in both law and politics, and helps to account for the major disjuncture experienced at the time of the Reformation, as religious change and accompanying social and political disruption were experienced as threats.

In seventeenth-century France, the *intendants* complemented existing mechanisms in serving the essentially traditional financial and military needs of
the government. Earlier work has been revised, and it is now widely agreed
that the *intendants* represented neither a major administrative transformation
nor an agency of despotic power and centralisation. Indeed, given the scale
of purchase of government office and of the right to pass on office in
seventeenth-century France, the extent to which the 'state' was subject to
the will of the ruler, as the traditional emphasis on *intendants* might imply,
is doubly questionable.

This sale of offices (venality), which was particularly important in France,[16]
represented a way to tap the wealth of those who otherwise made at best
a limited financial contribution to the costs of the state, in part through
tax exemptions, although many of the offices sold, in turn, brought new
exemptions. In part, as with tax-farming, the sale of offices represented a way
to obtain money at once, albeit at the cost of future revenues. Traditionally,
this has been criticised by scholars, not least for diverting investment income
from the productive economy; but, in practice, much twentieth-century fiscal
and monetary policy, particularly measures that contributed to inflation, served
the same ends, although they did not privatise office as venality did.

Furthermore, the sale of office was less indirect a means of raising revenue
from the prominent than taxing them indirectly by means of their reduced
capacity to earn rental income as a result of the taxation of their peasant
tenants. Venality of office encapsulated a world of shared crown–élite interests
that was subject to serious strains but, nevertheless, held together by the
exchange of status for service, a crucial form of both government and political
stability in this period.

The need for status at every level was far stronger than in the modern
world, and took the form not only of conspicuous consumption and display
– you are what, and how, you spend and appear – but also of a determination
to gain hereditary glory in the form of title. This reflected a social system
whose apex was a ruler capable of awarding status, and himself (or sometimes
herself) the living embodiment of status. This brought a field of governance
very different to that of bureaucracy into prominence. The ruler as dispenser
and maintainer of rank faced difficult tasks in responding to contradictory
pressures. In 1756, the Prince of Conti's claim that he had been dishonoured
by not being granted command over the French army that was preparing
to move into Westphalia – it went to a lower-ranking aristocrat – led Louis
XV to note that he was receiving too many similar complaints and that they
infuriated him.

This difficulty was underlined by the conspicuous character of promotions
in rank, and therefore honour, and by their importance to the politics of
aristocratic societies. The politics of titles have received insufficient systematic
treatment. They helped lubricate the world of patronage and patronage

demands, and linked crown and élite, court and localities. Where it occurred, the absence or removal of monarchy ensured a very different form of nobility. In the Dutch Republic, the rejection of Philip II removed the mechanism of ennoblement, thus leading to a decline in the number of nobles. A failure to permit sufficient ennoblement hit the ability of the nobility to sustain their position in the republics of Genoa and Venice. In France, where, in the early stages of the French Revolution, the National Assembly abolished noble titles in 1790, the attack on traditional respect for rank left the monarchy vulnerable.

The character of crown–aristocracy relations and the inchoate nature of most institutions ensured that politics were personal and that the calibre and effectiveness of government owed much to the direction provided by the monarch. This vindicates the scholarly possibilities of the biographical genre.

In, by relative standards, small states, such as Denmark, Portugal and Savoy-Piedmont, it was easier for a strong ruler to supervise government personally. A British memorandum of 1740 noted of Savoy-Piedmont,

> the laws are made by the King [Charles Emmanuel III, r. 1730–73]. He proposes a law in Council: They may advise against it, but if the King is still for it, their advice goes for nothing. 'Tis then sent to the Senate to be registered; who may offer their reasons against it; The King orders them to enter it, which they do, in such a case, with a clause, that the Senate does it *pour obeir* [to obey].[17]

However, even in what might seem today to have been small states, the difficulties of coping with factionalism among officialdom, and of inculcating notions of state service and efficient administration, were considerable, while the earlier discussion of Tuscany is instructive. In addition, the acceptance of regional differences among small states was widespread. It included, for example, the distinctive treatment within the papal states of Bologna, specifically the continued powers of the urban authorities there.

It is important to note the extent to which what are seen as small states were themselves often composite states. This was true of both Denmark and Savoy-Piedmont. Aside from important differences in rights, regulation and control between Savoy and Piedmont, there were others between additional possessions of the crown, which included the county of Nice and, in the eighteenth century, first Sicily (1713–20) and then Sardinia (1720), as well as gains from Lombardy in the 1730s and 1740s.

Furthermore, the assumption that unitary states were more successful than composite counterparts has to confront the extent to which states seen as successes, such as Savoy-Piedmont and Brandenburg-Prussia, retained such composite characteristics, as, to a lesser extent, did both Britain and France: Ireland retained a separate parliament until the close of the period. The variegated nature of French administration, without uniformity in taxation, local laws and local government, both reflected and encouraged a sense of regional identity. This variety extended into many spheres. For example, Alsace and Artois, both seventeenth-century gains of the French throne, fell outside the jurisdiction of the king's premier surgeon. More prominently, in the *pays d'états*, the most important of which were Brittany, Burgundy, Languedoc and Provence, each of which was a major province, taxes were levied only with the consent of the Estates (representative assemblies), and new demands from the crown were particularly strongly resisted.

The rulers of Savoy-Piedmont and Brandenburg-Prussia from the late seventeenth century were determined to give central direction, but were ready to work with established institutions and interests. Thus the policies of the rulers of Brandenburg-Prussia varied across their dominions, in response to the particular political cultures of the latter, with a more assertive policy in East Prussia and a greater willingness to accept limitations in the Rhenish possessions of Cleves and Mark. The General Directory, an institution created by Frederick William I (r. 1713–40) to supervise military, police and financial matters, was a means to increase royal control over provincial government and reflected a wish to match apparent increases in governmental capability in Austria and, even more, Russia. However, Frederick William's policies were successful in so far as they won over the traditional élite to a role within the absolutist state. Furthermore, the territorial organisation of the General Directory helped accentuate the tendency to respond to local circumstances that characterised Prussian, and indeed all, government. This variety was given bureaucratic form. For example, the instructions drawn up for the General Directory in 1748 included variations for the western provinces, while Silesia, the wealthy province conquered from the Habsburgs by Frederick the Great in 1740–41, was not placed under it at all. Instead, its provincial administration came directly under the control of Frederick.

Over most of Europe, clear hostility to the idea of despotism, and conventions of acceptable royal behaviour, limited the possibilities for monarchical action by setting restrictive limits of consent, in both theory and practice. These were less strong in Russia than further west, although, in 1730, an unsuccessful attempt was made to restrict the powers of the new ruler, Anna. Throughout Europe, tyranny was held up for condemnation, not least as un-Christian, and rulers who tested the limits were sharply criticised.

Like (governmental) corruption, the use of the term tyranny reflected the moral dimension of politics. This owed much to the extent to which politics and government were seen as having moral (as well as legal) dimensions, but was also a function of ambivalence about the nature of opposition to rulers who were not, in fact, acting in a tyrannical function. Royal rights and prerogatives, and the assumptions that guided responses to them, limited the space for political debate[18] and could oblige opposition to be strident, and disproportionate to the issues at stake.

The space for debate was, in turn, widened if royal powers could be presented as being wielded by minister-favourites, such as Buckingham, Strafford, Richelieu, Mazarin, Lerma, Olivares and, in the eighteenth century, Fleury, Pombal, Hoym, Menshikov, Munnich, Biron, Carteret and Bute, as well as less prominent individuals, rather than by the monarch. Such favourites were seen to challenge the rights and privileges of the many other participants in the processes of government and politics, including, in particular, aristocratic councillors who found themselves unable to influence policy. Favourites therefore accentuated the politics of faction. They also served as a means by which governmental power could apparently be increased by providing competent direction in the fashion necessary in a monarchical system, namely in the person of a 'substitute king'. From this perspective, the age of favourites in the early seventeenth century (not that favourites were restricted to that period) can be seen as playing a formative role in the development of absolutism.[19] Ecclesiastical favourites, such as William Laud, Archbishop of Canterbury in England under Charles I, could also be feared.

Tyranny represented the uncontrolled lust and passion that was so widely criticised in early modern culture. Monarchs were expected to win success and glory, but also to operate within a context of legality and tradition, and there was considerable support for the role and privileges of Estates.[20] This made new initiatives politically hazardous and administratively difficult, particularly as the widespread absence of policies and institutions for formal consultation ensured that it was hard to negotiate any extension in the scope of government. This was a classic instance of the weakness of authoritarianism, and it helped ensure that initiatives were regarded with suspicion and as justifying recourse to a right to revolt in support of established practices. Gaining the support of the aristocracy, while persuading them to abandon their former sponsorship of Estates, thus created long-term political and governmental problems; at the same time it ensured short-term stability, as well as according with a political culture that also put an emphasis on royal glory.

Whether or not Estates existed, encouraging a sense that monarchs could solve problems created an ideal, or at least an expectation, that posed unrealistic expectations on both rulers and the process of government, and this accentuated serious political problems at particular moments of tension. Britain's American colonies in the 1760s and France in the 1780s offered two dramatic examples. In the long term, however, all government faces problems at some stage, and it is naïve to think that difficulties can be divorced from rulership and statecraft.

In practice, most governmental initiatives in the period as a whole can be seen as a response to specific crises, rather than as a sign of a quest for more power, let alone a programme to strengthen royal authority. A recent study of Savoy-Piedmont, a state generally presented as an absolutism, and whose monarchs certainly pursued a clear programme of expanding territorial power, has concluded:

> It is questionable whether Victor Amadeus [II, r. 1675–1730] really wanted to create a uniform state. If the years between 1690 and 1713 saw an apparently more determined drive to extend central control and impositions at the expense of local liberty and exemptions it was the result less of a ducal blueprint for 'absolutism' than of a desperate search for money and men to wage wars.[21]

Church government and religious oversight were areas in which major change was forced on many governments. The Protestant Reformation and its Catholic response (the Catholic or Counter-Reformation) led to significant demands, not least in dealing with those who would not conform to the new orthodoxy, and, more generally, in trying to raise standards among clerics and their flocks to fulfil expectations of reform and to prevent a loss of support. In most states, this was a more serious threat to the integrity and strength of government than a failure to pay taxes. As toleration was seen as weakness, and authority as indivisible, heterodoxy represented a challenge to rulers. It was at the level of the state that the crucial political decisions were made about which faith was to be the established one, and how its worship was to be organised. Contemporary attitudes to ecclesiastical government and notions of toleration ensured that decisions, once made, had to be implemented through-out the state (unless specific privileges were at issue, as in Alsace once parts of it were gained by France from 1648) and with the assistance of the 'secular' government, in so far as such a distinction can be drawn.

Furthermore, the Reformation and the Counter-Reformation were chal-lenges that could not be met by standard responses, for much of the élite was, or might seem, unreliable. England for a while had no dukes after its sole one, Thomas, 4th Duke of Norfolk of the Howard line, a Catholic, was executed in 1572 for plotting against Elizabeth I, in favour of Mary, Queen of Scots, who had been driven from, first, her throne, and then Scotland in 1567–68 by a Protestant aristocratic league. William, Prince of Orange, one of Europe's leading aristocrats and a favourite of Charles V, was assassinated in 1584 at the behest of the latter's son, Philip II, for leading the Dutch Revolt. In France, aristocrats such as the Prince of Condé took up arms against the crown in the French Wars of Religion (1562–98). Whereas most medieval heresies had been restricted to marginals, Protestant and Catholic dissent spanned social spectrums or could be believed to do so.

Sigismund Báthory, a devout Catholic who, in 1586, became Prince of Transylvania, a state with powerful Protestant communities, was forced by the Diet that met in 1588 to expel the Jesuits. In 1591, the Diet insisted that the prince obtain the approval of the Council before taking major decisions, while it also pressed for control over both army and treasury. The Diet's refusal to back the prince's declaration of war on the Ottomans in 1594 led

Sigismund to abdicate, but he swiftly returned to power with the backing of the army.[22]

The challenge to authority and power posed by élite support for heterodoxy was made more serious by the ability and willingness of religious opponents to look abroad for external support, particularly from co-religionists. Thus, authority and sovereignty were doubly put at risk. English and Irish Catholics received Spanish help from Philip II while, nearly two centuries later, Protestants in the *Erblande* (Austrian Habsburg hereditary lands) were encouraged by the rulers of Prussia. In the eighteenth century, the Russians sought to win Orthodox support against Ottoman rule in the Balkans.

Yet, although having, in effect, assumed responsibility for deciding what constituted the true faith, and being challenged, in doing so, in this very serious fashion, governments could not react by creating effective new agencies for policing thought and activity. Both, instead, were largely left to ecclesiastical authorities, although the capacity of these for new activism was shown by the vitality of the Inquisition and Index in Catholic Europe, as well as the basic institution that was common across the confessional divide: the parochial system. Thus the Reformation posed serious challenges and, in some countries, led to a new ideology and practice of rulership, but it did not lead to a new governmental system.

The Reformation did, however, ensure that, in some states, distinctive religious arrangements became an expression and definition of national identity. The very process of creating state churches was a powerful and auspicious exercise of governmental authority. It represented a new definition of the state in Western Europe. The new practice was more similar to the states of Orthodoxy – medieval Byzantium and contemporary Russia – and to the Christian monarchy of Ethiopia, than to the states of pre-Reformation Western Europe, but it had a greater capacity for continued change than the Orthodox states displayed.

In England, the monarch from the 1530s was head of the Church, but the Church was also representative of a chosen people with a sense of divine mandate. Protestant England was seen as God's New Israel, with all the possibilities that this entailed of defining purposes and identities separate to those of the rest of Christendom. This national process of redefinition matched that of Protestant sects that saw themselves as the elect.

The Reformation also encouraged further debate on issues of obedience and authority. The radical consequences of resistance theory, which was most prominently advanced by Huguenot (French Protestant) writers during the French Wars of Religion in the late sixteenth century, but was also seen elsewhere, for example in Scotland, were countered in the seventeenth century. This helped create the intellectual background to what was to be called absolutism. Ideological developments, indeed, were as instrumental as crown–élite co-operation in forging absolutism; or, rather, they were an aspect of it. However, there were major differences between Catholic and Protestant political cultures, as well as important varieties within each: the different politics of say Poland and Portugal in the seventeenth century and, even more, the eighteenth century reflected these variations.

The education of future clerics and lawyers, many in Jesuit colleges, was important across Catholic Europe, especially in France, the *Erblande*, and southern Germany, and particularly in the seventeenth and early eighteenth century: students learned to venerate rulers and were taught the evils of resistance. There were 669 Jesuit colleges by 1750. By the time the rebellion known as the *Fronde* began in France in 1648, the bulk of the senior clergy and the *noblesse de robe* accepted the inviolability of the king of France. The *noblesse de l'épée* (nobility of the sword), however, were less well indoctrinated, and, partly in consequence, readier to defy the cardinal-ministers (Richelieu and Mazarin) in the 1630s–1650s. For them, subsequently, the implicit bargain of shared benefits presented by large-scale officership in the expanded wartime armies and, crucially, peacetime permanent forces of the late seventeenth century had to be offered alongside the indoctrination provided most effectively by education.

Indoctrination cannot be separated from issues of patronage, although, as with so many other aspects of early modern history, force also played a prominent role, especially on the front line between Protestantism and Catholicism, for example in the Rhineland in the 1580s and the *Erblande* in the 1620s. It is not surprising that in the Escorial, the palace-monastery built near Madrid to the instructions of Philip II, to serve, among other things, as a mausoleum to mark the dynasty's grandeur, there were two sets of paintings marking victories in the campaigns of Philip's army under the Duke of Parma in the Low Countries, including the siege of Maastricht in 1579. These triumphs destroyed the Protestant cause in what was eventually to become Belgium.[23]

Aside from supporting war, the ability to finance and otherwise support favourable clerics, religious foundations and clerical orders was important in the ideological politics of the period. This process encompassed the full range of clerical authority from Pope to priest: 'Philip II had succeeded in establishing a largely benevolent Spanish hegemony in Rome through the distribution of millions of Spanish ducats to thousands of Italian and Spanish churchmen and noble families.' This relationship was of great importance:

> the support of the papacy was critical to the political strength of the Spanish Empire as a whole ... That Spain retained papal support and the loyalty of many Roman nobles in the face of a much stronger France testified to the success of informal imperialism, to a form of political domination that relied more on the cultivation of a strong patron–client network than on military strength.[24]

Indeed, the failure of the French to play more of a military and political role in Italy despite major efforts to do so, particularly in 1635–59, was important not only to the politics of the peninsula, as well as those of Catholic Europe, but also to the subsequent character of Catholicism. A closer linkage with France would not only have helped Louis XIV in particular international and domestic junctures, especially the 1680s, but would also have encouraged different currents within Catholicism. Instead, Counter-Reformation, Tridentine, Baroque, Habsburg Catholicism was carried forward as Spanish power declined under Charles II (r. 1665–1700) because the Austrian Habsburgs took a triumphant role against the Ottomans in 1683–1718, in large part in co-operation with the papacy, particularly through the Holy League of 1684: Innocent XI (r. 1676–89) proved an especially energetic Pope.

Robert Evans's work on the *Erblande* makes a strong point about the political value of the education of the élite,[25] although there indoctrination had to counter a Protestant challenge not seen in Italy, and was, in large part, dependent on the military success of the Habsburgs in the 1620s. Had the varied opposing forces, which included the underrated Bethlan Gabor of Transylvania, been more successful, then it is possible that a more cautious account of the impact of education and indoctrination in Central Europe would have to be offered. Counter-Reformation political culture certainly had a far more limited impact in Hungary than in the *Erblande*, and this helped ensure the depth of aristocratic opposition to the Habsburgs in the Rakoczi uprising of 1703–11.

Education of the élite was also an issue of political influence in states where religious differences were not at stake. Thus in Catalonia, in north-eastern Spain, after Philip V (r. 1700–46) imposed his authority in 1714, the six traditional Catalan universities were suppressed, and a new pro-Bourbon one was created at Cervera in 1717.

Indoctrination was a matter not only of affecting élite attitudes, but also of those of the bulk of the population. Here, it is possible to view both Protestant and Catholic ecclesiastical and lay authorities as taking part in a similar process, a long Reformation, in which the people were subjected to increased supervision as part of a programme to improve their behaviour and strengthen their faith, and in direct response to the challenge of heterodoxy and the consequent danger that people would be tempted to dangerous error. This entailed policies of Christianisation for the population and orthodoxy for the clergy. The latter proved easier to introduce and enforce, not least as a result of improved education in seminaries for the next generation of clerics and more supervision by a revived episcopacy.

Christianisation for the people took longer, but in Catholic countries tended to be pressed from the 1560s in response to the Council of Trent (1545–63), which laid down the framework of Catholic reform. Thus, in rural Spain, there was an important drive, pushed by the Inquisition, in the 1560s and

1570s, although the rate at which, and extent to which, Tridentine reforms were implemented varied. Thus, in Italy there was felt to be a need for a fresh burst of reform under Innocent XI (r. 1676–89).

The enforcement of ecclesiastical sanctions underlined the nature of power in society and the public character of Christian sanctions. It also reflected the sense that religion and morality were not separable from each other, or jointly separate from secular life, nor spheres in which individual free will could play a role. At Wimborne Minster in England in the 1590s, presentments included 'the widow Sanders' for keeping 'a youth in her house', a breach of public propriety, and two men for conspicuously ignoring the demands of religious conformity: William Lucas 'for playing of a fiddle in the time of God's service', and Christopher Sylar 'for sitting by the fire in the sermon time and when we asked him if he would go to the church he said he would go when he listeth'. Protestantism might foster individualism and greater self-reliance in some respects, but there was, across Europe, also a strong emphasis on the corporate relationship of communities with God, and thus on discipline and compliance. If the authoritarian connotations of the term absolutism are applicable, it might be thought that this is the most pertinent example. Furthermore, this ecclesiastical dimension has direct bearing on the issues of governance and social politics, for the Churches taught obedience and drew heavily on the sponsorship of lay authorities.

The notion of a long Reformation in part presupposes a response to a late medieval crisis of Christianity supposedly compounded of clerical abuses and a lack of popular fervour. This has been overdone. While both were true, there was also much religious commitment in the fourteenth and fifteenth centuries. Hostility to the wealth and claims of the clergy was widespread, but far from new, and it was mostly directed to individuals who failed to meet standards. This hostility did not preclude extensive popular devotion, including much church-building and renovation, active support for local shrines and saints, and a continued and important role for monasteries, priories, nunneries and chantries in the spiritual, charitable and educational role of many communities. Religious vitality was also seen in local culture. The pre-Reformation Catholic Church was responsive to lay piety, with developments such as the rise of chantries and the spread of Corpus Christi festivals reflecting this shared effort.[26] The systematisation of objectives by the Council of Trent can be seen within a tradition of medieval reforming clerics, not least popes, and the same was true of the foundation of new religious orders.

Nevertheless, the process of clerical overhaul that characterised the long Reformation led to a stronger and more comprehensive ecclesiastical infrastructure. Furthermore, lay spirituality among Catholics was actively fostered by energetic preaching orders, as it was in both Catholic and Protestant Europe, by the revived parochial clergy. The importance of these developments was such that the Council of Trent (1545–63) can be seen as a turning point in early modern European history. The Churches also took a major role in improving the quantity and quality of educational provision.

Catholic (and, even more, Protestant) reform were more than simply institutional developments. The long Reformation was also central to a major cultural thrust, an attempt to inculcate a seriousness that restrained passions, and thus improved both individuals and the community, under the watchful eye of Church and state, in a world circled by divine injunctions. Again, there was much that was far from new. Taming the passions was a traditional Christian theme, and there is a danger that the reiteration of nostrums during the Reformation, and their ready availability as a result of the rapid spread of the medium of print, encourages an inappropriate suggestion of novelty. The depiction in the library of the Escorial of the denunciation of the Arian heresy at the Council of Nicaea of 325, instead, served to underline the extent to which the authority of the Church and the nature of Catholic orthodoxy had been challenged across the centuries.

Nevertheless, even if it was largely a question of traditional views being reiterated in sermons and other injunctions, as well as published, there was still an impact and authority derived from this expression. This was particularly true in Protestant countries for publications, which were increasingly seen as authoritative, as a consequence of the extensive publication of the Bible and of religious tracts and their impact through appearing in the vernacular.

The impact of the reiteration of the Christian message was driven home by compulsion. Regulations varied, but attendance at church services, as well as participation in rites, taking communion and being catechised, were all compulsory. Those who did not comply could anticipate humiliation and other punishments. This was more insistent than any lay regulation. In contrast to secular administrations, the actions of established Churches were more widespread, not least because their representatives were present generally in every parish and were overseen by regular hierarchical structures of ecclesiastical authority and jurisdiction. The need to offer a cure of souls gave these Churches a territorial structure and presence generally lacking in secular governments. Although Churches have, with reason, been criticised for concentrating their personnel and resources in towns, they nevertheless sought a comprehensive rural presence.

Indeed, the prime governmental success in early modern Europe was that of the creation, revival or strengthening of ecclesiastical structures and systems. These were more impressive than lay counterparts, and a tendency to neglect their role lessens our understanding of the culture of Europe, certainly until the major social changes of the nineteenth century. For example, in Catalonia, there was a new emphasis on the sacraments, and thus on priestly intercession. While, across Europe, prior to the Counter-Reformation, confirmation was rare, confession and communion might be attempted only once a year, and the Church did not necessarily play a role in marriage, the situation changed greatly in the early modern period, in part realising the hopes of earlier reformers who had remained Catholics. More frequent attendance at church and the greater emphasis on the sacraments increased the authority of Churches over their members, although, like other practices of authority, this entailed processes of negotiation that are frequently hidden from us due to the nature of the surviving sources. The personality of clerics was as important as their power.[27]

This regulation of the entire population owed much to a willingness, among both Protestants and Catholics, to regulate themselves. Both were matched by measures to encourage and channel enthusiasm, which was seen by both Protestants and Catholics, authorities and congregations, as opportunity and threat. The emphasis in late medieval piety on the inner life was a source of commitment, devotion and energy, but also a challenge to patterns of religious authority, both Catholic and Protestant.

The heterodox possibilities of lay piety were countered by the development of devotional confraternities and approved charitable foundations. These provided new networks of, in effect, kinship and means and forums of association that both replicated the patterns of established social structures, not least the segregation of women and the extent of hierarchy, and yet also presented new opportunities for linkage and social roles. This process was very important to the stability of, in particular, urban societies, as it provided ways for the ambitious and active to operate that supported the existing consensus. The total membership of confraternities was very large.

The goal of better behaviour had obvious political benefits, partly by encouraging restraint, while the enhancement of religious institutions and culture, with virtuous priests leading observant laity, ensured that ecclesiastical structures were better able to serve governmental functions, in particular in social welfare, education, health and moral policing.

The relationship was, however, more than instrumental, and here, as elsewhere, it is misleading to adopt a functional approach and to neglect ideological factors. Government was supposed to serve a moral purpose, and the state to possess and propagate a religious identity. This made the heterodox a problem. When crowned, monarchs swore to protect the Church and, generally, to extirpate heresy. The protection of established Churches gave rulers a divine purpose that underlay their rights to obedience. This protection encouraged many clerics to argue for the divine right of kings, but this right has to be understood as an aspect of proper authority. It was not an excuse for tyranny, which was un-Christian, and what would be expected if the devil seized the reins in Heaven.

In addition, there was no simple relationship between Church and state. The response of clerics – even those of established Churches – to rulers varied considerably, and not only among Protestants. The same was true of Catholics, with important differences of opinion reflecting the interplay of theological debate, institutional belief and political circumstances. Thus, in early-seventeenth-century France, aside from the tension between *politiques* and *dévots* (each of which group, or tendency, was far from united or uniform in opinion), there were important institutional tensions, for example between the Jesuits, who were keen on authority, and the Oratorians, who drew their support from the *Parlements* and the University of Paris.[28]

Furthermore, it was not only kings who could lay claim to an attribute of divine right as part of a world in which God's will was manifest. Other authorities could also seek to share in this source of validity and purpose. As a counterpart to the widespread character of 'godly' rule, the Renaissance ideal of good government was also pursued at different levels, by intermediate institutions as well as sovereign rulers.[29]

The protection of established Churches entailed restrictions on the public worship of other groups, and, as a consequence of the intertwining of Church and state, members of the latter encountered limitations on their political rights and on their ability to hold office. The revocation, in 1685, by Louis XIV of the Edict of Nantes, which had established Huguenot rights in 1598, was followed by a large Huguenot diaspora, including over 70,000 to the United Provinces, 50–70,000 to England, and 44,000 to the Empire. Thereafter, in law, all the French were Catholics, the only valid marriages were Catholic ones, and the children of Calvinist marriages were bastards. Although the laws were not systematically applied, they expressed the general attitude towards membership of the community and towards obedience. Although the revocation made Louis a hate figure across Protestant Europe, and has greatly affected his subsequent reputation, the response was very different within France. This provides an important clue to expectations about royal intervention and to the continued validity and popularity of sacral kingship. The anointment of monarchs with sacred oil was not some anachronistic curiosity, but a powerful affirmation of the nature of society and of the assertion of monarchy, alongside the Church, as God's instrument in a fallen world. Both were pledges of salvation.

Similarly, the Inquisition, although reviled in Protestant Europe, and criticised by 'progressive' Catholic intellectuals, appears to have enjoyed a considerable amount of popular support. In the lands of the Crown of Aragon in the late sixteenth and early seventeenth century, the frequent *autos de fe* (burnings) organised at the behest of the Inquisition were popular because those punished were mostly outsiders. However, the widespread tension between local interests and external agencies was shown by the hostility of local élites towards the Inquisition, particularly in Sicily, while the separate Aragonese Secretariat of the Inquisition was itself abolished in 1618.[30] Nevertheless, in the kingdom of Valencia, which was part of the Aragon crown lands, the Inquisition's attempts to repress the worst excesses of erroneous doctrine were seen as laudable, and it continued in the eighteenth century to demonstrate an impressive capacity to attract fresh recruits.[31] Religious tension in Spain had increased in the 1700s when, in the civil war that broke out there in 1704, as a result of the already contested succession to the throne, the clergy of Castile backed Philip V and proclaimed the conflict with the Habsburg claimant, 'Charles III' (later the Emperor Charles VI), a holy war: the Catholic Charles was backed by the Protestant British and Dutch.

Across Europe, hostile attitudes towards religious outsiders had existed prior to the Reformation, but were greatly strengthened by the problems it greatly amplified of dealing with the heterodox and of defining loyalty. The role of the ruler as the arm of the Church was markedly strengthened, at the same time as heterodoxy challenged the authority of rulers and Churches alike. As a result, the ideological framework of power was given new direction and energy for two centuries. This was more pertinent than abstract discussion over sovereignty, as the concepts of orthodoxy and heresy (if not always the issues) were easier to understand. Communion and the catechism had a meaning in every parish, and were aspects of a divinely ordained civil society that offered the prospect of redemption through Christ's suffering and the ministry of the Church to all believers. They had, in turn, to contain their passions, for, in resisting sin and the devil, they were, whatever their situation, making themselves fit for God's mercy. In Florence in 1729, earthquakes were blamed on the impiety of the population or the wickedness of the clergy, leading to penances, processions, and the end of the opera season.[32]

Divine judgment on human conduct was at once a drama and a bargain that was given cultural force across the range of arts. Painting, sculpture and sacred music all powerfully contributed, but so also did less durable forms, such as ceremonies, processions and theatrical productions, for example sectarian carnival and other celebrations seen at Dresden in the late sixteenth century or the puppet displays in churches the English tourist Richard Creed saw in Rome in 1700.[33] The arts offered instruction through admonition and example, helped raise and sustain religious consciousness, and also provided languages for spiritual awareness and solace. Religious images were particularly important, as their destruction by Protestant iconoclasts served to demonstrate to Catholics the attack on worship, both in an abstract sense and with reference to the devotional practices that gave individuals and communities a sense of identity and cohesion. Belief in the power of saints and the efficacy of images could also lead to a conviction that they would respond to attacks on them.

Calvinism, with its emphasis on predestinarianism, lacked this drama and did not employ the arts in the same fashion, although psalm singing was important to Calvinists. In the Calvinist psyche, God was more inscrutable and less to be propitiated, or even bargained with, through good acts. To that extent, he (and the Calvinist, like the Catholic, God was a he) was an absolute ruler, while his Catholic counterpart offered, in the sacraments and the stress on a good life, a host of opportunities for negotiation. Deference, order and good behaviour seemed a small price to pay for divine charity and mercy, at least to those who extolled divine mercy and demanded human compliance.

These demands could, however, be pushed too far, and many individuals found themselves unable or unwilling to match the standards exhorted from them. This was a challenge to authority in the local worlds of parish and congregation, but, generally, had no wider political impact. Despite the concerns of ecclesiastical and lay authorities, the same was true of individual dissidents whose heretical views could lead to accusations of sedition, for example Lucrecia de Leon. Put on trial in Spain by the Inquisition in 1590, accused of heresy and sedition, she was seen by her supporters as a divinely inspired seer. Her dreams criticised the government of Philip II. In three dreams in 1588, she saw a seven-headed dragon – the seven deadly sins – breathing fire across Spain.[34]

The Long Reformation is an aspect of the early modern and, even more, *ancien régime* state that is often overlooked. The mutual impact of this Reformation and of the governmental system summarised as absolutism requires extensive research. A clue to its importance is provided by the partial unravelling seen during the second half of the eighteenth century. This was not primarily a consequence of the varied anti-authoritarian intellectual movements given a misleading coherence by the term Enlightenment, although they challenged clerical authority, attacked the Counter-Reformation pillars of the Inquisition, of the Index and the Jesuits, and pressed for religious toleration. Nor was what has been seen as a 'post-Tridentine syndrome', in which the papal government suffered from a growing loss of energy,[35] more generally true of the Catholic and Protestant established Churches of the period.

The unravelling was, instead, a matter of a new relationship between government and established Churches that, in some cases, involved governmental assaults on the Churches. (Protestant) secularisation and (Catholic) concordats in the early sixteenth century indicated that these were far from novel, but in the eighteenth century there were attacks on the very practice of religious indoctrination and the concept of Church–state identity, and, in their place, attempts to offer a reconceptualisation of goals and community. This process began with Peter the Great's Westernisation policies, which included limitations of Orthodox domination. The Spiritual Regulation, published in January 1721, was a crucial step in Russia, not least because it made the role of state-directed change apparent, and thus made all ecclesiastical arrangements appear tentative. The Church was put under the authority of a college, or ministry, although this body rapidly altered its title to 'Most Holy Governing Synod'. The Spiritual Regulation emphasised the Tsar's authority over the Synod, and thus the bureaucratisation of sacral authority was one that was still ultimately personal in character. Finally abolishing the Patriarchate in 1721, Peter played the major role in the appointment of bishops.[36]

A new relationship of Church and state was taken forward across much of Europe in the second half of the century, as religious toleration was accepted, if not encouraged, in many states, including Austria, France, Scotland and Russia, while many rulers markedly increased their power over established Churches. This was particularly the case in Catholic Europe, where a determined anti-papal offensive imbued with a regalist ideology gathered pace from the 1760s. In addition, the abolition of the Jesuit order by Pope Clement XIV in 1773 reflected determined pressure from a number of rulers, particularly those of Portugal, France, Spain and Naples, in each of which the order was suppressed before the papacy had abolished it. In Spain, where a concordat of 1753 had confirmed the crown's right of presentation of the bishops and most of the secular (non-monks/friars) clergy, royal control was extended under Charles III (r. 1759–88), with royal permission being required from 1762 in order for papal documents to be published, and religious institutions banned from acquiring more property from 1765.

This regalist ideology was not new, and did not require rationalisation by progressive intellectuals. Instead, there were more traditional themes, particularly of greater royal control over ecclesiastical resources and of resistance to papal (and other extra-territorial) jurisdiction. Thus Peter the Great's decision to leave the patriarchate vacant in 1700, and his revival, the following year, of the Monastery Department to run Church lands, were, at least in part, designed to help in the mobilisation of resources for the war with Sweden, which had began badly that year. The suppression of the Jesuits provided spoils for those who took part. Maria Theresa made huge loans to aristocrats from the money gained, while the order's chief house in Vienna became the seat of the War Department.

These attacks were more important than the undermining of Christian orthodoxy by scientific advances. The latter had posed challenges throughout the early modern period, with the Copernican system contesting the Ptolemaic, displacing the notion of Earth's stationary and central position, or the notion of atoms raising questions about eucharistic doctrines.[37] Although unsettling, these ideas did not, however, sap the faith of more than a few, not least because of the variety of Christian intellectual strategies and the corresponding ability to make human knowledge seem to serve divine purposes.

It is misleading to draw a direct line from the dismantling of the indoctrinating institutions and practices of the Counter-Reformation to the outbreak of the French Revolution, but the multiple ideological tensions of Catholic Europe in the 1770s and 1780s, particularly in the Habsburg lands, in part related to the dismantling of the confessional state. A similar strand can be seen within the British Empire in 1775–1801, as the authority of the Church of England and the nature of confessionalism were challenged, with an important recurrence in the 1820s as Catholic Emancipation was pushed through the political process.

Whether or not that is regarded as necessary and/or progressive in a late-eighteenth-century context, the consequences of this dismantling throw light on the earlier value of such a governmental culture. Thus the confessional state should be seen as a vital adjunct of absolutism. This provides a way to re-examine the role of confessionalism in both the international relations of the period *c*.1550–*c*.1760 and also in domestic politics. As, more generally, with the relationship between crowns and élites, it is necessary to treat the ideological and cultural dimensions of this issue seriously and on their own terms, and not simply to adopt a functional and instrumental account of the situation.

The oversight of the crucial issue of religious homogeneity was, like corruption, an aspect of a governmental culture and system for which the modern connotations of the term 'bureaucracy' are inappropriate. Administrative organisations, both lay and ecclesiastical, reflected the values and methods of the social system. Appointment and promotion generally resulted from social rank, patronage and inheritance, which, in combination, defined merit. There was little in the way of a distinct bureaucratic ethos. Concepts of fidelity and clientage, characteristic of the aristocratic social system, illuminated policy and provided much of the texture of administration. Petitions for pensions for French military officials, for example, referred to patrons, family service and fidelity to the minister and his predecessors, and of obligations, in return, for protection and assistance. Across Europe, officials sought promotion to the aristocracy, not its replacement as a medium of power. The habit of regarding office as property, whether purchased or not, was deeply ingrained.

Attempts to alter the situation met with only limited success. Appalled at the scale of Russian corruption, Peter the Great (r. 1689–1725) created a network of procurators in 1722, but their effectiveness was limited, not least because of their abuse of power, the shortage of qualified candidates, and the difficulties of the task, including the impracticality of creating a system separate to the networks of local power. Prussian administration in the late seventeenth and eighteenth centuries has been seen as a model of efficiency, but it was still greatly affected by patronage and relatively unresponsive to the wishes of rulers.

Indeed, it is pertinent to note the claim that 'the lack of a responsible civil service undermined the cause of kings',[38] while adding that it also served this cause by restricting the possibility of unpopular government initiatives. Nevertheless, especially from the seventeenth century, the incessant nature of international competition led not only to attempts to utilise the resources of society – a traditional objective – but also to a wish to understand those resources and to appreciate the wealth-creating nature of economic processes and social structures. Such an appreciation was seen as a basis for the pursuit of measures to increase wealth.

These attitudes are generally called mercantilist or cameralist, although these were not identical. To the mercantilists bullion constituted and was the measure of wealth, whereas for cameralists it was principally a medium of exchange. The pursuit of measures to increase wealth required planning, information and a notion of secular improvement: the capacity of, and need for, humans to better their condition on earth, and one that could be achieved through state action. The notion developed of the state as an initiator of legislative and administrative rules designed to improve society and increase its resources: the theory and practice of cameralism. These two goals were seen as directly linked. Some writers envisaged a central role for the state, represented by an absolute sovereign authority assisted by a corps of professionalised officials. In this theory, the state's legislative scope was universal, covering the mores of subjects as much as their economic activity, because the ability of a subject to participate in the latter was held to be dependent on the former. Thus the equation would be disciplined society, plentiful resources and a strong military.

These ideas indicate the degree to which eighteenth-century Enlightenment attitudes towards government and the purposes of the state were prefigured by, and, in large measure, based upon the goals and practices of what has been termed the 'well-ordered police state'. The Enlightenment has been seen as giving theoretical validation to goals that had been set by a 'revolution of political culture' in the seventeenth century.[39] These goals and practices, in turn, drew on the corpus of legislation passed by medieval towns: there was a continuity of regulation and planning.

However, it is important not to translate this too readily into an account of what happened. Indeed, throughout the period, there is a very clear gap between initiatives and legislation and, on the other hand, implementation and administrative and social practice. The creation of new administrative bodies did not end this contrast. For example, the Florentine Health Board was established on a permanent basis in 1527. It can appear as a major new adjunct to government, not least because, although initially created to respond to the plague, it had become, by the early seventeenth century, a more wide-ranging body for the maintenance of public health. The board dispatched physicians to examine particular epidemics and also sought to use systematically collected information, demanding in 1622 that local authorities report on the state of sanitation. This reflected the view that open privies, stagnant water, and the failure to remove human and animal waste were responsible for 'miasmas' in the air, thought to cause epidemics. However, neither the local authorities nor the people were ready to respond to the advice of the board. Policy-making in public health was not greatly carried forward in Tuscany during the sixteenth and seventeenth centuries.[40]

Efforts elsewhere to control the plague and other epidemics, for example in the French city of Bordeaux in the first half of the seventeenth century, were also generally unsuccessful. It was difficult to enforce quarantine regulations. Attempts to control prostitution also had little success. This was another sphere in which the focus of public action was urban and represented a continuation of medieval efforts to impose regulations. These attempts did not face opponents equivalent to the rats and other natural vectors of disease, but, similarly, they found it difficult to translate edicts into observance.

Whatever its limitations, the potential of government, particularly as a means to mobilise the resources of society in order to maximise the public welfare, however defined, was increasingly discussed and grasped from the seventeenth century. Pressure for stronger and more uniform administration clashed with traditional concepts of rulership as mediated through a governmental 'system' reflecting privileges and rights that were heavily influenced both by the social structure and by the habit of conceiving of administration primarily in terms of legal precedent, with the latter, in part, represented by Estates.

Rulers varied in their willingness to exchange the traditional foundations of royal authority in legal precedent and a particularist social order for a new conception of government. However, it is important neither to present too black-and-white a picture nor to overstate a clash or conflict between cameralism and traditional institutions and views; not least because it seems clear that cameralists sought to work through such institutions, while clashes generally arose from the customary royal demands for more funds. Rather than seeking to monopolise power, central governments co-opted subordinate institutions, which issued ordinances as well as implementing them. It is also pertinent to note that sovereignty is a problematic term, and that early modern European sovereignty, at once theoretically irresistible and limited at the same time, was different to the modern sense of the term.

Potentially, there was a clash between a mechanical/unitary/natural law concept of monarchy, and one that was traditional/sacral/corporate/confessional. But this did not become readily apparent until the mid-eighteenth century. Earlier, the former was very much in check, except, under Peter the Great, in Russia, where corporate and intermediate institutions were generally lacking. Instead, many of the reforms in early modern European government can best be understood as habitual responses to problems that focused on the attempt to make existing practices work better.

Government in the early modern period cannot any longer readily be discussed or explained in terms of modernisation, because the concept has ceased to be clear-cut. In particular, since the 1980s, there has been a reaction against public ownership, centralisation and state direction across much of the world. There have also been frequent calls for government to seek the assistance of 'pillars' of the local community, for example against crime. These 'community leaders' are not the descendants of the landed élite, but the analogy is instructive. As yet, these developments have not been fully incorporated into historical perspectives on earlier ages, but that is a fruitful approach that may well lead to sustained revisionism.

In the early modern period, the dominant note was the continuation of earlier practices of government and response with scant sense, particularly outside the circles of ministers, that they were redundant or could be replaced. This was a constant theme, to which particular distinctive movements, moments or periods of political and governmental activity were subordinate.

The emphasis here is instructive, not least because it deals with the more general question as to how far a particular generation in early modern Europe could alter the situation, and therefore addresses the issue of the scope of change. Thus, with the thesis of the Military Revolution, generally dated to *c*.1470–*c*.1660, there is the question of how far, in practice, it dramatically altered the legacy and continuing process of late medieval circumstances and development.[41] If there was, in fact, no new dramatic, or at least revolutionary, development in military capability to fund in this period, particularly (although not only) in the span of one generation, this has important implications for our understanding of early modern European government as a whole.

More generally, analysis of the relationship between early modern changes and long-term tendencies is a useful tool that can also be directly applied to the questions of government. In the case of absolutism, it is possible to emphasise the role of new ideas about authority and government in ministerial circles, not least those that sought to define new theories of the purposes, roles and rights of the state and to abstract it from inherited legalistic suppositions. It is also possible to stress the pressing need to fund warfare and the impact this had on rulers coping with heavy levels of indebtedness. Military preparations and, even more, the resort to war made it unacceptable to cope with the financial situation by shifts and expedients. Instead, there was pressure to tap new sources of capital, income and credit. Yet both of these theories have to take due note of the extent to which the power of the landed aristocracy continued to establish the contours of government.[42] Furthermore, the emphasis, in much of the work on social history, on the strength of family and kinship underlines the continued political importance of patronage.

It is also possible to shift the focus of attention by moving from the social politics and government by clientage seen in settled regions with relatively clear allegiance, and, instead, consider the related issues of government in regions whose allegiance was less clear, and the imposition of authority in them. The 'state', again, has an ambivalent role, as in this case it can be employed, functionally, to include the landed orders and other groups with influence, such as the Church. These groups could all pull in the same direction, but, in other instances, the authority of the ruler was challenged most clearly by these very groups.

Frontier zones were far more widespread than in modern Europe, due not only to the number of polities, but also to the range and number of jurisdictions. The latter helped to make precise mapping difficult, and this, in turn, ensured that frontiers were understood as zones rather than in linear terms. Frontier zones provided particular cover for often large-scale brigandage. The financial and judicial authority of rulers was rejected and their agents ignored, intimidated or challenged. Banditry and feuding were not easy to suppress. In Italy, for example in Lombardy and the Veneto, there was a rise in violence and a revival of feuds at the close of the sixteenth century. Brigandage, frequently associated with the social élite, remained a marked feature of Sicilian society. In the kingdom of Aragon, there were serious feuds, including that in the 1570s and 1580s between the Count of Chinchón, a leading minister, and the Duke of Villahermosa, the most prominent noble. This struggle encompassed rivalry at court and fighting in the localities, a reminder that patronage links did not always serve the causes of peace and authority. At the same time, feuds could serve to foster royal or princely authority, with aristocratic officials serving (at least ostensibly) the interests of their rulers, as well as their own goals, when they engaged in feuds.[43] Like duels, feuds reflected the potency of honour as a motive for aristocratic conduct.[44]

The economic downturn of the early seventeenth century, which was general throughout Europe, put additional strain on nobilities, as indeed on most of the community, encouraging aristocratic lawlessness. However, the extent of this was, in part, lessened by the series of international conflicts that began in 1618. They provided employment for aristocratic energies. It would be easy to present this as another instance of the rise of the state understood as a product of crown–élite co-operation. In part, the armies and navies of the period indeed reflected just such a co-operation, but, in the Thirty Years' War (1618–48), the extent to which military entrepreneurs followed their own views and made their own terms encourages caution about any simple links between war, state formation and crown–élite cohesion. Furthermore, although fictional, the representation of the commission of array at work in Shakespeare's *Henry IV Part II*, involving Bullcalf, and so on,[45] was not a depiction of a well-oiled administration.

In the closing decades of the seventeenth century, this relationship between war, state formation and crown–élite cohesion appears more clear-cut, not least as leading rulers increased the size of their armies, while minor rulers, particularly in Germany, raised permanent forces of their own. Both thus provided a focus for aristocratic loyalty and honourable service, at the same time as the development of the notion of rank based on service, for example in 1671 in Denmark (where the obligation on nobles to provide soldiers ended in 1679)[46] furthered this process.

This socio-institutional change – rulers and élite joined in larger armies – was more important than the technological development represented by gunpowder weaponry. The latter has traditionally been seen as an adjunct of the stronger state – all those cannon battering down castle walls – but the position was considerably more complex. Developments in technology were mediated through existing social and political structures, such that, in some areas, they contributed to a strengthening of the authority of the ruler; in others, to its lessening, and, in the majority, to the need for the partnership between rulers and élite to confront new challenges.

The ambiguous impact of military developments was not restricted to Christian Europe. In Morocco, they helped enable the Sa'adian rulers to further the process of state consolidation – against domestic and international competitors – but also provided potent weaponry for subjects to use when defying authority.[47]

The same was true for Europe, in that, in the late sixteenth century, both the Dutch Revolt and the French Wars of Religion showed how new military techniques (weapons, fortifications, tactics, training) could be used to help resist royal authority. A variety of political and military problems (not least the burdens of war finance and other commitments) helped ensure that Philip II and Philip III were unable to suppress the revolt in the northern provinces of the Low Countries, while, in France, Charles IX, Henry III and Henry IV, although the last was more successful, particularly against the Huguenots, had to accept compromise terms at the conclusion of successive conflicts. These problems included the advantage the defence gained by advances in fortification. Major fortresses could still be taken, as was Antwerp spectacularly by the Spanish Army of Flanders in 1585, and Amiens by Henry IV in 1597, but the resources and time required to mount successful sieges, and even assaults, placed a heavy burden on states. Indeed, the Huguenot stronghold of La Rochelle was not captured until 1628.

That was an important date that marked the shift towards a situation in which military developments worked to the advantage of states, understood as central governments, but, to be stable, as England showed in 1655–60, this had to be with the co-operation of the landed interest. To gain Paris in 1594, Henry IV famously had had to embrace Catholicism the previous year, and this was a public act, not a mere matter of private conscience.

It would be a mistakenly instrumental approach to see a tipping point towards state power as stemming from military developments, whether the cannon of the 'Renaissance monarchies', or the new-model Dutch and Swedish forces of Michael Roberts's century of military revolution (1560–1660), however much its dates have been adjusted by subsequent scholarship. Instead, military developments worked to the advantage of states, generally, only if it was possible to win local co-operation and, generally, only in the absence of sustained external intervention. The fall of La Rochelle can be combined with the fate of other cities, including the inability of both the Catholic League and, later, the *Frondeurs* to retain Paris, of rebels against Philip IV of Spain to retain Messina, Naples and Palermo, and of opponents of the republican government of Commonwealth England to retain Edinburgh, Wexford and Drogheda. Each case, however, was different, and, in all bar the last, it would be dangerous to abstract the military dimension and attribute success largely to military capability.

The raising of armies can be seen as lessening the need for nobles to turn to banditry. Furthermore, frontier zones, such as the Volga valley, the Western Isles of Scotland, and Ulster,[48] were brought under government control, particularly with the suppression of rebellions, although also as a result of longer-term social, political and economic developments. Looked at differently, the 'psychic space' of areas where central government had been weak increasingly had to encompass royal authority as an aspect of the arbitration of worth and honour,[49] although this was more an issue for nobles than for villagers.

Banditry remained a common feature in many rural regions of Europe, including Apulia, Calabria, Sicily and Jülich.[50] Troops were used for many policing purposes, particularly in rural and frontier areas, where police forces were generally weak and the task of maintaining order difficult, even without attempting the harder problem of enforcing law on a systematic basis. The violence involved in some policing, and the size of possible problems, encouraged the use of troops. The British, French and others used troops against smugglers, for example France in Dauphiné in the early 1730s and on Belle Île off Brittany in 1764.

This was not, however, an easy solution, for, in the absence of local support, troops could achieve relatively little. Officials in the French border province of Roussillon found little support for their struggle with smugglers in the early 1770s, and the army argued that local complicity made it impossible to pursue bands in the interior of the province. This was not simply a frontier problem. Piedmont has been seen as endemically lawless, until the experience of Napoleonic rule in 1801–14 brought a new attitude and a new gendarmerie.[51]

Throughout the early modern period, force was used in some frontier areas in order to establish, enforce and strengthen sovereign control. In 1763, Tillot, the leading minister in the Duchy of Parma, organised a small expedition against Mezzano, an episcopal fief whose population resisted integration with the duchy. In 1767–68, he took similar police measures over the Corti di Monchio, a mountainous region on the Parmesan–Tuscan frontier, where the privileges and immunities of the local ecclesiastical lord had also created difficulties. Like other frontier regions, this one contained many deserters and smugglers.

The role of force and the prevalence of brutality in securing control serves as a suggestion of the more generally conditional character of obedience and deference. The importance of this rises the more the emphasis is placed on ideological factors when explaining stability and control. It is necessary to emphasise that a degree of disorder and disobedience is to be expected in any state, but, allowing for that, the extensive character of brigandage and of other, sometimes related, aspects of disobedience, for example smuggling, is worthy of note. It can be seen as another dimension of a fundamental political process, that of presenting grievances for redress, with the grievances, in these cases, seen as regulations that were to be circumvented by those who felt that their own actions were crucial to gaining redress. The role of popular attitudes is further highlighted by the situation in countries, such as Tudor and Stuart England, where the rise in litigation testified to a public willingness to turn to the state in order to seek arbitration of their disputes. In such instances, there appears to have been a powerful sense that community pressure needed to be complemented by the authority of the law.[52]

The use of force to help ensure control in frontier areas was taken further in the 1790s as the successive governments of Revolutionary France sought to suppress opposition. The Jacobins by 1794 also sought to purge the language of regional *patois*. The divisiveness of France's linguistic inheritance was seen as a source of weakness in the patriot project.[53]

Alongside discussion of aristocratic military service or banditry in the early modern period in structural terms, it is also pertinent to note both the importance of particular conjunctures – both geographical and temporal – and the extent to which the aristocracy was not a homogenous bloc. However much they might be articulated by marital links, patronage and other factors, such as provincial identity, there was also tension within nobilities. These had a variety of causes and forms, including rivalries between factional groups, between old and new nobles, between nobles from particular areas, and between the wealthy and the less affluent. These rivalries provided much of the content and dynamic of politics, and created problems as well as opportunities for rulers. This can be seen in France with tensions between the nobility of the sword and that of the robe.

The same was true in England, where there was a shift of emphasis in politics in the late sixteenth century away from a focus on relations between crown and aristocracy, and, instead, towards relations between crown and gentry. At the centre, although the royal court remained the major focus of politics and society, this led to a greater (albeit grudging) role for Parliament and a stress on ideas of representation, and, in the localities, to the growing importance of the gentry, not least as justices of the peace. The rise in England of a more numerous and independent gentry, with a sense and obligation of public duty focused at the national level, was linked to the failure of the peerage to be the prime beneficiary of the socio-political changes of the period. This had been unclear in the years of 'mid-sixteenth-century crisis' arising from the minority of Edward VI, the succession of Mary, and the uncertainty of the early years of Elizabeth, years in which 'a polity built on the foundation of personal and dynamic monarchy' had to cope with its absence or limitations.[54] In the event, the creation of stronger crown links with this gentry was fundamental to the achievement of the Elizabethan period and was demonstrated on royal progresses, although the troubled politics of the 1590s indicated that this could not prevent serious problems.[55]

The emphasis on Parliament and the gentry under Elizabeth I (r. 1558–1603) contrasted markedly with the earlier situation in England, particularly in the second half of the fifteenth century, where politics was far more arranged in terms of aristocratic clientage systems, and contrasted also with that in contemporary France and Spain where such systems remained powerful. Most of the continental states did not witness such linkages with the gentry or lesser nobility until the major expansion of standing armies from the late seventeenth century, although earlier episodes when military service was combined with religious homogeneity, for example Spain under Philip II and Sweden under Gustavus Adolphus (r. 1611–32), provided opportunities for such linkages.

It is necessary throughout to qualify general remarks, many of which have a schematic character, by drawing attention to the limited nature of the scholarly coverage of many topics and, moreover, the extent to which work on those that have been covered has been subject to debate, with the clear implication that other topics that have been tackled are ripe for re-examination. This can be seen by considering a crucial moment of constitutional power and display in France, the *lit de justice*, the occasion on which the king made a ceremonial visit to the *Parlement* of Paris. In 1983, an important work argued that the importance of the medieval *lit de justice* had been exaggerated by Jean du Tillet, Chief Clerk to the *Parlement* from 1530 to 1570, this corresponding to a more general search for the authentication and authority of age. Instead, it was claimed that the *lit de justice* became important only from 1537, while it was from 1597 that it became the occasion when the monarch (initially, Henry IV) enforced the registration of controversial legislation. Thus the *lit de justice* was a consequence of Renaissance monarchy, creating a distinctive early modern constitutional arrangement focused on greater royal power and with the monarch taking the initiative.[56]

More recent scholarship, however, has argued for more consistency with medieval roots, certainly from the 1320s, including a positive re-evaluation of Jean de Tillet's account. Instead, the emphasis has been on differing political contexts. In place of an occasion when monarch and *Parlement* co-operated, the *lit de justice* came to play a different role in a more tense, if not adversarial, situation from the Wars of Religion of the late sixteenth century.[57]

This issue indicates the problems of discussing chronological change and, more specifically, of assessing what is to be analysed. The extent to which constitutional forms and ideas were moulded by political needs and circumstances directs attention not only to the difficulty of establishing patterns of cause and effect, but also to the questions of what extent and why the early modern period should be seen as different to that of the fourteenth and fifteenth centuries.[58] This question is not restricted to political issues. Similarly, for example, the transformation of rural society in Eastern

Europe towards a 'second serfdom', with heavy labour services provided by the peasantry, can be seen as a response to the commercial opportunities of early modern grain export to other parts of Europe, but appears also to have been, at least, prefigured by fifteenth-century changes, as lords, who had gained private possession of public jurisdictions, responded to the economic problems of the late medieval period, particularly fixed cash incomes.[59]

Other economic trends that were of long duration included the spread of the money economy, with an increasing emphasis on the use of coins for transactions such as rent, instead of the provision of food or services. In Eastern Europe, the 'second serfdom' held back this trend, but it was pronounced in the rural economy of Western Europe, and was particularly important to the world of towns and markets. This made the entire economy more responsive to changes, such as inflation and deflation, and accentuated the social impact of such developments.

Again, the 'Long Reformation' of the early modern period can be seen as another stage in the long-term project of Christianisation, with a more specific clear parallel to the attempt following the Fourth Lateran Council in 1215 to disseminate the Christian faith and way of life and to ensure uniformity in both, while popular movements for reform and renewal were also prefigured. These continuities were readily apparent to contemporaries, and were given added force by the longevity of most Catholic institutions. In France, the crusade against the heretical Albigensians in the early thirteenth century was employed as an example, in the late sixteenth century, by Catholics arguing the case against religious pluralism.

There are many other examples of continuity. For example, there are few signs that attitudes towards women's role in society changed greatly, and this was an important aspect of a patriarchal, male-centred society that took inequality and hierarchy for granted, and was also reverential of age. The Christian moral code continued to be the basis of social and legal injunctions, with an emphasis on monogamy, heterosexuality and birth within marriage, and with the force of legal prohibitions added to denunciations of those who did not abide by the code.

In political terms, there was also much continuity with medieval circumstances. Opposition to the hegemonic pretensions of the Emperor, both within and outside the Empire, was scarcely new. Furthermore, attempts by territorial rulers to enhance their authority and power at the expense of other bodies were long-standing. Moreover, the claim of the state to a monopoly of war was not new.

A more systematic attempt to integrate late medieval developments with those of the early modern period is required before the novelty of the latter can be boldly asserted. This is not simply a matter of considering continuity between say the fifteenth and the sixteenth centuries, but also one of asking how far the sixteenth century can be seen in terms of a resumption of

European development after the long demographic, political and psychological crisis stemming from the crises of the fourteenth century, of which the Black Death was only the most prominent. Thus the so-called new or Renaissance monarchies of the late fifteenth and early sixteenth centuries can be seen as another stage in a long-term development of order and public authority; not identical with, but similar to, thirteenth-century monarchies.

This perspective can be extended by treating the varied crises of the seventeenth century, and, in particular, the protracted end to population growth, as a return to the fourteenth century. Comparisons can, of course, be made too easily. There were, for example, important differences between the problems Charles I of England encountered with Parliament in the late 1620s and the early 1640s and those faced by Richard II (r. 1377–99). But, at the same time, a consideration of the sixteenth and seventeenth centuries, at least in part, in terms of a longer cycle of growth and decline, not only helps us recover the perspective of most contemporary commentators, and appreciate their frequent reference to past examples, but also captures an important truth about the limitations of the notion of change simply in one direction.

This is an important revisionist perspective. So also is the emphasis on co-operation: co-operation, *not* consensus. The latter is pressed by some scholars who term themselves revisionists, but it is a description that gives less than due weight both to what was often an inherently problematic relationship between rulers, élites and subjects, and to the extent of internal disorder in the period. In place of a choice between consensus and conflict, it is helpful to emphasise compromise and the way in which more or less lasting compromises solved or lessened disputes between rulers, élites and local communities.

These compromises were provisional but some became the basis not only for a degree of stabilisation, but also for organisational development. The latter was the case in early modern Europe, but became even more so in the nineteenth and twentieth centuries. Prior to the late nineteenth century, much of Europe was an agricultural society in which organisations (including, but not only, governments) could directly involve only a small minority of the population; although some militaries employed several per cent of the male population, while the Churches provided a comprehensive structure and an ideology that elicited much activity and support.

Notes

1. C. Durston, *Cromwell's Major-Generals: Godly Government During the English Revolution* (Manchester, 2001).

2. J.-C. Waquet, *Corruption. Ethics and Power in Florence, 1600–1770* (Oxford, 1991), p. 96.

3. W. Beik, *Absolutism and Society in Seventeenth-Century France. State Power and Provincial Aristocracy in Languedoc* (Cambridge, 1986); J. Bergin, *Cardinal Richelieu: Power and the Pursuit of Wealth* (New Haven, CT, 1985).

4. Waquet, *Corruption*, p. 143. For another example, L. L. Peck, *Court Patronage and Corruption in Early Stuart England* (1990).

5. J. K. Brackett, *Criminal Justice and Crime in Late Renaissance Florence, 1537–1609* (Cambridge, 1992); G. Benadusi, *A Provincial Élite in Early Modern Tuscany. Family and Power in the Creation of the State* (Baltimore, MD, 1996).

6. D. Potter, *War and Government in the French Provinces: Picardy, 1470–1560* (Cambridge, 1993).

7. R. H. Hilton, *English and French Towns in Feudal Society: A Comparative Study* (Cambridge, 1995).

8. J. B. Collins, *Fiscal Limits of Absolutism: Direct Taxation in Seventeenth-Century France* (Berkeley, CA, 1988) and *The State in Early Modern France* (Cambridge, 1995). With reference to recruitment in Castile in the 1630s, R. Mackay, *The Limits of Royal Authority. Resistance and Obedience in Seventeenth-Century Castile* (Cambridge, 1999).

9. B. Mundy, *The Mapping of New Spain: Indigenous Cartography and the Maps of the Relaciones Geograficas* (Chicago, IL, 1996).

10. H. M. Scott (ed.), *The European Nobilities in the Seventeenth and Eighteenth Centuries* (2 vols, 1995); J. Dewald, *The European Nobility, 1400–1800* (Cambridge, 1996).

11. B. Meehan-Waters, *Autocracy and Aristocracy: The Russian Service Élite of 1730* (New Brunswick, NJ, 1982); L. Hughes, *Peter the Great* (New Haven, CT, 2002), pp. 165–7.

12. R. R. Harding, *Anatomy of a Power Élite. The Provincial Governors of Early Modern France* (New Haven, CT, 1978); D. J. Sturdy, *Louis XIV* (Basingstoke, 2000), pp. 46–9.

13. G. T. Matthews, *The Royal-General Farms in Eighteenth Century France* (1958).

14. W. Hubatsch, *Frederick the Great of Prussia: Absolutism and Administration* (1973); C. B. A. Behrens, *Society, Government and the Enlightenment: The Experiences of Eighteenth-Century France and Prussia* (1985); D. McKay, *The Great Elector* (Harlow, 2001).

15. M. C.'t Hart, *The Making of a Bourgeois State. War, Politics and Finance During the Dutch Revolt* (Manchester, 1993).

16. W. Doyle, *Venality. The Sale of Offices in Eighteenth-Century France* (Oxford, 1996). For England, where venality was less important, G. E. Aylmer, *The Crown's Servants. Government and Civil Service Under Charles II, 1660–1685* (Oxford, 2002), pp. 87–92.

17. London, Public Record Office 30/29/3/1 fol. 15.

18. For the background, W. M. Spellman, *European Political Thought 1600–1700* (Basingstoke, 1998).

19. J. H. Elliott, *Richelieu and Olivares* (Cambridge, 1991); J. M. Elliott and L. W. B. Brockliss (eds), *The World of the Favourite* (New Haven, CT, 1999); A. Feros, *Kingship and Favoritism in the Spain of Philip III, 1598–1621* (Cambridge, MA, 2000).

20. M. A. R. Graves, *The Parliaments of Early Modern Europe* (Harlow, 2001).

21. C. Storrs, *War, Diplomacy and the Rise of Savoy, 1692–1720* (Cambridge, 2000), p. 312.

22. G. Barta et al. (eds), *History of Transylvania* (Budapest, 1994), pp. 293–4.

23. The best introduction to the reign is H. Kamen, *Philip II of Spain* (New Haven, CT, 1997).

24. T. J. Dandelet, *Spanish Rome 1500–1700* (New Haven, CT, 2001), pp. 217–18.

25. R. J. W. Evans, *The Making of the Habsburg Monarchy 1550–1700* (Oxford, 1979).

26. R. N. Swanson, *Religion and Devotion in Europe, c.1215–c.1515* (Cambridge, 1995).

27. H. Kamen, *The Phoenix and the Flame. Catalonia and the Counter Reformation* (New Haven, CT, 1993); M. A. Mullett, *The Catholic Reformation* (1999).

28. C. Williams, *The French Oratorians and Absolutism, 1611–1641* (New York, 1988).

29. A. Calabria and J. A. Marino (eds), *Good Government in Spanish Naples* (New York, 1990).

30. S. Haliczer, *Inquisition and Society in the Kingdom of Valencia 1478–1834* (Berkeley, CA, 1990). See, more generally, J. Edwards, *The Spanish Inquisition* (Stroud, 1999).

31. W. Monter, *Frontiers of Heresy. The Spanish Inquisition from the Basque Lands to Sicily* (Cambridge, 1990).

32. Stephen Fox to Henry Fox, 2 July 1729, BL. Add. 51417 fol. 24.

33. H. Watanabe-O'Kelly, *Court Culture in Dresden. From Renaissance to Baroque* (Basingstoke, 2002), pp. 20–1; January 1700, Creed journal, private collection.

34. R. Kagan, *Lucrecia's Dreams. Politics and Prophecy in Sixteenth-Century Spain* (Berkeley, CA, 1990).

35. H. Gross, *Rome in the Age of Enlightenment. The Post-Tridentine Syndrome and the Ancien Regime* (Cambridge, 1990).

36. J. Cracraft, *The Church of Peter the Great* (Stanford, CA, 1971).

37. P. Redondi, *Galileo: Heretic* (1989).

38. A. Calabria, *The Cost of Empire. The Finances of the Kingdom of Naples in the Time of Spanish Rule* (Cambridge, 1991), p. 132.

39. M. Raeff, *The Well-Ordered Police State: Social and Institutional Change through Law in the Germanies and Russia, 1600–1800* (New Haven, CT, 1983).

40. C. M. Cipolla, *Miasmas and Disease. Public Health and the Environment in the Pre-Industrial Age* (New Haven, CT, 1992).

41. See, for example, G. Phillips, *The Anglo-Scots Wars 1513–1550* (Woodbridge, 1999).

42. J. Miller (ed.), *Absolutism in Seventeenth-Century Europe* (1990).

43. H. Zmora, *State and Nobility in Early Modern Germany. The Knightly Feud in Franconia, 1450–1567* (Cambridge, 1997).

44. V. G. Kiernan, *The Duel in European History. Honour and the Reign of Aristocracy* (Oxford, 1989).

45. *Henry IV Part II* (III, ii), first performed probably in 1598.

46. K. J. V. Jespersen, 'Social Change and Military Revolution in Early Modern Europe: Some Danish Evidence', *Historical Journal*, 26 (1983), pp. 4–13.

47. W. F. Cook, *The Hundred Years War for Morocco. Gunpowder and the Military Revolution in the Early Modern Muslim World* (Boulder, CO, 1994).

48. J. M. Hill, *Fire and Sword. Sorley Boy MacDonnell and the Rise of Clan Ian Mor 1538–90* (1993). For a more benign spread of control, L. Wolff, *Venice and the Slavs. The Discovery of Dalmatia in the Age of the Enlightenment* (Stanford, CA, 2001).

49. M. Greenshield, *An Economy of Violence in Early Modern France: Crime and Justice in the Haute Auvergne, 1587–1664* (University Park, Pennsylvania, 1995).

50. U. Danker, 'Bandits and the state: robbers and the authorities in the Holy Roman Empire', in R. J. Evans (ed.), *The German Underworld* (1988), pp. 75–107.

51. M. Broers, *Napoleonic Imperialism and the Savoyard Monarchy, 1733–1821. State Building in Piedmont* (Lewiston, NY, 1997).

52. C. Muldrew, 'The culture of reconciliation: community and the settlement of economic disputes in early modern England', *Historical Journal*, 39 (1996), pp. 939–41.

53. D. A. Bell, *The Cult of the Nation in France. Inventing Nationalism, 1680–1800* (Cambridge, MA, 2001), p. 175. For another area where language was linked to identity, M. Stoyle, *West Britons: Cornish Identities and the Early Modern British State* (Exeter, 2002), p. 14.

54. S. Alford, *Kingship and Politics in the Reign of Edward VI* (Cambridge, 2002), pp. 203–6.

55. J. Guy (ed.), *The Reign of Elizabeth I: Court and Culture in the Last Decade* (Cambridge, 1995).

56. S. Hanley, *The Lit de Justice of the Kings of France: Constitutional Ideology in Legend, Ritual and Discourse* (Princeton, NJ, 1983).

57. E. A. R. Brown and R. C. Famiglietti, *The Lit de Justice: Semantics, Ceremonial and the Parlement of Paris 1300–1600* (Sigmaringen, 1994).

58. For an important argument for continuity, H. Zmora, *Monarchy, Aristocracy, and the State in Europe, 1300–1800* (2001).

59. R. C. Hoffmann, *Land, Liberties, and Lordship in a Late Medieval Countryside. Agrarian Structures and Change in the Duchy of Wroclaw* (Philadelphia, PA, 1989).

CHAPTER 3

A States System?

§ ANOTHER explanation of modernisation is that of a competitive states system. This argument would suggest that, although regimes might seek a continuation of traditional methods of government, the pressures of participating in a competitive states system, specifically of maintaining substantial armed forces and engaging in war, were such that change was forced on them. Frequent warfare is seen as the consequence of the multipolar nature of European statehood: as both cause and product of this multipolarity. In contrast, there were fewer states (particularly in ratio to population) in East, South and South-West Asia.

Linked to this is a Darwinian notion that international competition registered the strengths and weaknesses of particular governmental forms and ensured that the weakest were destroyed, while it also provided much of the pressure on both governments and people that lay behind specific political events. Thus the extensive warfare of the period from 1618 to 1660 can be presented as testing the political systems and social stability of European states, leading, in part, to the successive crises of the 1640s and 1650s that are, together, referred to as the mid-seventeenth-century crisis.

This analysis tends to have a teleological dimension, not that this is necessary. There is a focus on the development of unitary (rather than composite) states. These apparently represented, particularly to nineteenth-century writers imbued with the values and perspectives of nationalism, not only the future, but also the present, understood as the states best able to survive in the highly competitive international relations of the period.

Such an analysis has been pushed harder in recent years as the role of war in state development has been stressed, both in detailed scholarship and by generalists, such as Charles Tilly, while the role of international competition in comparative state development has been profitably emphasised by political scientists, such as Brian Downing and Thomas Ertman.[1] The interaction between geopolitics, war and state formation has been seen as crucial. It offers not only an account of the play of contingency, but also an explanatory model that apparently can differentiate between the differing fate of types of states and particular polities, as well as a political *longue durée* (long term) that replaces that of economics in accounting for developments and, indeed, for the very process of state evolution.

This approach addresses the question of the competitive advantage of respective states and governmental systems. This issue was of concern to contemporaries, as in comparisons of seventeenth-century England and the United Provinces, or of Britain and France in the eighteenth century. Consideration of the advantage of particular governmental systems played a role in discussion of the early American constitution and of the revolutionary Polish constitution of 1791. The typology of statehood can also be discussed by modern commentators in terms of relative success, inviting an exposition that is teleological. Such an exposition focuses on the mobilisation of resources for conflict and for military preparedness, an image that draws on a modern military vocabulary.

This mobilisation has been seen as central to success in international relations and, indeed, in the case of Poland, which was partitioned out of independent existence in 1772–95, to a failure to survive. In this analysis, politics is designed to serve war; and the effectiveness of political structures is measured by the size of armies and navies. The 1791 Polish constitution provided for an army of 100,000 men, a force that would have helped Poland to preserve its independence. In contrast, after the old constitution was re-imposed under Russian pressure, the army was reduced to 15,000 men, a tiny army by contemporary standards.

Russian military capability repeatedly had a crucial impact on Polish developments, and this has been seen as demonstrating that states lacking a highly centralised and ultimately repressive form of government survived on the military sufferance of those under such a rule.[2] In 1755 Frederick II 'the Great' (r. 1740–86) replied to a suggestion from his ally France that Augustus III of Saxony-Poland (r. 1733–63) be encouraged to prevent the possible movement of Russian troops through Poland in order to attack Prussia, by arguing that the Poles would be able to resist for a fortnight only, that they would fail, and that the consequence would be the ruin of the state.[3] Frederick II's concern about Russia was a clear instance of the response to the practicalities of power. Like his father, Frederick William I (r. 1713–40), Frederick II was prepared to defy Russia, but, in general, Prussia's concern encouraged caution.

This was an aspect of the hegemony that Russia managed to win in Eastern Europe. Indeed, it would be misleading to contrast European international relations with those elsewhere and imply that the multipolarity resulting from numerous independent states in Europe was completely different to the hegemonic systems in East and South-East Asia stemming from the power of China and Mughal India respectively. Instead, in early modern Europe, as earlier, there was a tension caused by the attempts of some rulers to gain a hegemonic position. This continued until the defeat of Napoleon in 1812–15, after which there was no such hegemony within Europe during the nineteenth century. In Eastern Europe, however, Russia continued to enjoy the hegemony created by its earlier absorption of Ukraine, Lithuania and much of Poland, and its defeat of Sweden and the Ottoman Empire. This hegemony, created in 1708–74, although stemming from longer-term international and domestic developments, lasted until the early 1990s, albeit with serious interruptions in 1917–20 and 1941–44.

In analyses focusing on the relationship between state-building and war, success in either was seen as mutually reinforcing, while, conversely, external pressure interacted with internal division. Far from eighteenth-century Poland being a united but vulnerable victim, Russian ends were furthered by divisions among the Poles and by their willingness to seek external assistance. In 1754 Frederick II noted that the divisions were incessant, and had such an impact that it was unnecessary for him to intervene through bribery in order to prevent possibly unwelcome steps from a forthcoming Diet.[4]

There is in fact a latent politicisation in much of this analysis, with debate, dissension and the division of power being associated with weakness. As with the case of privatised government functions discussed in the previous chapter, this assumption can be questioned in terms of modern understandings of contemporary political effectiveness and success. Furthermore, in the early modern period, the notion of progress was politicised for contemporaries, and it is important not to lose sight of this in modern discussion. In the case of the United Provinces (modern Netherlands), for example, was political progress in the seventeenth and eighteenth centuries to be associated with a more centralised state and/or with the domination of the House of Orange, and how far was it advanced or compromised by particular domestic and foreign policy strategies?

This is an appropriate example because the United Provinces lacked the strong centralised institutions and sense of national identity that were subsequently to be regarded as necessary, but was still a major power capable of deploying a large army and, in 1590–1713, of playing an effective role, successively, against Spain, England and France. The relationship between the federal, decentralised character of Dutch politics, the strength of mercantile and entrepreneurial elements and ethos, and the strong commercial economy which helped the republic sustain a large long-term public debt, was a dynamic one.[5]

Politically, the United Provinces was unstable with important rivalries between and within provinces, and major differences over policy. However, the existence of a federal structure, while giving these rivalries the continuity of institutional form, also made it possible to run a pluralistic political system.[6] This contributed to the contemporary debate about the value of republicanism as a form of government.[7] Like Poland, the elective quality of Dutch government helped to ensure that the problem of minister-favourites was uncommon.

Again like Poland, religious toleration was encouraged in the United Provinces. It gave a particular character to Dutch society, especially in the towns, and was also valuable as a means to draw on different economic and financial networks, particularly those of European Jewry. Toleration also made it easier to retain control over areas conquered from Spain, from 1590, that had a Catholic majority.

However, at times, tensions in the United Provinces reached a point where violent solutions were sought or followed. In 1618, disagreements between the *Stadtholder* (governor) of five of the provinces, Maurice of Nassau, Prince of Orange, who was also Captain-General of the army, and the Grand Pensionary of the States of Holland, Jan van Oldenbarneveldt, focused on the states' attempt to raise their own militia, although religious differences over Calvinist orthodoxy also played a role. Oldenbarneveldt was executed for treason in 1619. In 1650, control over the army and its size were central issues in a dispute between Maurice's nephew, William II, and the States of Holland. William responded to the states' attempt to demobilize regiments after the end of the Thirty Years' War by trying to seize Amsterdam, only to fail and, soon after, die. In 1672, however, violent mobs helped lead the Orangists to power in Holland. Whether three episodes of violent political crisis in a century, all of which were short-term, should be regarded as a sign of weakness or, rather, as one of the strengths of Dutch political life, is open to debate.[8]

A similar point can be made about the Holy Roman Empire. This was long treated as an anachronism. This was the tradition encouraged by German nationalist scholars from the nineteenth century and it reflected both the apparent failure of the Empire to resist French expansionism and the sense that a continued Austrian/Habsburg role in Germany through the Empire and the status of successive Habsburg rulers of Austria as Emperor was redundant, not only because it was unsuccessful but also because other forms of state development were progressive. This argument appeared to receive backing from the confessional division of Germany in the sixteenth century, and its culmination in the Thirty Years' War (1618–48). This conflict led to a serious devastation of much of Germany that later served as a demonstration of the apparent failure of the Empire. The devastation was the work of both German and foreign forces, and could therefore be used to criticise the Empire on both heads, first for failing to prevent conflict between German rulers, and, second, for not stopping foreign invaders who captured leading German cities in an unprecedented fashion: in 1631, Gustavus Adolphus of Sweden took Mainz, following this with Munich in 1632. Swedish forces continued to operate deep into Germany until the end of the war. In the 1640s, French and Swedish forces both campaigned in southern Germany. Devastation stemmed in large part from the weakness of contemporary logistics, and the consequent need for armies to live off the land. This also encouraged devastation as a means to deny resources to opponents.

Subsequently, it was also argued, the Westphalian peace settlement that ended the war in 1648 kept Germany weak and a prey to external attack, particularly by allowing territorial rulers to ally with foreign powers, as in the French-backed League of the Rhine in the 1650s. In addition, the Empire's internal constitutional structures were presented as anachronistic, involving archaic legal cases, rather than effective decision-making. In this approach, the four Austro-Prussian wars between 1740 and 1779 (1740–42, 1744–45, 1756–63, 1778–79) exposed the fundamental weakness of the Empire, and its eventual destruction by Napoleon was both long overdue and a fundamental stage in the evolution of a modern Germany.

All the above suppositions have been questioned by recent scholarship. In place of an emphasis on confessional division has come a stress on the ability of the Empire's federal structure to cope with many of the resulting difficulties. Indeed, conflict within the Empire between 1555 and 1618, particularly prior to 1600, was less, and less serious in its consequences, than conflict in that period in France, the Low Countries or the British Isles.

Clearly this was not the case with the Thirty Years' War, but it would be misleading to attribute all the problems of 1618–48 to the imperial constitution and German politics. Both were at issue, but, from the outset, the crisis owed much to the intervention of outside powers, particularly Spain, the United Provinces, Denmark, Sweden and, most decisively for protracting the struggle, France, officially in 1635, although earlier in practice.[9] This intervention can be seen as the consequence of the failure of the imperial system, but that is a case that cannot also be made for other states that suffered external intervention, including France repeatedly during the Wars of Religion, particularly from Spain in the 1590s, and Britain in 1688. In all these cases, there was a readiness on the part of at least some prominent members of the élite to seek external support, combined with the problem that this was offered on unwelcome terms. Thus the Dutch lent support to German Protestant co-religionists, but also saw north-west Germany as a field for manoeuvre against Spain and seized fortresses accordingly. In 1688, William III of Orange similarly invaded England in order to ensure its support against Louis XIV of France, and, indeed, led it into a costly war with the latter (1689–97). The collapse or defeat of resistance to William, first in England and then throughout the British Isles, does not prove the failure of the British political system, but, rather, demonstrates the need to consider governmental capability in terms of particular conjunctures.

The Westphalian settlement can be positively re-evaluated, like its predecessor, the system that followed the Peace of Augsburg of 1555. They were different, not least because the Westphalian settlement followed a protracted conflict and involved foreign guarantors: France and Sweden. These monarchs were, also, now rulers of territories within the Empire: part of Alsace, and a series of territories in northern Germany – Wismar, the former ecclesiastical principalities of Bremen and Verden, and Western Pomerania – respectively. Nevertheless, the two peace settlements had in common a determination to make a federal system work and, in particular, to retain an imperial constitution with an Emperor who was unable (simply as Emperor, as contrasted with the strength derived from his hereditary possession) to wield power comparable to that of other sovereign rulers. In addition, the extent to which the later Austro-Prussian wars reflected and caused the breakdown of the imperial system is questionable, as is the need for its eventual collapse. The Empire avoided the revolutionary breakdown that destroyed Bourbon France in 1792, although it could not survive the crisis caused by failure against Napoleon.[10]

Examination of individual points throws light not only on the imperial constitution, but also on other aspects of authority and power in the period. For example, the extent to which imperial princes were willing to co-operate with the Emperor can be seen not simply as a response to the power politics of the Empire, and, indeed, of Europe, but also as a consequence of a powerful political culture that encouraged loyalty and searched for reasons to remain obedient and to settle differences through mutual agreement.

This is the best explanation for the conduct of successive Electors of Saxony, the most powerful German Protestant ruler, for most of the late sixteenth and seventeenth centuries. The desire of the Electors to co-operate with the Emperor reflected not craven weakness and personal self-indulgence, but a conservative wish to maintain the imperial constitution. This ensured that the Electors saw their leadership of the *Corpus Evangelicorum* (Protestant body in the Empire) not as a reason to seek political chaos in order to foster Lutheranism, but as an opportunity to contribute to the stability of the Empire. The Peace of Augsburg was regarded as an acceptable settlement by the Electors, not least because it guaranteed both the survival of Lutheranism and the liberties of the German nation. The ability of imperial institutions and German rulers to settle the disputes that arose over the interpretation of the peace appeared to justify confidence in the constitution.

In contrast, the formation of the Protestant Union in 1608 by Protestant rulers ready to respond with a confessional league to the increase in religious tension in the 1600s focusing on the city of Donauwörth was unwelcome to Saxony, as was the rising in Bohemia against the Habsburgs in 1618. John George I of Saxony (r. 1611–56) refused the Bohemian throne, and took part in the campaigning against the Calvinist Frederick V of the Palatinate, who accepted it, being rewarded with Lusatia (part of the Bohemian crown lands) by the Emperor, Ferdinand II. As the latter's power increased in the 1620s, the Saxons refused to join other Protestant opponents to him; and this was a vital help to Ferdinand. The Saxons only joined the Swedes, their co-religionists, in 1631 when put under military pressure by the advance both of Gustavus Adolphus and of the army of the Catholic League, and John

George was happy to negotiate a reconciliation with the Emperor by the Peace of Prague of 1635.

Saxon policies can be seen as a valuable reminder of the ability of loyalty to overcome confessional difference. This was an important guide to a widespread ethos of the period, both within and outside Germany, as well as to the specific strength of both the Empire and a slowly developing sense of German nationhood. These could also be seen in the clauses of the Westphalia Settlement. Territorial rulers within the Empire were allowed to raise and maintain their own troops, but the reasons given were to protect the Empire and maintain internal peace; while permission to negotiate alliances with other states came with the caveat that these were not to harm the Empire.

The notion, familiar in much of the political science literature, that the Westphalian system represented a new development in the theory and practice of international relations, with a stress on sovereign nation states, has little relationship to the more circumspect shift in the relationship between Emperor, Empire and princes actually seen in the peace. Furthermore, international relations in the century after Westphalia were not too different from those in the preceding century. There was a similar variety in state forms and powers, a continuation of the struggle between France and Spain that had been important from the 1490s, an adjustment by neighbouring powers to the quasi-hegemonies in Western Europe gained by first Spain, then France, and, further east, the shifting relationships of Russia, Poland, Sweden, the Ottoman Empire and other polities. The impact of the Reformation on the practice and atmosphere of international relations over the following century was more important than that of Westphalia. In terms of power politics, the defeats of the Ottomans from 1683 were of greater consequence than those of the Habsburgs in the Thirty Years' War, principally in 1631 and, again, in 1636–48. The latter defeats largely reaffirmed the long-established constraints on imperial power, and marked the reversal of short-term Habsburg gains in the 1620s and mid-1630s.

Aside from consideration of Westphalia, there is a need to give due weight to the ability of imperial institutions to discharge functions, and also to the capacity of the system to engender new responses. This can be seen with the creation, in the early sixteenth century, of the ten *Kreise* (imperial circles) which provided a valuable intermediate level, intended for co-operative purposes, between the Imperial Diet and the individual territories of the Empire.[11] Although the effectivness of the *Kreise* varied, and they were subject to the power politics of the local territorial states, they did provide a way to focus regional interests, to ensure that earlier regional leagues did not become a disruptive model for German politics, and to utilise the ambitions of territorial rulers for wider goals. This was seen in Swabia where, in an area with a large number of weak rulers, the *Kreis* played an important role in organising support for the defence of the Empire against the French and the Ottomans in the late seventeenth century.[12] The memory of the Thirty Years' War remained powerful and helped shape German political assumptions, encouraging the view that effective co-operation between German rulers was necessary in order to prevent the recurrence of such a calamity. There was scant reason for contemporaries to be confident that such a challenge would not be repeated, and, indeed, it occurred at the hands of France in 1792–1813. Furthermore, the *Kreise*, like the Empire in general, remained relatively effective into the late eighteenth century.[13]

There were serious challenges to imperial harmony, not least the Habsburg attempt to increase the jurisdictional powers of the Emperor Charles VI in the 1720s;[14] his exclusion of Saxon and Bavarian claims on the imperial succession with the Pragmatic Sanction; the impact of war between Bavaria and Austria in 1741–45, as Charles VII, Charles Albert of Bavaria, lay claim to parts of the Habsburg inheritance; the Prussian challenge to Maria Theresa, which included a revival of confessionalism; and the hostile response to the Emperor Joseph II's plans, particularly for the Bavarian succession, in 1777–79 and, even more, 1785. The last led to the creation of a *Fürstenbund*, or league of princes, that was particularly disturbing for Joseph II, as it included Catholics as well as Protestants and was pushed hard by Frederick II of Prussia. Again, the novelty of this should not be overrated. From the 1550s, the French had developed a strategy of seeking to overcome confessional divisions in organising opposition to the Habsburgs. In the late 1720s, they had joined Britain–Hanover in trying to create an alliance system that encompassed the Protestant Landgrave of Hesse-Cassel and the Catholic Wittelsbach Electors.

Nevertheless, as also indicated elsewhere in this book, it is important to distinguish between crises and breakdown. It is the durability of the imperial idea that emerges clearly, not least in response to what were seen as attempts to infringe the rubric and meaning of the constitution, as with opposition to Ferdinand II in 1631, Charles VI in the 1720s, and Joseph II in 1785. In addition, most of the Empire rallied behind the Emperor against both Louis XIV and the Ottomans.

The most serious crisis between the Peace of Westphalia (1648) and the outbreak of the French Revolutionary Wars in 1792 occurred in the early 1740s, when the failure of Charles VI to ensure a male heir, a serious problem in all monarchical systems, provoked a crisis in which the dynastic strategies of the leading princely powers, each of which was an electorate, led to a civil war within the Empire. As in the Thirty Years' War, this was greatly complicated by international intervention, although confessional differences were less important than in the earlier conflict. The War of the Austrian Succession, however, was more swiftly resolved in the Empire, as Frederick II of Prussia was bought off in 1742 (and, again, in 1745) with recognition of his conquest of Silesia, while the Austrians were militarily successful against Bavaria in the winter of 1741–42 and were then helped by the impact of

British entry into the war in 1743 on French priorities. Charles VII's death in 1745 led to a return to the norm of a Habsburg emperor as other candidacies proved abortive.

The viability of the Empire was an issue separate from that of the Austrian Habsburg composite state, but, as the Austrian Habsburgs were emperors throughout, except during the brief reign of Charles VII (1742–45), the two were not completely separate. Instead, the imperial title was the most glorious of the panoply of Habsburg possessions, positions and claims, while Habsburg power helped give more force to the imperial position. Habsburg forces played an important role in resisting French pressure on the Empire, and the range of Habsburg interests could also serve to help win foreign support to the same end. The prestige of the Emperor contributed to that of the Empire.

The image of the Emperor Leopold I (r. 1658–1705) benefited greatly when the defeat of the Ottoman Turks outside Vienna in 1683 was followed by successful campaigning in Hungary,[15] which, when resumed under his son Charles VI (r. 1711–40), had, by 1718, brought major gains for Christendom. Between 1683 and 1720, the Austrian Habsburgs, Leopold I, Joseph I and Charles VI, although rulers of a composite state, benefited from a spectacular increase in territorial power, a growth surpassed in Europe only by Russia under Peter the Great. In Italy, the Habsburgs gained Naples, Sicily, Mantua and the Milanese; in the Balkans, Hungary, Transylvania, Little Wallachia and much of Serbia; and, further west, the Spanish Netherlands. Accompanying this expansion was a growth in military strength and reputation, and a determination to enforce imperial authority and Austrian power in every area possible. Military service provided opportunities for aristocrats across the Habsburg dominions and beyond. Jacob van Gansinot, the Wittelsbach envoy in The Hague, wrote in 1725 that Charles VI was the most powerful Emperor since the foundation of the Holy Roman Empire.[16] The concerns of British, French and other diplomats about Austrian power scarcely suggested any confidence in the redundancy of composite monarchies.

Furthermore, simply in terms of international relations, it is misleading to assume that because, for example, the Empire was dissolved at the behest of Napoleon in 1806, Poland was successively partitioned out of existence in 1772–95, and the independence of Geneva, Genoa, Venice, the Swiss Confederation, and the United Provinces, all republics, were all destroyed in the 1790s, the future therefore lay with states lacking representative institutions, and, more particularly, powerful unitary states. The French, who were responsible for the destruction of the independence of all of these states bar Poland (Austria also played a major role in the destruction of Venice), in addition defeated Austria, Prussia and Spain, all states without important representative institutions, in 1792–1809. The complications of the relationship between government system and international success is further indicated by the fact that the French might have conquered Britain had it not been an island.

Earlier, the Swedish Age of Liberty had arisen from the ruins of the defeat of a more autocratic system during the Great Northern War (1700–21). The United States of America was an eighteenth-century creation, and it did not become an autocracy. The issue of how best to secure and control national resources was, however, a significant source of dispute in the early Republic, as it was also to be, in the nineteenth century, in the newly independent states of Latin America.

In the nineteenth century, nation states, such as France, Germany and Italy, were not obviously more successful than multi-ethnic states, such as Austria, Russia or Britain (which then included Ireland). It is mistaken to assume that the more or less centralised national state was, in any way, superior to the composite monarchy in the early modern period. The Habsburg monarchy survived until 1918, and its demise was perhaps not as much of a foregone conclusion as has often been assumed in the past. Moreover, the Habsburg monarchy did not fare worse in the Napoleonic era than smaller more homogeneous states in defending itself against France.

In addition, federalism proved an effective way to construct a composite state, both on the small scale of Switzerland and the United Provinces, and on the larger scale of the United States, where the declaration of independence was issued in 1776. In the Habsburg monarchy, the failure to produce a strong confederal Estates system in the early modern period was crucial to its politics: only the Habsburg rulers created administrative institutions covering all their lands.[17]

In the late eighteenth century, the composite monarchy as a special type of state seemed anachronistic to some rulers and ministers who wished to expand governmental power, while, subsequently, in the last two crisis decades of the century, the British and Habsburg composite monarchies did experience serious problems. For Habsburg reformers, it seemed less plausible than in the past to have several principalities and kingdoms united under one ruler but with several languages. A system that had worked in the seventeenth century no longer seemed appropriate. Joseph II, Emperor 1765–90 and sole ruler of the Habsburg dominions in 1780–90, therefore attempted to introduce centralising measures, including the imposition of German as an official language in most of his dominions, with disastrous results, especially in Hungary.

Earlier in the eighteenth century, such states and situations had not seemed unusual or anachronistic, although, in an important shift, the Habsburgs had abandoned the practice of dividing the *Erblande* between members of the family. The Pragmatic Sanction of 1713 declared the inheritance indivisible, albeit in response to the need to confront the problems created by the absence of a male heir. As a further reminder of the ability of traditional systems to change, elective monarchy ceased to be the practice in the early modern period in Bohemia, Denmark, Hungary and Russia.

The Empire was not the sole area in which states were challenged by more powerful counterparts, leading to questions about the relative capability of particular systems. This was also an issue in Italy, where the republics of Genoa and Venice were challenged by the power of Austria, France and Spain, while the local princely states, such as Mantua, Parma and Tuscany, were also overawed, as were the Papal States.

The issue of international competitiveness as a test of political systems is especially pertinent in the eighteenth century in the case of Saxony-Poland (1697–1763), Hanover-Britain (1714–1837), and, to a lesser extent, Hesse-Cassel-Sweden (1720–51), composite states that were challenged by the rise, first, of Russia and, then, of Prussia as well. These rises led to a testing degree of pressure and volatility in northern European and, more particularly, northern German politics, before which all the projects of personal union failed to achieve their ambitions. However, Prussia itself, in part, represented just such a project, the realisation of the Hohenzollern family diplomacy that brought Brandenburg, East Prussia, Cleves and Mark under one ruler. In addition, Prussia had an army designed to maximise the war-making potential of the close links between the Hohenzollerns and the landowners.

Prussia continued to expand in this fashion in the eighteenth century. Ansbach and Bayreuth, the dominions of the Franconian branch of the Hohenzollern family, were acquired thus in 1791; similarly, the extinction of branches of the Wittelsbach family in 1685, 1742, 1777 and 1779 led to a process of amalgamation. These were important gains obtained without war and thus attracting insufficient scholarly attention. Indeed, the contrast between the amount of scholarly attention devoted to the conquest of Silesia from the Habsburgs in 1740–42 and that to the acquisition by Prussia of East Friesland (1744), Ansbach and Bayreuth suggests, as least in part, an emphasis on the role of force that is misleading as an account of the factors affecting territorial growth. Against that view, it can be argued that peacetime gains owed something to a willingness to fight on other occasions, and this was certainly true of East Friesland. George II of Hanover (also King of Britain, r. 1727–60) had a claim on East Friesland, but was not in a position to pursue it.

A focus on state-building through war and competitive diplomacy does not have to assume a modern state system. There was a prevalence of traditional objectives and methods, both of which may be summarised in terms of dynasticism, although it is necessary to note important variations in what that entailed. These objectives and methods subvert attempts to advance a systemic model of a state system understood in modern terms.

In addition, a modern 'realist' model of international relations is too readily assumed in the discussion of the period, but specialist work repeatedly challenges it, not least by noting the role of idealist conceptions. For example, the intervention of Christian IV of Denmark (r. 1588–1648) in the Thirty Years' War in 1625 is commonly ascribed to purely territorial interests, a determination to annex prince bishoprics in north-west Germany.

Recent scholarly work has taken a more favourable approach to Christian's presentation of his motives, has stressed the consequences of his position as a German territorial ruler as well as king of Denmark, and has argued that Denmark's involvement in the war was conditioned by his *Reichsfürst* mentality, specifically his concern for princely liberties in the face of what he saw as an inexorable Habsburg advance.[18]

State-building is a less helpful and clear-cut concept than is frequently appreciated. In so far as there was a sense of identification with states or, other than in loose terms, nations, it was less widespread than in the nineteenth and twentieth centuries, and also less dominant among the number of overlapping identities (kin, locality, province, religion) that vied for attention and negotiation at the individual and communal level.

Furthermore, the dynastic imperative ensured that the creation of states was subordinated to a patrimonial proprietorship that encouraged such practices as dividing inheritances among members of the ruling family. This was seen not only with the inheritance of Charles V, but also with subsequent divisions among the Austrian Habsburgs, such that the Tyrol was separately governed for much of the seventeenth century. Other inheritances, such as that of Hesse in the sixteenth century, were also divided, helping to establish a long-standing division between Hesse-Cassel and Hesse-Darmstadt, not least over the future of the weaker branches: Hesse-Marburg and Hesse-Rheinfels. In 1652, John George I of Saxony divided his lands, giving his three younger sons principalities: Saxe-Weissenfels, -Merseburg, and -Zeitz.

More generally, the role of younger sons and other relations was an important complication in dynastic politics. Gaston, Duke of Orléans (1608–60), brother of Louis XIII of France (r. 1610–43) and, until the birth of the future Louis XIV in 1638, his heir, was an example of a prince who was an important and independent political figure, able to raise forces and willing to conspire against the crown. Francis, Duke of Alençon, and then of Anjou (1554–84), brother of Henry III, was an earlier instance of the same process. Like Gaston of Orleans, Alençon took an independent line in Franco-Spanish relations.

Similar policies were adopted by prominent princely and aristocratic houses, such as those of Guise, Nevers, Orange and Sapieha, the interests of which frequently spanned 'states'. This was a particular problem where states were small. Princely and aristocratic houses had then to respond to different rulers, and this division of loyalties created problems for rulers, and gave their prominent subjects room for manoeuvre. The house of Orange had a role in German as well as Dutch politics, although the principality of Orange in southern France was taken from them. In the mid-sixteenth century, the Guise had interests in France, Lorraine and Scotland.

As with other issues, there is room for a debate about evidence. More particularly, there is the degree to which the idioms of the pursuit of dynastic advantage concealed a shift towards a more modern and 'rational' state system and one in which the essential units were states, with a clear notion of state interest, rather than dynasties. In addition, the choice of sources can suggest different conclusions. A focus on those produced by central governments can lead to a misleading emphasis on states.

The continued currency of succession disputes in international relations certainly highlights the importance of dynastic factors, and serves to link the sixteenth and eighteenth centuries. The eighteenth century saw not only the Wars of the Spanish, Polish, Austrian and Bavarian Succession, but also confrontations or conflicts that essentially rose from then: in Europe, the Seven Years' War essentially rose from an attempt to contest Prussia's conquest of Silesia at the outset of the War of the Austrian Succession. Dynastic competition over successions also played an important role in a number of disputes that came close to war, and that were prominent in the international relations of the period, for example over Tuscany and Parma in the late 1720s and early 1730s, and, in the Empire, over Jülich and Berg in the late 1730s.

Indeed, there was still a major element of dynastic competition in the 1800s and 1810s, with Napoleon seizing or creating kingdoms and principalities, including Holland, Italy, Naples, Spain and Westphalia, for himself and his family, while his opponents sought to cement his defeat with a territorial order based on a number of states whose rationale was essentially dynastic: the Austrian, Prussian and Dutch monarchies from 1815 were internally divided, over religion and/or linguistically. To the British government, the establishment, as a result of the Congress of Vienna (1814–15), of the house of Orange in a Dutch monarchy that also ruled Belgium appeared to be the best way to keep the French out of the Low Countries; while the new presence of Prussia in the Catholic Rhineland also acted as a barrier.

The continued role of dynastic issues was not the sole limitation to the nation-state approach. Nationalism or proto-nationalism was also weak, and was such into the early nineteenth century. This was particularly the case in Germany. Within the German Confederation, as earlier within the Holy Roman Empire, the political system opposed an overarching constitutional and cultural sense of common German identity to a reality of conflicting territorial policies. In so far as there was a sense of German identity, it was more important in arousing and sustaining a degree of popular animosity against outsiders than in influencing policy. Animosities could also be strongly developed within the German and Italian 'nations', for example between Bavaria and the Tyrol.

Thus, throughout the period, the expansion of armed forces and engagement in war can be seen as measures that served traditional goals, rather than a new agenda. The frequent references to glorious past leaders, for example Henry IV in France, served to underline this continuity. So also did hostility to the idea of hegemonic power that constituted a central assumption of much European thought about international relations, albeit an assumption whose language and images changed, giving rise, in the eighteenth century, to the idea of a mechanically natural balance of power.

This idea seemed, and seems, very modern, particularly with its commitment to quantifying power and thus offering an apparently rational way to arrive at a scientific analysis of international relations. Once quantified, power could be understood in mechanistic terms that corresponded to those being popularised for Newtonian physics. The notion of the balance assumed that hegemonic power would meet with a matching reaction, rather as Sir Isaac Newton had revealed that the action of a force created an equal and opposite response.

However, the theory of the balance of power had many deficiencies. There was the important question of whether it was descriptive, explaining what happened naturally, or prescriptive, explaining what ought to happen but required human volition to take effect. Indeed, the role of balance of theory literature in calling for policies supposedly in pursuit of such a balance underlines its role as polemic as much as analysis. Aside from this point, there was the extent to which power could not be readily measured. The balance also carried with it the concept of natural interests: goals that stemmed from inherent characteristics. This again had problems, not least a belief that there was only one natural policy, and a related failure to allow for differences in opinion.

The concept of natural interests challenged the idea that monarchs (or any other leaders) were best placed to choose policies and to change them. Instead, the assumption that monarchs could neglect natural interests was increasingly encouraged, most particularly with France's alliance with Austria from 1756, which was attributed within France to unwarranted pressures around the crown, including the most influential of Louis XV's mistresses, Madame de Pompadour, and also Louis XVI's wife, Marie Antoinette, the daughter of Maria Theresa of Austria.[19] Similarly, there was criticism in Britain of what were seen as the Hanoverian commitments of monarchs from 1714, while Philip V's quest for Italian gains for Spain and for the children of his second marriage to Elizabeth Farnese was criticised as a distortion of Spanish interests.

Current analytical models of state development that assume some mechanistic search for efficiency and, in the case of warfare, a maximisation of force, do violence to the complex process by which, in the early modern period, interest in new ideas and methods interacted with powerful elements of continuity. The notion of effectiveness was framed and applied in terms of dominant cultural and social patterns. For example, a stress on the value of morale and the importance of honour came naturally to the aristocratic order that dominated war-making, and traditional assumptions about appropriate conduct were important in force structure and tactics.

The pursuit of traditional goals did not, however, necessarily prevent either the expansion of armed forces or war from having a modernising impact. It has, for example, been argued that the fiscal demands of the European military system helped to drive forward a development in state mechanisms.

A degree of care is required in making such claims. First, it was frequently the case that resources were raised, in whole or part, from traditional forms of expropriation, rather than from their modern counterparts of taxation and loans. At one extreme, much of the wealth obtained by Henry VIII of England's seizure of the monasteries in 1536–40 was promptly employed to pay for war with France and Scotland. More generally, armies operated by means of 'contributions' – levying demands for supplies under the threat of devastation – and these had a major impact on operational goals and methods, most notoriously during the Thirty Years' War, and, more generally, in the sixteenth and seventeenth centuries; although less so in the eighteenth, as a result of an improvement in logistics. The participation of France and other states in the Thirty Years' War revealed fundamental administrative limitations, placed heavy burdens on the people,[20] and did not readily achieve military goals.

After the Thirty Years' War, there was a greater tendency to try to develop institutional provision of supplies and to use taxation or loans to that end. This helps explain the growing popularity (with governments) of excise taxes from the late seventeenth century, for example in England and in German principalities. These taxes were raised by state officials or farmed out to private contractors, but, whichever system was followed, they were not a function of the produce or control of the land. They did not tax the largest industry and source of employment, agriculture – and, instead, ensured that a heavy fiscal burden was borne by manufacturing, commerce and consumers – but excises were not dependent on landowners for their implementation, and this helped central government.

The larger standing (permanent) armies which were developed from the mid-seventeenth century, and the permanent state navies, that were created in the same period, both required constant revenue streams, and these can be seen as crucial to a shift in governance. The impact of war and militarism on society could also be considerable. This was particularly true of Eastern Europe, where conscription, with its concomitant regulation and data gathering, was crucial in changing the relationship between state and people. In Western Europe, in contrast, there was far less conscription, serfdom and labour control. The relationship between the three was only partial. Poland had serfdom, but lacked a large army or conscription. Nevertheless, although the methods of control varied, a general feature of Eastern Europe was a degree of social control lacking further west, linked to external goals, whether production for external markets, as in Poland, or war.

The control that the Polish landlords wielded over their peasantry was matched, in the eighteenth century, by the Partitioning powers (Austria, Prussia and Russia), but, unlike Poland, their social structures and political practices served the pursuit of military strength. Resistance to attempts to increase royal power in the 1650s and 1660s prevented political support for the development of a more effective Polish army. Whatever their deficiencies as politico-governmental systems, Austria, Prussia and Russia were, by Polish standards, centralising monarchies able to make a major impact in international relations.

Attempts to create aspects of such government in Western Europe met with resistance, in large part due to the nature of intermediate institutions, as well as to different political cultures, varying leadership skills, and contrasting degrees of international intervention. Between 1550 and 1750, it proved easier to increase central governmental authority and power in Denmark, France and Spain than in Sweden, Britain and most of the Holy Roman Empire; although that did not mean that the former were necessarily more effective in international relations, and Denmark proved less successful than Sweden.

It is also necessary to give due weight to contingencies. Their impact can be seen in Eastern Europe. As a state on Europe's open frontier, Muscovy/Russia faced problems and opportunities. Had it succumbed to its Islamic opponents, then Poland-Lithuania would have been the major frontier state and, if successful, the dominant power in Eastern Europe. This might well have affected not only contemporary views about political best practice but also subsequent views about relative capability. The struggle between Russia and the Tatars was long-standing, and it was far from clear which was likely to be the more successful. For example, in 1521, the Crimean Tatars had organised a pan-Tatar league that ousted the pro-Russian Khan of Kazan. The same year, the Crimean and Kazan Tatars advanced on Moscow from the south and the east, and the city was saved only by an attack on the Crimea by the Tatars of Astrakhan.

The situation in the Empire also indicated the role of circumstances. In Württemberg, as in Prussia, institutional development and ruler–Estate relations were both fuelled primarily by the duke's fiscal requirements which rose essentially from competitive international relations, but the Dukes of Württemberg failed totally to emulate the rulers of Prussia. Most lesser German princes were not prepared to surrender the initiative to their more powerful neighbours, and the conditions of the Empire after the Peace of Westphalia (1648) made it imperative that they continue to play an active role if they sought to maintain their status and autonomy. Although the Empire provided a protective framework for its weaker members, it did not allow them to retreat into passivity because the rights and privileges defining a territory's position had to be protected from the ambitions of neighbours.[21]

More generally, rulers had a need not only for constant and predictable revenue, but also for a greater amount of information on which to base revenue demands. Thus international competitiveness can be linked to the cadastral, cartographic and demographic surveys that became more prominent in the eighteenth century. Nevertheless, the argument that such competitiveness led to change and modernisation has been overplayed. In many instances, financial demands, instead, led to a degree of reliance on existing interests that limited options for change. In the United Provinces, the serious financial strains caused by seventeenth-century military expenditure helped to sustain a political system based on provincial particularism and the power of urban oligarchies,[22] although this also accorded with the dominant political culture and there was only limited interest in a more centralised political system. In 1672, 1747 and 1787, when the Orangists came to power in the province of Holland, they did not take the opportunity to create a new governmental system. In France, the sale of offices (and of the right of reversion to them) was, like other fiscal expedients, pressed hard in times of war. In the 1790s, the forces of Revolutionary France resorted to brutal expropriation in Germany, Italy and indeed France, while their Austrian and Prussian opponents were heavily dependent on British subsidies. Yet, in the meanwhile, there had been a development in governmental capability to which we shall return in Chapters 5 and 6.

This capability was primarily devoted to international competition, one of the major consequences of which was a territorial expansionism that helped create diverse realms even if they did not take the form of composite states. The incorporation of peoples of very different ethnicities and belief gathered pace in the eighteenth century, creating fresh problems of adjustment. Russia's westward expansion into the Baltic region, Ukraine and Poland brought many Lutherans, Uniates and Catholics within its borders. Austrian expansion into the northern Balkans brought an engagement with Orthodoxy and Islam, although this was lessened by defeat, particularly the reversal of 1739, when Belgrade, northern Serbia and western Wallachia, all of which had been ceded to Austria in 1718, were returned to Ottoman rule. In 1775, the Ottoman Turks ceded Bucovina to Austria, in large part as a return for Austrian backing (short of fighting) during the Russo-Ottoman war of 1768–74, and Joseph II then made extensive changes to the Orthodox Church there. Prussian expansion into Silesia (1740–41) and Poland (1772–95) swept many Catholics into its fold, and more were to follow, in 1814–15, with gains in Germany thanks to the Congress of Vienna, particularly in the Rhineland. Imperial expansion by Britain and France added another dimension to this problem, especially when the British conquered Catholic territories where the population remained and its religion had to be accepted: Minorca (1708) and Québec (1759–60). In contrast, the French Catholic population of Nova Scotia, the Acadians, were expelled in 1755, when they refused to promise loyalty in the developing conflict between Britain and France. Their lands were given to British settlers.

The problem of religious diversity was in part reconceptualised in the eighteenth century by rulers who were less concerned than their predecessors about rebellion and more anxious about maximising resources for war. Concern that religious dissidents were being excluded from contributing to the national military and economic stock began to outweigh fears of the political instabilities hitherto seen as an axiomatic product of internal diversity, and frequently only accepted due to necessity, and sometimes at the cost of civil war (for example France 1598–1685, Swiss Cantons).

Where religious disabilities prevented groups from serving the state (or might hinder their accumulation of wealth that could be productive and be taxed), then disabilities came to be seen in the eighteenth century, at least by central governments and enlightened opinion, as liabilities. This owed much also to a related doctrine that saw religious persecution as an unproductive restriction on trade, while the monarchs' own self-image as the modernisers and liberators of their societies was also important. This was particularly apparent with Peter the Great. Following contemporary theories about the effects of intolerance on the economy, Joseph II invited the heterodox to revive trade in depressed areas of his empire. At Ostend, Protestants were allowed to worship freely inside the town as a means of regenerating the port. His rival, Frederick II of Prussia, while continuing his father's policy of stirring up Protestant unrest in Habsburg territories and benefiting from the presentation of his conquest of Silesia as a blow for Protestantism, also respected Catholic rights in his conquests. There, Protestant minorities had to continue paying tithes to Catholic priests, while Frederick gave refuge to Jesuits, and allowed a Catholic church to be consecrated in Berlin.

More generally, the relationships of government, religion and war remained dynamic, and also dependent on particular rulers and circumstances. This looked towards the problems that both Revolutionary France and Napoleon were to encounter. Religious fervour and a sense of threat from secularist foreigners helped engender support for their opponents, for example in the kingdom of Naples in 1798. This brought an important popular dimension into international relations, although the novelty of this should not be exaggerated. Guerrillas had already played a considerable role in Iberian operations during the War of the Spanish Succession (1701–14). Marshal Berwick, who led the Franco-Spanish invasion of Portugal in 1704, was surprised by the weakness of organized resistance, but equally amazed by the vigour of the peasants in attacks on his communications and in fighting back in the villages.

When the French under Napoleon invaded and occupied much of Spain in 1808–13, they repeatedly defeated their poorly armed opponents, but Spanish regular and guerrilla operations denied them control over the countryside and hit their communications and logistics. The insurgents were neither bandits questing for booty nor patriots simply fighting for crown, church and country, although both elements played an important role. Instead, as in Navarre, they were also landowning peasants fighting to protect both their interests and a society that did so. Thus there was no simple transfer of allegiance to invaders: ideological factors took precedence over the idea of the state as a protection system whose conquest led to a ready renegotiation of obligations. The latter did occur in some areas – for example, repeatedly in the vulnerable Spanish Netherlands when the French overran them in the late seventeenth century – but exceptions underline the weakness of systemic accounts.

The abolition of Navarre's privileges by the French under Napoleon, their efforts to reform society and their rapacity all aroused hostility in 1808–13.[23] This should not be seen as something that was new. Indeed, there were examples of popular political consciousness and activism in the Middle Ages leading to successful military action, including in northern Italy in the twelfth century, Scotland and Flanders in the early fourteenth, and Bohemia in the early fifteenth. Each of these cases also involved other factors, but they indicate the extent to which it is seriously misleading to write popular roles out of the centuries prior to the revolutionary crisis of the late eighteenth century.

The extent to which this perspective needs to be integrated into an assessment of the early modern period is unclear. It does suggest that there was an additional level of consent to that offered by the élite, a consent that was more a case of compliance but that, nevertheless, also posed the problem of resistance if it was absent. From this perspective, the frequency of wars and the increase in the size of armies can be seen as providing employment for active young males who might otherwise have been a major cause of disruption, although this relationship can also be presented in a much harsher light.

This is a reminder of the extent to which international competition was not in some way separate from the concerns and activities of the bulk of society, but, instead, an ever-present source of demands and costs. At the level of individual states, the unpredictabilities of such competition ensured that there was an unsettled dynamic to politics. At the level of Europe as a whole, the impact of such competition provided characteristics to society and politics, and offers modern scholarship a way to approach the chronology and causation of developments.

Notes

1. C. Tilly, *Coercion, Capital and European States AD 990–1990* (Cambridge, MA, 1990); B. Downing, *The Military Revolution and Political Change. Origins of Democracy and Autocracy in Early Modern Europe* (Princeton, NJ, 1992); T. Ertman, *Birth of the Leviathan* (Cambridge, 1997).

2. J. Lukowski, *Liberty's Folly. The Polish-Lithuanian Commonwealth in the Eighteenth Century* (1991), and *The Partitions of Poland: 1772, 1793, 1795* (1999).

3. *Politische Correspondenz Friedrichs des Grossen*, XI, 282.

4. *Politische Correspondenz*, X, 278, 421.

5. J. Glete, *War and the State in Early Modern Europe. Spain, the Dutch Republic and Sweden as Fiscal-military States, 1500–1660* (2002), pp. 140–73. The best introduction to early modern Dutch history is J. I. Israel's lengthy *The Dutch Republic: Its Rise, Greatness and Fall, 1477–1806* (Oxford, 1995).

6. J. L. Price, *Holland and the Dutch Republic in the Seventeenth Century. The Politics of Particularism* (Oxford, 1994).

7. E. Kossmann, *Political Thought in the Dutch Republic: Three Studies* (Amsterdam, 2000).

8. J. L. Price, *Dutch Society, 1588–1713* (Harlow, 2000).

9. R. Asch, *The Thirty Years War. The Holy Roman Empire and Europe, 1618–1648* (Basingstoke, 1997).

10. J. Gagliardo, *Reich and Nation. The Holy Roman Empire as Idea and Reality 1763–1806* (Bloomington, IN, 1980); T. C. W. Blanning, 'The French Revolution and the modernization of Germany', *Central European History*, 22 (1989), pp. 109–29.

11. M. Hughes, *Early Modern Germany 1477–1806* (1992); P. H. Wilson, *The Holy Roman Empire 1495–1806* (Basingstoke, 1999).

12. T. Scott, *Regional Identity and Economic Change. The Upper Rhine, 1450–1600* (Oxford, 1997); J. A. Vann, *The Swabian Kreis. Institutional Growth in the Holy Roman Empire 1648–1715* (Brussels, 1975).

13. P. H. Wilson, 'The politics of military recruitment in eighteenth-century Germany', *English Historical Review*, 117 (2002), p. 568.

14. M. Hughes, *Law and Politics in Eighteenth Century Germany: The Imperial Aulic Council in the Reign of Charles VI* (Woodbridge, Suffolk, 1988).

15. M. Gouloubeva, *The Glorification of Leopold I in Image, Spectacle and Text* (Mainz, 2000).

16. Gansinot to Ferdinand, Count Plettenberg, leading minister to the Elector of Cologne, 22 December 1725, Münster, Staatsarchiv, Deposit Nordkirchen NB. 259.

17. R. J. W. Evans and T. V. Thomas (eds), *Crown, Church and Estates. Central European Politics in the Sixteenth and Seventeenth Centuries* (1992).

18. P. Lockhart, *Denmark in the Thirty Years' War, 1618–1648. King Christian IV and the Decline of the Oldenburg State* (Selinsgrove, NJ, 1996).

19. G. Savage, 'Favier's heirs: the French Revolution and the *secret du roi*', *Historical Journal*, 41 (1998), pp. 225–58; T. Kaiser, 'Who's afraid of Marie-Antoinette? Diplomacy, Austrophobia, and the queen', *French History*, 14 (2000), pp. 241–71.

20. R. J. Knecht, *Richelieu* (Harlow, 1991).

21. J. A. Vann, *The Making of a State: Württemberg 1593–1793* (Ithaca, NY, 1984); P. H. Wilson, *War, State and Society in Württemberg, 1677–1793* (Cambridge, 1995).

22. M. C.'t Hart, *The Making of a Bourgeois State. War, Politics and Finance during the Dutch Revolt* (Manchester, 1993).

23. J. L. Tone, *The Fatal Knot. The Guerrilla War in Navarre and the Defeat of Napoleon in Spain* (Chapel Hill, NC, 1995).

CHAPTER 4

Social Dynamics

§ THE emphasis of this book is on government–élite relationship, the state as an expression of this relationship, and politics as a consequence of its difficulties. It is also important to set these issues in their social context and to consider its dynamics and challenges. In particular, it would be foolish to offer an unproblematic account of élite hegemony.

The contours of the social and economic history of the period have been ably discussed,[1] although a number of issues remain in need of further clarification. These include the economic interaction of the different parts of Europe, and the social and political consequences of this interaction. This offers the possibility of probing differences in order to understand the nature of the different Europes that it is all to easy to underrate. The misleading customary focus on the baton-passing analysis, in which leading powers are understood in sequential terms, has led to a stress on Spain (c.1500–c.1640), the Dutch and France (seventeenth century), and Britain, Russia and Prussia (eighteenth). The remainder of Europe is then understood in terms of impact, echoes and responses, with a particular emphasis in economic models on a subordinate, if not exploited, relationship.

This approach risks underrating, if not misunderstanding, the complexities of relations between regions, as well as the autonomous development of those not seen as leaders. This is particularly the case with the Mediterranean and, more specifically, Italy; although in practice much, if not most, of Europe is underrated in this perspective and it is a problem at all scales. It is, for example, not simply a question of the Mediterranean in the early modern period, but also of Eastern Europe. As Larry Wolff has shown,[2] this tendency was not simply a product of modern assessments but, instead, a result of the structuring and restructuring of the European spatial imagination in the early modern period, particularly in the eighteenth century. At the more local scale, there was also the question of traditional assumptions about the respective value of areas of arable agriculture and nucleated settlement, contrasted with the less intensive pastoral and forest regions, where settlement was less concentrated and social discipline generally less.

The presentation of Italy repays study as it is symptomatic of the more general issues of perception and emphasis at the regional level, and relates to the issue of assessing capability as well as to the social dynamics of state power.

As Atlantic states created empires that spanned the oceans, it is easy to overlook the Mediterranean, or at least to treat it as an inconsequential backwater. While, in the sixteenth century, Magellan and Drake explored Europe's 'dark side of the earth', or Cortes, Pizarro and Legaspi blazed the trail for Spain's empire in the New World and the Philippines, the Mediterranean no longer appeared the centre of what Edward Gibbon was to call, in the eighteenth century, the 'world question'. By the end of the sixteenth century, although the Ottoman advance had been largely stopped, the interaction of politics and economics that was important to economic development was no longer working to the advantage of Christian Mediterranean societies.[3] Venice was apparently sinking into decay, and the key routes of trade and cultural interchange no longer ran across and around the blue sea.

As with most commonly accepted historical interpretations, there was, and is, a measure of truth in this, and it would be foolish to pretend that the Mediterranean played as central a role as hitherto. Yet there is also much that is misleading, if not wrong, about the standard neglect of the sea and its surrounds.

This can be seen in economic terms. Exports from the Mediterranean, such as salt and cultural services, could not compete with the value of the trans-oceanic goods brought to Atlantic Europe, particularly, but not only, tea and ceramics from China, cotton cloth from India, sugar, cocoa, coffee and tobacco from the New World, and gold from Brazil. The import of these goods reflected the growing strength of European consumer demand as well as the possibilities offered by European-dominated trading systems,[4] although that demand was satisfied in large part by slave labour. Nor did the Mediterranean produce the industrial goods that were of increasing value from the late eighteenth century: the iron products of forges and steam-driven equipment that were starting to come from Britain.

As a consequence, trade was increasingly a matter of the penetration of the Mediterranean by foreign goods and by foreign merchants bringing these goods and seeking raw materials, such as salt, for exploitation. The English and Dutch made a major impact from the late sixteenth century, although the extent to which they took over trade, particularly carrying trade and trade in the eastern Mediterranean, has been qualified.[5] Attempts by Italian rulers to free trade from duties in order to encourage its growth did not greatly help local economies. Livorno's prominence as a trading centre owed much to its designation as a free port in 1675, but such measures could not transform the economy. Livorno was not to lead to a Tuscan industrial revolution. Instead, it became an important port for the Atlantic traders who took over commercial links between the Mediterranean and the Atlantic. These traders also helped change the economic fortunes and activities of other parts of Europe. Thus Dutch demand for timber had a major impact on Norway from the seventeenth century.

Although a revisionist perspective would find it difficult to portray, say, a Balkan industrial revolution in the late eighteenth century, gloom about Mediterranean Europe has to be put in perspective. There is a serious problem of hindsight, in particular of reading back from the nineteenth century, and of underrating the extent to which there was considerable economic activity and development in the sixteenth, seventeenth and eighteenth centuries. For example, Southern Europe was affected by the improvement in communications that was an important help to trade in the eighteenth century. Portugal signed postal conventions with England in 1705 and Spain in 1718. However, in 1763, only about 12 kilograms of mail a month was going from Portugal to Spain, and the most important international link from Portugal within Europe was with Britain, and an aspect of its imperial economy. Similarly, in Northern Europe, improved communications focused on the major Atlantic commercial centres. In 1693–94, for example, Saxony inaugurated a weekly post from the United Provinces and improved the service with Germany's leading port, Hamburg, so that a reply could be received in eight days.

Nevertheless, as most of Europe did not experience large-scale industrialisation and significant economic transformation until the twentieth century, it is helpful only to a limited extent to think in terms of regional failure. For example, there was no particular Mediterranean reason for Livorno's 'failure' to touch off a Tuscan industrial revolution. Elsewhere in Europe, successful ports, such as La Rochelle, Cadiz, Hamburg, Cork and Bristol, led to enclave economies,[6] rather than economic transformation.

In addition, it is far from clear that the criteria adopted to define and describe economic progress give due weight to the variety of activity in this period. Research on a number of areas not generally seen in terms of economic development, such as Lombardy[7] and the Veneto in the seventeenth century, or Venetian trade and the Veneto's industry and agriculture in the eighteenth century, or Spain in the last years of the reign of Charles II (r. 1665–1700) and in the eighteenth and nineteenth centuries,[8] has, in fact, indicated a considerable degree of resilience, adaptability and growth that suggests that an economic geography of Europe portraying the South as backward is unhelpful, although it would be mistaken to ignore difficulties. For example, in Spain, the weak state of Castilian agriculture limited the potential for urban expansion, and technological change was unable to overcome this until well into the nineteenth century.[9] For northern Italy, Peter Musgrave's analysis of the Valpolicella in the Veneto reveals that the economy there was growing strongly after a crisis in the early sixteenth century and that it did not have a stagnant 'anti-enterprise' society, as is sometimes suggested of Catholic societies:

this was an economy which was changing its patterns of production and apparently concentrating more on market production ... without at the same time reducing its food production – an economy ... which was able to respond to the problems and challenges presented by a changing world without evidently changing its social or economic structure in a revolutionary sort of way ... The means the South [of Europe] adopted were different and, since they did not involve fundamental restructuring of societies and economies, must be judged by eighteenth-century criteria to have been both more efficient and more beneficial than those adopted by the North.[10]

The last is an important point, which both directs attention to contemporary assessments of the costs and benefits of changes and underlines variations in the acceptability of these costs. This point is of more general applicability, and undermines attempts to adopt a schematic account that assume a similar willingness both to change and to make assessments of costs on the same basis.

The Valpolicella's economy was one 'in which all the parts have to be seen fitting together on an equal basis',[11] rather than an economy based on specialisation. There was a stress on the avoidance of risk and over-commitment that reflected the difference between modern and pre-modern views of specialisation. It was not until the nineteenth century, when 'the law of comparative advantage finally drove out of profitability most of the complementary sources of income ... and placed a growing premium on specialisation in both production and employment',[12] that the economic system of the Valpolicella declined; and, indeed, across much of Europe, economic change was limited until the nineteenth century.

More generally, the varied response by scholars to 'proto-industrialisation'[13] – the movement of industry to some rural areas – indicates the conceptual problems of discussing economic growth. This shift, which sought to bene-fit from lower labour costs and less restrictive labour practices than in the towns, has been seen as progressive; but has also been presented as a system that lessened the prospect of economic transformation. It certainly made the economy, and thus the social dynamics, of some rural areas different to those where agricultural work was the prime form of employment. Proto-industrialisation was a long-term process with important medieval roots. An emphasis on it discourages a stress on a more revolutionary character for industrial change, most commonly presented in terms of the revolutionary impact of a coal-based steam technology.[14] An emphasis on proto-industrialisation also ensures an understanding of the multitude of often complex links between towns and countryside. Although relations between them could be adversarial, this was yet another field in which compromise and negotiation were present alongside, and often as aspects of, less happy relations.

Aside from the conceptual issues, there are also problems posed by the sources. It is very difficult to gain widespread reliable indices for living standards, returns on investments, or the other economic data series that are necessary in assessing the appropriateness of past economic strategies. A small number of series, particularly the Sound Tolls that recorded traffic between the Baltic and the North Sea, and the shipments of silver from the New World into Spain, are frequently cited, but it is unclear that they bear the weight of the wider applicability. In addition, work on the silver shipments has suggested problems with the reliability of the records. It is not possible to discount evasion of customs duties by treating it as a constant factor, because rates of evasion varied, in part as a consequence of the patchy character of administrative effectiveness. Most economic series relate to trade, and there is a danger that large areas of the rural economy, especially those that focused on auto- or local consumption, are underrated.

A reconsideration of the economic success of particular sectors and regions, and an awareness of the continued importance of local variations and identities,[15] undermines any facile ranking of comparative advantage by country or culture, and challenges many of the assumptions about the reasons for the economic development of Atlantic Europe. It is also possible to present the societies of the remainder of Europe as far from stagnant in their economic activities and social assumptions.

As yet there has been no systematic attempt to integrate the repositioning of respective success in the economic world with the comparable debate about state formation and development, but a common theme is readily apparent. The growth of Atlantic Europe remains clear, but the limited value of employing more widely criteria essentially devised to discuss the Atlantic economies is apparent. In the case of state formation, there is less clarity, due, in large part, to divisions about the value of centralisation and bureaucratisation, but it is apparent that the decline of the Mediterranean, specifically of Spain and the Italian principalities, has been overdone. This is more readily clear if the cultural and intellectual life and values of the period are also considered.

The same case about an exaggeration, and undue anticipation, of decline has also been made for the Ottoman Empire. Aside from the need to criticise the teleological aspect of much writing about the Empire, there is also a case for understanding decentralisation there in a benign fashion. Rather than being seen as consequence and cause of weakness, it has been claimed that this permitted a more broad-based political structure, and one with beneficial economic results.[16]

Across Europe, an understanding of the variety of paths of development contributes to a richer assessment of the social dynamics of particular regions. Detailed research reveals very varied patterns of social-political activity and related tensions.[17] These contributed to the character of local political worlds, or what has been termed cultural provinces,[18] and provided the context within which the demands of central government were received.

For example, in the province of Holland, the nobility did more than survive the Dutch Revolt. They also played a major role in a province, and state, too often seen as simply 'bourgeois'. Instead, the conservative and particularistic character of the revolt helped enable Holland's nobility to adapt to the new politics of the United Provinces. The nobles now shared in the sovereignty that had fallen to the States [Parliament] of Holland: they composed its first member and were the only representatives of the countryside. The nobles continued to hold the greatest share of the manors and, as manorial lords, played a major role in the government of the countryside. Such seigneurial jurisdiction was indeed important across most of Europe, but tends to be underrated because public courts receive more attention. The nobles of Holland also played a disproportionately large role in the administrative colleges of the province. Their place in the political élite that governed Holland was in co-operation with that of the urban oligarchs, although social rapprochement was limited: the nobles continued to inter-marry and to retain a way of life that was distinct from that of the urban oligarchs.[19]

As in the case of ruling dynasties and inter-'state' relations, the family strategies of leading landowners played a major role in shaping the system of power in Europe's localities. This was true, for example, of Brescia in the Venetian-ruled *terra firma*. There, the families that sustained the city's most important governmental responsibilities owed their political pre-eminence to family continuity, antiquity, both in terms of time served on council and in terms of social status, wealth, professional standing, and beneficial marriage connections. All five factors were tied to the behaviour of household and lineage. The stability of these families was important to the maintenance of political order. Family ties were crucial in both alliances and disputes among the Brescian élite. They also proved a formidable challenge to the effective administration of justice, and thus to Venetian control. Powerful families at the fore in municipal government sought to run aspects of it, such as the judicial apparatus and the grain provisioning system, in their own interests. In 1640–45, a dispute between the Brescian oligarchy and the Venetian state over the fiscal demands of the latter provided the occasion for a campaign from within Brescia by well-off, but disenfranchised, groups (not the lower orders) challenging the élite and proposing a more broadly based government. The Venetian state eventually chose to compromise with the local oligarchy, and the Brescian protesters, who anyway lacked self-confidence, cohesion and popular support, were rendered powerless by this decision. Thus, the political system of the *terra firma* – local particularism, and, especially, the power of urban aristocracies – continued to prevail, notably in peripheral areas where Venetians themselves owned few properties, such as Brescia and the Friuli.[20]

The resilience of the aristocratic order emerges from research on many other areas. In Aix-en-Provence in France, old and new aristocratic families were readily assimilated in a reasonably fluid social structure. The city offered a variety of sources of income and investment, particularly the opportunity to purchase office, to old and new families alike. Far from there being clear divides within the élite, old families bought offices to nearly the same extent as new families, and they invested in bonds even more. Conversely, new noble families purchased fiefs, and thus expanded their landed profile. Division and hierarchy in Aix were based on the extent, not the nature, of a family's wealth, and on factions and politics, not functions. Marriage encouraged factionalism, but also promoted assimilation and kept the social structure flexible.

The interaction between these local worlds and central government was far from fixed in its character and provided much of the content of politics. Rulers tended to seek to establish their officials as the intermediaries between themselves and the localities, but they encountered resistance from nobles and others who wanted direct representation at court, although this difference was not necessarily a cause of tension and it was possible (and indeed usual) to accommodate both approaches.

In Aix, the first half of the seventeenth century saw the nobility seeking to prevent a further extension of royal authority in Provence, a response to the unpopularity of the Richelieu and Mazarin ministries. However, the 1660s on 'witnessed a cooperative effort between local nobles and that same central authority, a development that ... both accommodated the state-building programs of Louis XIV and promoted the political power of factions within the local urban nobility'[21] – a conclusion similar to that of William Beik on the province of Languedoc.

This process had implications for the nature of local politics. It has been argued that there was a re-creation of the urban community, as 'vertical' ties between social groups broke down and the élite, instead, turned their backs on communal traditions and increasingly looked outwards. This shift has been dated from the late seventeenth century in the major French city of Toulouse. There, economic conditions aggravated social discord, the central government became a more important focus of élite loyalty, and traditional forms of political participation were destroyed.[22] This thesis of the élite turning from communal values has been widely applied, not only in political and social matters, but also with reference to a supposed abandonment of a common world view. The thesis has been linked to a supposedly more scientific approach among the élite, with formerly shared views now labelled as magic. Changing élite attitudes and strategies certainly have to be seen as more than political. There were also important issues of identity that cannot be explained in terms of simple political or socio-economic reductionism.

A common theme in government is the very limited role played by those outside the élite. That did not, however, preclude an important degree of full or partial self-government for many of them. This was a consequence of traditional rights, historical privileges, and the extent to which both central governments and local élites relied on delegation and compromise, and were willing to seek a social consensus that encompassed much of the population. Thus, in Burgundy, village communities played a major role, and the crown strengthened its position by integrating village assemblies into the state's political structure, thus deepening the linkage between rural society and the crown. Influential village figures made up much of what has been seen as a 'middling sort' in society.[23] In addition, friendship ties and other linkages that spanned kinship and patronage helped link 'middling men' to the 'public sphere'[24] in eighteenth-century England and elsewhere.

In cities, those outside the élite had a greater political role than their rural counterparts, such that 'almost every male adult who headed his own household was included in the political system ... they were citizens'. In contrast, women, servants and the poor lacked any real role in political life.[25]

When the élite fractured and sought to mobilise support in civil conflict, as happened repeatedly as a consequence of the religious divisions of the sixteenth century, then those outside the élite could play a more direct role in the political process. Furthermore, the role of popular participation in religious change – 'a dynamic process of engagement between government and people'[26] – could not but have encouraged a wider practice of participation. This was not, however, a break from the situation in the late medieval period, and, in addition, did not cause a political breakdown as long as it did not lead to major disruption.

Nevertheless, the extent to which civil conflict helped disrupt the social hierarchy encouraged crown–élite cohesion, although other reasons also played a major role in this containment of adversarial élite politics. Powerful social tensions led to a series of major peasant uprisings throughout the period, from the German Peasants' War of 1524–25 to those in Bohemia (1775), Transylvania (1784) and France (1789), as well as to a more insistent pattern of local disputes and disaffection, although there were relatively few major peasant risings in the period 1680–1760.[27] The German Peasants' War was a serious conflict motivated by social tension and economic discontent, and encouraged by the volatile atmosphere in Reformation Europe. The forces of princely power and seigneurial authority restored control, although they had to fight full-scale battles to achieve this end. In the early stages, the princes were often forced to rely on fortified positions, but, in the end, mercenaries, cannon and military experience were decisive in the field.

Popular uprisings faced crucial problems. Political ambiguity about the notion of rebellion ensured that there was often a fatal confusion of purpose, while it proved difficult in rebellions to sustain 'vertical links' – between élite and others – without which it was difficult to achieve political and military goals. This proved to be a serious problem in the Dutch Revolt. The developing radicalism of the Protestant cities of Brabant, especially Bruges and Ghent, led, in 1577, to a collapse of the revolt's precarious unity, with the bulk of the nobility moving towards the restoration of the authority of Philip II. In addition, radical goals alienated élite support from the revolt in Naples in 1647–48, a revolt that saw a high level of popular participation and social division.

Some popular risings focused on opposition to local landowners, but others, for example those in France in 1636–37 and 1639, were more a product of the consequences of governmental fiscal demands. If supported by local landowners, these risings were a particular challenge to the power and rationale of the state. Thus the *croquants*, who rose in Gascony in 1636–37, were particularly menacing because they were led by some local gentry. The danger that religion would encourage such action helps explain why the victorious Austrian Habsburgs were so keen to drive Protestant nobles into exile from Austria, Bohemia and Moravia in the 1620s. The frequency of peasant uprisings ensures that it is misleading to think of social stability in terms of quiescence.

Poaching provided a more continuous instance of the same point, although it is unclear how far this should be seen as more than a search for food. At the same time, poaching, like other evasions of regulations, led to an active defiance of the existing order, and one that involved not only poachers but also those that benefited from their activities. In some areas, this was just a matter of family and friends, but, in others, poached meat was sold, ensuring that the benefits and the responsibility were more widely spread. There is no comparative study of poaching in early modern Europe, and information about it is limited and bitty, in large part a matter of episodic judicial activity. Thus the political views of poachers cannot really be recovered.

It might be tempting for some commentators to see them as social warriors who were active members of an alternative society, an approach that has been adopted for pirates and, more generally, sailors,[28] but such an approach has flaws. Aside from the grave lack of necessary information, it was also the case that, operating individually or in small groups, poachers lacked cohesion. Furthermore, the extent to which evasion and defiance of the injunctions of the existing order reflected full-fledged social conflict is unclear.

More generally, the often ambiguous relationship between social stability and quiescence is an issue throughout. It is important to any consideration of the world of the early modern poor, while, as a separate issue of relations, power and authority, there is also the question of gender.

For all groups, new developments were assimilated through the existing contours of society. Thus, factors of consumption and demand, which were so crucial to economic activity, were mediated through notions of honour and reputation. This can also be seen with printing. Although education had played a major role already in late medieval cities without any connection to printing, its importance as a means to approach and use the world of print encouraged a greater emphasis both on education and on the role of learning in education. This was also socially and politically divisive, for access to learning developed in terms of existing social structures and practices. As books, treatises, pamphlets and other printed forms became the principal media for public dispute, the majority of the population were excluded for reasons of cost and/or literacy,[29] and, in some areas, because they spoke a language, such as Gaelic, that was poorly catered for in the world of print.[30]

Furthermore, the culture of print brought new authorities and processes of authorisation. This was a matter not simply of censorship, but also of the way in which contents reflected social expectations. Thus the concerns and experiences of the bulk of the population were excluded, while the standardisation that printing helped bring to writing imposed additional norms. Works produced in regional varieties of languages such as Italian were revised and standardised,[31] and the role of *patois* in speech was not matched in print. Most people could neither read nor afford books, most men and, even more, women, lacked formal education, and the inability of the poor to express themselves equally was accentuated.

More generally, the social politics of Reformation Europe ensured that the population was not consulted on religious change (or its absence); although their attitudes played a major role in the reception of change. However, when there was popular pressure, in response to what were deep-seated and divisive changes in ideology and culture, it was often brutally repressed. The bulk of the population had only a limited participation-stake in the system.[32] If the economic system provided them with work, they had only a limited ability to affect the terms and security of this engagement; although it is important not to underrate the determination with which rights and interests could be maintained, and the extent to which some peasants and artisans not only enjoyed rights, but also were able to group together to maintain them.

However, there was an appreciable section of the population that was scarcely accommodated even in this fashion. This group was the poor understood as a problem, a protean mass which, it was widely feared, constituted an under-class, able and willing to irrupt into the social world.

This had both direct and indirect consequences for governance. The argument that élite cohesion and a willingness to look sympathetically to central government stemmed from concern about the poor is less easy to demonstrate than the simple extent of public response to poverty in terms of major programmes for public welfare. By modern standards, they were gravely limited in terms of coverage, intention and impact, but, aside from the intractable quality of modern poverty, it is worth noting that this effort was being made by a far poorer society. Furthermore, the related public order responses to the poor, while harsh, were less so than those in some other parts of the world.

Slavery was all too much a feature of the European presence in the New

World, where it was crucial to the plantation economies that produced great wealth, and enslavement was used by African rulers keen to dispose of prisoners. This was not the remedy followed in Europe, although the inmates of prison workhouses may not have been confident about the distinction, while galleys were manned, in part, by prisoners kept in slave conditions, and others were deported as forced labour to Europe's colonies.

The emphasis in Christian Europe was on containment of the poor, with coercion being reserved for those judged criminal. A widespread process of institutional provision for the poor joined voluntary and ecclesiastical efforts with governmental intervention.[33] Much of the latter was municipal, with central government playing very little role, although this role became more prominent in the eighteenth century.[34]

Poverty posed serious problems for the effectiveness of government. This was a major question of bureaucratic organisation, but there were wider issues about the capability of the state, not least the limited ability of public authorities to create new jobs. Yet some success was possible in ensuring grain supplies in times of dearth. This reflected a view that dearth should be seen not simply as a natural hardship that was a product of the divine order, but as, at least in part, the result of human action, specifically the manipulation of markets to their own profit by middlemen. Action against middlemen was not new, and, again, there was a continuation from medieval urban regulations to the policies of territorial states, not least in their attempts to combine moral and utilitarian rationales and responses. Information was needed for the planning and pursuit of social welfare policies. In England, commissions were issued to ensure grain supplies and, from 1586–87, this policy was based on attempts to ensure information on the distribution of grain and the size of households.[35]

In so far as it can be assessed, governments proved more effective at controlling the poor than at containing poverty, although the extent of this control was limited. Control of the poor involved the categorisation of those judged unacceptable, with those seen as the needy or virtuous poor distinguished from those treated as problems, although, alongside charity care and humanity, the treatment of the former could be hard and focused on control, or at least segregation. Legislation outlined a categorisation that was also publicised in sermons and by the use of such techniques as providing tokens and passes to those seen as acceptable, and/or by obliging them to wear distinctive clothing. In Scotland there was a licensed begging system, a blue badge granting the right to beg in one's home parish. The less fortunate were regarded as public criminals, and treated accordingly in a society that made plentiful use of corporal punishment.

The two processes were combined when the criminalised poor were publicly designated and stigmatised through branding, whipping and the use of the pillory.[36] This process of public shaming was an important aspect of the power of authorities, both lay (whether public or seigneurial) and ecclesiastical, in the period, but one that was challenged when the sense of community was weakened or when authorities sought to enforce new controls and injunctions. Many of the criminalised poor were also incarcerated in harsh conditions.

Most of those who suffered thus were men, but the treatment of women was also part of the social dynamics of power. In its broadest sense, Europe was part of a world that put an emphasis on male authority and stereotypes, and that, in large part, defined femininity in terms of what masculinity was not expected to fulfil. Male authority was seen not only in state and community, but also in the household.[37] The beating of wives was commonplace, and was part of a system that treated them, alongside children and servants, as dependants and, therefore, inferiors.

There were changes in the position of women in the period, especially those stemming from the Reformation, but it is important not to exaggerate them. Much remained traditional, as in the different standards applied to male and female pre-marital and extra-marital sex, and the limitations on the economic opportunities of most women. The status and wealth of women continued to be derived from their husbands and fathers, and thus defined by them. Many marriages continued to be arranged, while wives' control over their dowries was limited and they were not normally allowed to make wills.[38]

At the same time, gender relations were subject to the play of personality and to the often complex expectations of family and kinship, and, in practice, women enjoyed more control over aspects of their own lives than legal codes or prescriptive literature might enjoin. The very openness of legal processes to women also offered a way in which they sought more control.[39] In general, women were active in the legal process, and thus had more control over their lives than patriarchal nostrums might suggest. Possibly this contributed to what has been seen as 'a general feeling of anxiety among men regarding the gender order in the sixteenth and seventeenth centuries ... that certainly in part was due to the new assertiveness of women',[40] although that may, in part, be due to the greater availability of sources thanks to the spread of printing.

The Reformation provided new opportunities for female spirituality, and some women were able to claim and exercise a right to conscience and self-determination in religious matters. These opportunities did not, however, fully transcend gender limitations. The attitudes of Protestant sects reflected traditional social ideals and practices, and few women rose to positions of authority within them. Instead, there was an emphasis on the home as the proper place for female religiosity.

Furthermore, convents, which had provided women with a world with some autonomy, were dissolved.[41] Nuns were probably the group that lost most from the Reformation. Within Catholic Europe, the currents of Counter-Reformation were, in part, shaped by women, particularly at the level of individual households and communities. Women also played a major role in the social welfare dimension of Catholic society, a dimension that linked spiritual injunctions to charity with the practical needs of communities.

The Reformation did lead to a more sympathetic attitude towards marriage and towards sexual love within marriage, one that was reflected and strengthened by the fact that, in Protestant Europe, clergy now could be married, whereas, in Catholic states, such as Bavaria, there were campaigns to end clerical concubinage (informal marriages). Across Europe, concern about the disruptive nature of sexual desire focused on single and adulterous women, but these sexual standards appear to have reflected female as well as male views, suggesting that women, to some degree, supported the maintenance of patriarchy. The extent to which the tensions, compromises and variety that characterised the authority of heads of households can usefully be compared with those of princely rulers is unclear, but both focused anxieties about order and stability at the same time that they represented sites for negotiation. Whereas rulers were readily compared to God as images of authority, the comparison of the latter with heads of households was limited by the absence of a married deity.

Women punished as witches by male-dominated legal systems suffered terribly. However, women were not simply the victims of witchcraft accusations: they were also actively involved in bringing prosecutions and in acting as witnesses and as searchers for marks supposedly revealing witches. Belief in witches reflected the widespread conviction that forces of good and evil battled for control of the world, and throughout the world, and that this battle could be personalised, although the difficulty of creating a comprehensive account of popular beliefs is such that there is undue emphasis on the reports of inquisitors.[42] This was a world that was shadowed by a world of spirits, good and bad, and these spirits were seen, and believed, to intervene frequently in the life of humans. This belief brought together Christian notions, in particular providentialism, a conviction of God's direct intervention in the life of individuals, the intercessory role of saints, sacraments, prayer and belief, and the existence of heaven, purgatory, hell and the devil, with a related and overlapping group of ideas, beliefs and customs that were partially Christianised, but also testified to a mental world that was not explicable in terms of Christian theology. This was a world of good and evil, knowledge and magic, of fatalism, of the occult, and of astrology and alchemy.

The true path of Christian virtue and salvation was challenged not only by false prophets laying claim to the word of Jesus, but also by a malevolent world presided over by the devil. Witches were allegedly prominent among his followers. The Christian world-picture provided much ground for fear, with millenarian, apocalyptic and eschatological anxieties drawing heavily on the Book of Revelation.[43] These anxieties appear to have become stronger in the sixteenth century as a consequence of the Reformation, although this process may owe something to increased surveillance by anxious authorities combined with the greater evidence provided by printing. It is widely argued that concern about the devil as a powerful malign force directing an empire of evil, including, in particular, witches, increased from the sixteenth century, before declining from the late seventeenth or, in some areas, early eighteenth, century.

This fearful world could be only partially countered by Christianity and, indeed, other forms of white magic, but the very sense of menace and danger helps to account for the energy devoted to religious issues and the fears encouraged by violent and/or enforced changes in Church belief and practice, for example the despoliation of shrines and ending of pilgrimages. The range and depth of popular responses to religious challenges serve as a reminder of the need to consider the populace as more than a passive recipient of policies and initiatives from the more powerful, and is a more general instance of the need to avoid considering religious issues as separate from those of politics and society. These religious issues were part of a world that cannot be thus disaggregated for discussion without doing considerable violence to contemporary attitudes. In addition, study of religious issues provides a way to understand other aspects of the period. The wearing of crucifixes, the frequency of prayers, by individuals, families and communities, the making of the sign of the cross, and the reverence shown to religious images and, in Orthodox Russia, icons, were all aspects of a world in which the doings of the day were suffused with Christian action and thought.

These concerns and responses were focused by preachers, and, in Catholic and Orthodox Europe, this was part of a world whose needs were, in part, met by pilgrimage shrines, relics, processions and saintly clerics. All of these facets of religious activity were given new energy during the Counter-Reformation. 'Living saints' included visionaries, stigmatics, mystics, miracle-workers, curers and exorcists, and they fought the devil and other foes of the Church. Thus, Catholic victories in battle, seen as God-given, were regarded as arising from saintly intercession: both that of the Virgin and those of prominent religious figures, such as Dominicus a Jesu Maria, a Carmelite who was present at the victory of Catholic forces over the Bohemians at the White Mountain in 1620.

It is important not to present popular religiosity as static, geographically uniform, and simple. Concepts such as popular religion and terms such as traditional beliefs carry with them such a presumption, but it is misleading.[44] The very vitality of popular religious practices, and their close interaction with more established currents, helps underline the depth of the psychological crisis caused by the Protestant Reformation, and also the problems faced by those trying to enforce the new religious settlement.

The Protestant Reformation, with its emphasis on a vernacular Bible, ensured that good and evil became more literary and less oral and visual than hitherto, but that did not diminish the need for people to understand their world in terms of the struggle between the two: indeed, it may even have encouraged it. The Reformation shattered some important traditional patterns of faith, and thus posed new psychological demands. The belief in the efficacy of prayers for the souls of the dead in purgatory was fundamental to monasticism as well as to chantries. Its disappearance, or at least its discouragement, represented a major and disturbing discontinuity in emotional and religious links between generations. The ending of masses for the dead destroyed the community of the living and the dead, although this relationship had not been free from shifts of emphasis during previous centuries.

Protestantism had little time for sacred places, such as holy wells and shrines, but that did not lessen the sense of direct providential intervention, and of a daily interaction of the human world and the wider spheres of good and evil. Evil, malevolence and the inscrutable workings of the divine will seemed the only way to explain the sudden pitfalls of the human condition. Fatal accidents and tragic illnesses frequently snuffed out life with brutal and unpredictable rapidity.

Belief in a powerful and remorseless devil[45] and concern about witches gained a new prominence in the sixteenth century, and bridged élite and populace, Church and state, although there was a contrast between the category of witchcraft imposed by the law and less-defined traditional religious and folklore beliefs. The frequency of curses in disputes and the concern to which they gave rise focused attention on the power of bewitchment and its ready impact on individual lives. Most witch charges arose from personal quarrels rather than inquisitorial action by governing agencies.[46] Accusations of witchcraft arose from a range of causes, including refusals to give charity, but fear of real evil was the core. It was believed possible to cause harm to person and property using magical means, as part of a rejection of society and Christianity.

These beliefs were not swept away by the Renaissance, the Reformation, or the supposed onset of the modern age. Indeed, they did not decline in impact until the late seventeenth or eighteenth century. Across Europe – Protestant, Catholic and Orthodox – belief in prediction, astrology, alchemy and the occult was especially strong in the early seventeenth century, as was fear of witchcraft, although in some areas, such as the Electorate of the Palatinate in Germany, witch trials did not occur. The Emperor Rudolf II (r. 1576–1612) was very interested in astrology and the occult, while, in Britain, James VI and I wrote against witches. This was also a period of rising confessional tension. The Sacred Congregation for the Propagation of the Faith, founded by Pope Gregory XV in 1622, marked an upsurge in Catholic proselytising efforts.

James VI and I's writings were an aspect of the way in which news of witches was spread in the new culture of print: in learned treatises, chapbooks, printed ballads and engravings. Information was increasingly shaped as a commodity by the culture of print, which, in turn, ensured its wide dissemination, although written newsletters also played a similar role, especially for political news.[47] Rather than treating this process as an unproblematic aspect of modernisation, it is important to note the extent to which information was as much about strange providences, for example interventions by divine or diabolical agencies or sightings of peculiar animals, as about a more secular account of life. Similarly, the heretical Italian miller Domenico Scandella was able to get hold of literature that expanded his horizons, although it is unclear how far his unorthodox views on creation and theology were widely held or whether they can be seen as a sign of a deeply rooted subordinate religious culture.[48]

The scientific revolution has enjoyed much scholarly attention, and the inventions, ideas and intellectual systems arising from, or associated with, the work of Galileo (1564–1642) and Newton (1642–1727) in particular represented both major advances in European thought and also a development that, in the long term, was of global consequence. It helped ensure that, in a world that was to be increasingly understood in scientific terms, and manipulated accordingly, these terms were European and linked to other aspects of Western culture. The laws on scientific reactions developed by Newton, Boyle (1627–91) and others sought to establish clear causal relationships with universal applicability. There was clearly in the seventeenth century an important intellectual development that also had a long-term impact on Christian Europe's capability in economic and military developments relative to those of other societies. The emphasis on observation, experimentation and mathematics seen in astronomy, chemistry, physics and other branches of science provided encouragement for information-gathering and the use of data to help both decision-making and cycles of testing policies and then amending them.[49]

However, recent work has indicated the extent to which new scientific ideas were frequently heavily dependent on the earlier learning.[50] Ptolemaic geocentrism remained important, as did the Aristotelian ideas that had been prominent at the close of the Middle Ages. Whichever scientific ideas were followed, it is unclear how far they affected attitudes towards government. It is attractive to draw a linkage between the definition of 'the natural world as a harmonious and rational order, guided by clear underlying principles' and political assumptions,[51] but the process was far from clear-cut.

Most of the population was unaware of the new science. It was still widely believed in the eighteenth century that astrological anatomies and zodiacs were keys to character and guides to the future, that extra-terrestrial forces intervened in the affairs of the world, particularly human and animal health and the state of the crops and weather, and that each constellation presided over a particular part of man, guidance being provided by almanacs. Although it is generally argued that belief in magic and divine intervention declined in the early modern period,[52] this thesis rests on insufficient research to be considered as applicable across the whole of Europe. Moreover, many did not accept the new cosmology.

At the important level of interaction between clergy and people, an interaction where beliefs were shaped and where religious ideas played a major role, Richard Creed noted of the Church of Nicolas of Tolentino in Rome, which he visited in March 1700:

> the fathers make little cakes as big as a farthing, and stick seven of them together; and so call them the seven loaves; they bless the flour and make them with holy water and so give them to the people to eat when they are sick; and if they recover they say the cakes cured them; if they die they say the cakes saved their souls.[53]

The apparent poisoning, or, more probably, contamination of the communion wine on 12 September 1776, the General Day of Prayer and Repentance, in Zurich's main church, which became a major episode in German thought in the period, led to much discussion of the nature of evil, and indicated that what counted as valid evidence and interpretation was a matter of controversy. Johann Lavater (1741–1801), a leading Zurich preacher, claimed that attacks on traditional Christian faith had undermined the foundations of morality, and were therefore responsible for the crime. Johann Waser, another pastor and a critic of the nature of oligarchic rule in Zurich, was executed in 1780 because he was falsely accused of being entangled in the affair.[54] Lavater himself was to die of wounds received during the French occupation of Zurich.

The use of the culture of print for preserving tradition and traditional learning, as well as for disseminating new ideas and influences, is a reminder of the ability of traditional influences to respond to new opportunities, and of the dynamic possibilities of traditional learning. The same was true of Catholicism. Printed propaganda was far from being a Protestant prerogative. Instead there was an extensive Catholic printed propaganda that included, in Bavaria, pilgrimage books that provided explanations for the origins and miracles of local shrines.[55]

The troubled character of the popular imagination was not one that readily lent itself to a conviction of the superior value of earthly government. Similarly, the desire for inexhaustible supplies of food and wealth central to many folk tales was not one that could be fulfilled by economic growth. Indeed the combination of these beliefs reflected the hardship of the life of the poor and their need to turn to magical solutions.

This was scarcely surprising. The poor were under great pressure, because 'social dynamics' were more a question of élite demands on the poor than of pressures from the poor on the élite. The demographic expansion of the sixteenth century put pressure on living standards, while economic growth could not provide sufficient employment for the rising numbers of poor. The labour shortages, high wages and low rents of the late medieval period were replaced by a price inflation that had an even greater effect since it followed a period that had known scant inflation. In many areas, rents and food prices rose faster than wages. This hit both tenants and those with little or no land. In this volatile and tense situation, agrarian capitalism became more intense. Landlords tried to increase the yield of their customary estates and to destroy the system of customary tenure.

In general, in the seventeenth century, stagnation replaced demographic and economic growth. Far from improving the lot of the bulk of the population, this led to widespread economic difficulties, as well as serious fiscal strains on states that were also bearing the burdens of lengthy conflicts. The allocation of the resulting costs of the economic downturn by the political and social structures of the period was such as to bear heavily on the bulk of the population.

In Eastern Europe, a determination, and ability, to control labour in an area where it was in short supply, as well as to contain labour costs and to profit from the opportunity to export grain to Western Europe, led to the spread of serfdom, although this was not a new process: serfdom had been spreading from the fifteenth century. Peasant rights were lessened, for example in the Russian legal code of 1649, and, prior to the eighteenth century, rulers in Eastern Europe made few attempts to see that surviving rights were observed. The attitudes and powers of landlords in Eastern Europe, not least the character of their seigneurial jurisdiction, were crucial to the spread of serfdom. A similar process has been seen as occurring in southern Italy, although there the emphasis is on refeudalisation, whereas, in much of Eastern Europe, this was not a return to an earlier situation.

Even where serfdom was not at issue, peasants found that they were put under serious pressure due to landlord demands, taxation, debts, market insecurity and the climate, which deteriorated in the seventeenth century, affecting crop yields. This deterioration has been attributed to sunspot activity. The appropriation, sometimes by simple seizure, of common land by more powerful landowners was a widespread problem, for example in Italy and in England, where it led to enclosure riots. This was an aspect of the more general attempt by landlords to use their position for their profit. Even when these issues were not to the fore, peasant holdings suffered from a lack of capital, and from difficulties in gaining access to distant markets and to the opportunities they presented.

As with rulers in both international and domestic relations, landlords' economic and seigneurial positions could variously lead them to a wish to fix rights and, alternatively, to an attempt to leave them imprecise. The extent to which both methods could be seen as ways to advance interests reflected the social and political practice of the age, as well as the tension between attempts to establish, fix and sustain conventions and regulations, and the more inchoate and less rigid nature of practices and attitudes. The prevalence of litigation was an aspect of this tension.

Social and economic pressures helped lend urgency to the process of asserting and expanding rights, and these pressures did not only affect the poor. Indeed landowner debt, and even more the prospect and fear of debt, were powerful factors encouraging economic and social pressures throughout society. These debts arose in part from conspicuous consumption, but were also a consequence of other aspects of status, particularly the costs of service to the crown. This helped to increase divisions among the nobility for those who accumulated debts through service, or who were unable to alleviate the burden of debt by service, felt bitter towards more fortunate counterparts. The latter were frequently the allies and dependants of favourite ministers, and thus debt helped register political opportunity and dissension among the élite. Thus the improvement of government finances was of great interest to the nobility as it lessened the need for states to transfer part of the cost of government, in particular of raising and maintaining troops, to them.[56] At all levels, those who lacked access to power found that litigation and other means of arbitration did not serve them as well as their powerful counterparts.

More generally, throughout the early modern period, economic problems led to social pressure on the weaker members of the community and those judged most marginal, for example to measures against illegitimacy and bridal pregnancy, to the insistence on formal church weddings as the sole source of marital legitimacy, and to attempts to prevent the poor from marrying. Concern about alleged witchcraft developed in this context of social tension and coercion.

The poor were harshly treated by man and nature alike. They ate less, and less well, than the wealthier members of the community, and their housing was of far lower standard, and generally less long-lasting. The malnutrition of the poor reduced their resistance to ill-health, as well as ensuring that, had they been willing, they were less able to challenge authority. Growth was stunted and energy levels hit. Poor diet particularly encouraged parasitic infection, hepatitis and salmonella. Ill-health affected fertility and also maternal fitness during pregnancy. Although rich and poor alike were hit hard by the diseases of the period, the demographic regime of the poor was less favourable. Child mortality figures were also higher among the poor because the social pressures that led to infanticide were far more common among them.

While the wealthy might choose to seek compromise in their disputes with each other, they generally showed less willingness to do so in disputes with their social inferiors. Social, political, economic and moral intimidation were frequently the lot of the poor. The able-bodied unemployed were regarded as lazy or greedy, and were treated harshly as rogues and vagabonds. The visual and literary image of these groups was negative. They were often presented as bestial or semi-bestial. In much of Eastern Europe, serfs were routinely beaten for real or alleged misdemeanours,[57] while landlords' torture chambers were not unknown. The treatment of native peoples and imported slaves in European colonies provided a more pronounced picture of attitudes to labour control, but it shared some of the characteristics of serfdom.

Yet, alongside an emphasis on top-down structures of authority and drives for reformation and control, it is important to emphasise the extent to which demands and changes were negotiated as well as imposed, such that the 'state' was the expression of a wide stratum of society.[58] Furthermore, there was a considerable degree of activity and innovation stemming from the bulk of the population. This can be seen in Counter-Reformation religious sensibilities, and, more generally, in the nature of popular religion. The local community was the nerve centre of everyday religion, and was capable of maintaining its own identity, while at the same time absorbing, adapting and rejecting external pressures for reforms. In Catalonia, some of the most important Counter-Reformation developments, such as the Rosary and the confraternities, took root in popular culture, as did new saints and a more sacramental religion.[59] Indeed, it is often not helpful to propose a clear division between official and popular Catholicism. In south-west Germany, Catholicism became increasingly dependent on the role of the parochial clergy, but this 'clericalisation' occurred in part due to popular pressure.[60] Furthermore, variations in popular needs and desires helped ensure that the character of Catholic confessionalism varied greatly.[61]

Most peasant unrest was directed not so much at changing the system as at more specific causes, thus conforming to the general patterns of political activity in early modern Europe. Opposed to innovations, such as new obligations, and to what were construed as abuses of authority, much peasant action was aimed at conservative redress through direct action that would elicit a sympathetic response or favourable royal intervention. This can be interpreted as reflecting a lack of revolutionary consciousness, although at times, as in Transylvania in 1784–85, when the abolition of the nobility was sought by the rebelling serfs led by Horea, goals were very radical.

More than prudential concerns about what could be achieved was at stake. There was also a political dimension to peasant activity. The identity of the oppressor in the more violent risings was frequently ethnic or religious. In Transylvania in 1595 the nobles brutally suppressed the Székelys, an ethnic group, many of whom were serfs who had been offered their liberty by the prince the previous year if they helped against the Ottomans. This led the Székelys to help the Voivode of Wallachia when he invaded Transylvania in 1599. He restored Székely liberties, only for them to be revoked in 1600 when an imperial army gained control. The major peasant rising in Upper Austria in 1626 was in part a response to Counter-Reformation pressures, the Golden Charter of the 1768 rising in the western Ukraine ordered the killing of Poles and Jews, and, in the Pugachev rising in the Volga valley in 1773–74, there was support for the Old Believers and cultural antipathy to the Westernisation of Russia, as well as hostility to the aristocracy.

The extent to which social identities and fault-lines were religious and ethnic as much as class-based, indeed that religion and ethnicity should, at least in this respect, be seen as social contexts, was not only important to domestic tensions. They also played a role in the configuration of political control. The stress in most states on religious homogeneity, and the treatment of toleration as a weakness, ensured that some religious and ethnic groups were marginalised, becoming an aspect of the categorisation of an internal hierarchy, as well, sometimes, as an apparent problem of control and order.

More generally, religious policy and practice need to be seen as central to what has been presented as a politics of paternalism, with the reciprocities that the latter entailed. This has led to a call for 'a developmental typology of paternalist constellations of authority reaching back into the fifteenth and sixteenth centuries, which might do more justice to the compromise-rich transitional character of the early modern period than the scholastic controversy over the – limited – scope of state modernisation efforts'.[62]

Governments did not attempt to play off religious and ethnic groups in order to maximise their own power and room for manoeuvre. Instead, there was a close process of identification between crown and state, religion and society, which arose directly from the sacral character of kingship and the sense of the indivisibility of religious truth. These ideological factors were important to the culture of authority, and thus to the range of options available to rulers as they engaged with the social dynamics of their dominions. They also ensured that challenges to orthodoxy and religious authority called sacral governance into question.[63]

Notes

1. The literature can be approached through J. DeVries, *The Economy of Europe in an Age of Crisis, 1600–1750* (Cambridge, 1976), R. S. Duplessis, *Transitions to Capitalism in Early Modern Europe* (Cambridge, 1997), T. Scott (ed.), *The Peasantries of Europe from the Fourteenth to the Eighteenth Centuries* (Harlow, 1998), and H. Kamen, *Early Modern European Society* (2000).

2. L. Wolff, *Inventing Eastern Europe: The Map of Civilization on the Mind of the Enlightenment* (Stanford, CA, 1994). See also J. N. Hillgarth, *The Mirror of Spain, 1500–1700: The Formation of a Myth* (Ann Arbor, MI, 2000).

3. J. K. J. Thomson, *Decline in History. The European Experience* (Oxford, 1998).

4. J. J. McCusker and K. Morgan (eds), *The Early Modern Atlantic Economy* (Cambridge, 2000).

5. M. Greene, 'Beyond the northern invasion: the Mediterranean in the seventeenth century', *Past and Present*, no. 174 (February 2002), pp. 46–52 and *A Shared World: Christians and Muslims in the Early Modern Mediterranean* (Princeton, NJ, 2002).

6. K. Morgan, *Bristol and the Atlantic Trade in the Eighteenth Century* (Cambridge, 1993).

7. D. Sella, *Crisis and Continuity. The Economy of Spanish Lombardy in the Seventeenth Century* (Cambridge, MA, 1979); G. Pagano de Divitiis, *English Merchants in Seventeenth-Century Italy* (Cambridge, 1998). For a recent emphasis on decline, G. Hanlon, *Early Modern Italy, 1550–1800: Three Seasons in European History* (Basingstoke, 2000).

8. J. Georgelin, *Venise au siècle des lumières* (Paris, 1978); D. R. Ringrose, *Spain, Europe, and the 'Spanish Miracle', 1700–1900* (Cambridge, 1996); B. Y. Casalilla, 'City and Countryside in Spain: Changing Structures, Changing Relationships, 1450–1850', in J. A. Marino (ed.), *Early Modern History and the Social Sciences. Testing the Limits of Braudel's Mediterranean* (Kirksville, MO, 2002), p. 57.

9. D. S. Reher, *Town and Country in Pre-Industrial Spain, Cuenca 1550–1870* (Cambridge, 1990).

10. P. Musgrave, *Land and Economy in Baroque Italy: Valpolicella, 1630–1797* (Leicester, 1992), p. 75.

11. Musgrave, *Land*, p. 180.

12. Ibid., pp. 183–4.

13. S. C. Ogilvie and M. Cerman (eds), *European Proto-Industrialisation* (Cambridge, 1996).

14. D. Rollison, *The Local Origins of Modern Society, Gloucestershire 1500–1800* (1992).

15. X. de Planhol, *An Historical Geography of France* (Cambridge, 1994), pp. 293–320.

16. A. Salzmann, 'An *ancien régime* revisited: "privatization" and political economy in the eighteenth-century Ottoman Empire', *Politics and Society*, 21 (1993), pp. 393–423.

17. For social strains in Italy, C. Black, *Early Modern Italy: A Social History* (2001).

18. C. Phythian-Adams (ed.), *Societies, Cultures and Kinship, 1580–1850. Cultural Provinces and English Local History* (Leicester, 1992).

19. H. J. K. van Nierop, *The Nobility of Holland. From Knights to Regents, 1500–1650* (Cambridge, 1993).

20. J. M. Ferraro, *Family and Public Life in Brescia, 1580–1650: The Foundations of Power in the Venetian State* (Cambridge, 1993). For the role of family links and marriage, S. Chojnacki, *Women and Men in Renaissance Venice: Twelve Essays on Patrician Society* (Baltimore, MD, 2000).

21. D. Bohanan, *Old and New Nobility in Aix-en-Provence, 1600–1695: Portrait of an Urban Élite* (Baton Rouge, LA, 1992), p. 97.

22. R. A. Schneider, *Public Life in Toulouse, 1463–1789. From Municipal Republic to Cosmopolitan City* (Ithaca, NY, 1990).

23. H. L. Root, *Peasants and King in Burgundy: Agrarian Foundations of French Absolutism* (Berkeley, CA, 1987); K. Wrightson, 'The politics of the parish in early modern England', in P. Griffiths, A. Fox and S. Hindle (eds), *The Experience of Authority in Early Modern England* (Basingstoke, 1996), pp. 10–46; Hindle, *The State and Social Change in Early Modern England, c. 1550–1640* (Basingstoke, 2000); D. Luebke, *His Majesty's Rebels: Communities, Factions and Rural Revolt in the Black Forest, 1725–1745* (Ithaca, NY, 1997); W. te Brake, *Shaping History. Ordinary People in European Politics, 1500–1700* (Berkeley, CA, 1998). For the relationship between socio-economic change and absolutism, T. Munck, *The Pesantry and the Early Absolute Monarchy in Denmark, 1660–1708* (Copenhagen, 1979).

24. N. Tadmor, *Family and Friends in Eighteenth-Century England. Household, Kinship and Patronage* (Cambridge, 2001), pp. 216–36, 277.

25. C. R. Friedrichs, *Urban Politics in Early Modern Europe* (2000), p. 73; M. Walker, *German Home Towns* (Ithaca, NY, 1971).

26. E. H. Shagan, *Popular Politics and the English Reformation* (Cambridge, 2002), p. 309.

27. T. Scott, 'Peasant revolts in early modern Germany', *Historical Journal*, 28 (1985), pp. 455–68; T. Barnett-Robisheaux, 'Peasant revolts in Germany and central Europe after the Peasants War', *Central European History*, 17 (1984), pp. 384–403; H. Gabel and W. Schulze, 'Peasant resistance and politicisation in Germany in the eighteenth century', in E. Hellmuth (ed.), *The Transformation of Political Culture* (Oxford, 1990), pp. 119–46.

28. M. Rediker, *Between the Devil and the Deep Blue Sea: Merchant Seamen, Pirates, and the Anglo-American Maritime World, 1700–1750* (Cambridge, 1987); P. Linebaugh and Rediker, *The Many-Headed Hydra. Sailors, Slaves, Commoners, and the Hidden History of the Revolutionary Atlantic* (2000).

29. M. Van Gelderen, *The Political Thought of the Dutch Revolt 1555–1590* (Cambridge, 1992); E. Eisenstein, *The Printing Revolution in Early Modern Europe* (Cambridge, 1993).

30. T. C. Barnard, 'Protestants and the Irish language, c.1675–1725', *Journal of Ecclesiastical History*, 44 (1993), pp. 270–2.

31. B. Richardson, *Print Culture in Renaissance Italy: The Editor and the Vernacular Text, 1470–1600* (Cambridge, 1994).

32. R. Po-Chia Hsia, *Social Discipline in the Reformation. Central Europe 1550–1750* (1989).

33. C. Fairchilds, *Poverty and Charity in Aix-en-Provence, 1640–1789* (Baltimore, MD, 1976); C. Jones, *The Charitable Imperative: Hospitals and Nursing in Ancien Regime and Revolutionary France* (1989).

34. R. Schwartz, *Policing the Poor in Eighteenth-Century France* (Chapel Hill, NC, 1988).

35. T. Gray (ed.), *Harvest Failure in Devon and Cornwall: The Book of Orders and the Corn Surveys of 1623 and 1630–1* (Redruth, 1992).

36. R. Jütte, *Poverty and Deviance in Early Modern Europe* (Cambridge, 1994).

37. M. E. Wiesner, *Women and Gender in Early Modern Europe* (2nd edn, Cambridge, 2000); J. G. Turner (ed.), *Sexuality and Gender in Early Modern Europe: Institutions, Texts, Images* (1993); O. Hufton, *The Prospect Before Her: A History of Women in Western Europe, I: 1500–1800* (1996).

38. J.-L. Flandrin, *Families in Former Times: Kinship, Household and Sexuality* (Cambridge, 1976); O. Hufton, *The Prospect Before Her: a History of Women in Western Europe I* (1996).

39. J. Kermode and G. Walker (eds), *Women, Crime and the Courts in Early Modern England* (1994); J. M. Ferraro, *Marriage Wars in Late Renaissance Venice* (Oxford, 2001), p. 158.

40. E. B. Weaver, 'Gender', in G. Ruggiero (ed.), *A Companion to the Worlds of the Renaissance* (2002), p. 203.

41. N. Z. Davis, *Society and Culture in Early Modern France* (Stanford, CA, 1965), p. 119.

42. R. Briggs, *Witches and Neighbours: The Social and Cultural Context of European Witchcraft* (Oxford, 1996).

43. A. Cunningham and O. P. Grell, *The Four Horsemen of the Apocalypse: Religion, War, Famine and Death in Reformation Europe* (Cambridge, 2000).

44. T. Johnson, 'Holy fabrications: the catacomb saints and the Counter-Reformation in Bavaria', *Journal of Ecclesiastical History*, 47 (1996), pp. 274–97, esp. pp. 274, 294–7.

45. D. Oldridge, *The Devil in Early Modern England* (Stroud, 2001).

46. J. Barry, M. Hester and G. Roberts (eds), *Witchcraft in Early Modern Europe. Studies in Culture and Belief* (Cambridge, 1996).

47. H. Duranton and P. Rétat (eds), *Gazettes et Information Politique sous l'Ancien Régime* (Saint-Étienne, 1999); A. Bellany, *The Politics of Court Scandal in Early Modern England. News Culture and the Overbury Affair, 1603–1660* (Cambridge, 2002), pp. 75–135.

48. C. Ginzburg, *The Cheese and the Worms* (1992).

49. R. Porter and M. Teich (eds), *The Scientific Revolution in National Context* (Cambridge, 1992); P. Dear, *Revolutionizing the Sciences: European Knowledge and Its Ambitions, 1500–1700* (Basingstoke, 2001).

50. S. S. Genuth, *Comets, Popular Culture and the Birth of Modern Cosmology* (Princeton, NJ, 1997).

51. P. H. Wilson, *Absolutism in Central Europe* (2000), p. 17.

52. The most prominent exponent of this approach is K. Thomas, *Religion and the Decline of Magic* (1971).

53. Creed journal, private collection.

54. J. Freedman, *A Poisoned Chalice* (Princeton, NJ, 2002).

55. P. M. Soergel, *Wondrous in His Saints. Counter-Reformation Propaganda in Bavaria* (Berkeley, CA, 1993).

56. For the prevalence of this, D. Parrott, *Richelieu's Army: War, Government and Society in France, 1624–1642* (Cambridge, 2002).

57. A. Kahan, *The Plow, the Hammer and the Knout: An Economic History of Eighteenth-Century Russia* (Chicago, IL, 1985).

58. P. Blickle (ed.), *Resistance, Representation, and Community* (Oxford, 1997).

59. H. Kamen, *The Phoenix and the Flame. Catalonia and the Counter Reformation* (New Haven, CT, 1993).

60. M. R. Forster, 'Clericalism and communalism in German Catholicism', in M. Reinhart (ed.), *Infinite Boundaries. Order, Disorder, and Reorder in Early Modern German Culture* (1998), p. 75.

61. Forster, 'With and without confessionalization. Varieties of early modern German Catholicism', *Journal of Early Modern History*, 1 (1997), pp. 341–3.

62. N. Schindler, *Rebellion, Community and Custom in Early Modern Germany* (Cambridge, 2002), p. 299.

63. D. K. Van Kley, *The Religious Origins of the French Revolution: From Calvin to the Civil Constitution, 1560–1791* (New Haven, CT, 1996).

CHAPTER 5

Chronological Perspectives

§ HAVING outlined the structural aspects of the situation, it is necessary to look at how they changed over time. It is particularly appropriate to discuss how religious divisions, the mid-seventeenth-century crisis, and absolutism fit into this analysis. In part, the analysis hinges on expectations about the nature of political culture. If tension is seen as a normal feature of political society, not a sign of crisis or incipient crisis, then it is possible to present a different emphasis to one that focuses on divisions and crises. It is also important to avoid a teleological account, and, instead, to offer one that incorporates regional and sectoral variations.

Beginning in 1550 ensures that the initial crisis of the Reformation is not discussed, but also that the period under discussion begins with a half-century in which conflict within states took place across much of the Continent. This was particularly, but far from only, the case in France, the Low Countries, Scotland, Ireland and England, in each of which rebellion was linked to religious disaffection, although other factors also played a role – particularly in France and Scotland, tensions within the élite. In Germany there was a serious, but short-lived, crisis in 1552 when a French-backed rebellion by a group of Protestant princes led by Maurice of Saxony drove the Emperor Charles V from Germany. The crisis was resolved in 1555 when the Peace of Augsburg accepted the position of Lutheranism, at least to the extent of allowing Lutheran territorial rulers within the Empire to make Lutheranism the religion of their territories. This was symptomatic of the need to consider political factors (and, also, the type of political factor that had to be considered) when seeking to settle religious issues. Other Protestant faiths were not tolerated under the peace.

The nature of this settlement was important. Far from the terms of the settlement being a privilege and the Emperor giving a religious peace that re-created harmony, this settlement was the product of hard bargaining at a Diet, and set the basis for decades of contention that would challenge imperial authority and political cohesion. Indeed, there was to be conflict, particularly in dioceses, such as Cologne, where the prince-archbishop sought to become a Protestant and introduce secularisation.

Imperial authority had for centuries been contested in Germany and northern Italy. These conflicts had been essentially political in character, but, from the Investiture Crisis of the late eleventh century, there had also been an important ecclesiastical dimension with struggles between the authority of Emperor and Pope interacting with disputes over control of Italy. On several occasions, Emperors sponsored anti-Popes who contested the authority of the Pope, but the idea of a universal Pope and an undivided Catholicism was not challenged, and on each occasion schism was resolved.

The Reformation, however, introduced a major ideological barrier to the renewal of papal and imperial authority. This undermined the possibilities flowing from contingent events. These included the discovery of large quantities of exploitable silver in the New World territories of the Habsburgs, and the Ottoman defeat of the Hungarians in 1526, which put the Holy Roman Empire itself under threat, and offered the possibility of rallying support around the Emperor.

The most dramatic breakdown of authority occurred in France, where the Wars of Religion (1562–98) led to a collapse of royal authority, followed by social strife and foreign intervention. The origins of the wars lay in the fragility of the monarchy after the death of Henry II following a jousting accident in 1559, but religious differences provided much of the agenda of the subsequent conflicts. Henry's sons, Francis II (r. 1559–60), Charles IX (r. 1560–74), and Henry III (r. 1574–89), were unable to control the factionalism of the leading nobility as Francis I and Henry II had succeeded in doing. During the earlier reigns factionalism had been intense, but the king had been able to remain the focus of authority and power, in part by refusing to surrender the means and fruits of patronage to any one faction.

Their successors were unable to follow suit, but the rise of religious difference among the nobility made a policy of balancing advantages, let alone compromise, difficult; while the strength and range of factional links[1] made any resulting disputes serious. Furthermore, religious disputes provided occasions for conflict. The First War began after the most prominent Catholic aristocrat, Francis, Duke of Guise, with his affinity, was involved in a dispute with a Huguenot (French Protestant) congregation at Vassy that led to the massacre of the latter. A prominent aristocrat travelled in peacetime with numbers of supporters sufficient to start a conflict. Once blood had been shed, particularly of prominent nobles, then the struggle in part took on the aspect of a blood feud, while, as the struggle persisted, the *noblesse seconde* (lesser nobility) were also drawn more directly into it.

The French Wars of Religion were marked by a series of peace treaties and truces. Although some of the subsequent periods of peace lasted only a few months, this was not true of all of them. Nevertheless, the root causes of dissension remained, and, whatever their length, periods of peace were characterised by a degree of mutual suspicion that helped fan the flames when conflict resumed. There was a genuine popular dimension to the wars: they were not simply a matter of the struggles of king, nobles and their affinities. Instead, particularly in the towns, there was a high level of engagement with the confessional struggle. This led to outbursts of mass violence, as well as to a degree of independence from aristocratic leadership among both the Catholic League and the Protestant towns. Royal power and authority collapsed during the crisis, reaching its nadir in 1589 when Henry III was assassinated while unsuccessfully besieging his capital.

The eventual success of his successor, Henry IV (r. 1589–1610), in restoring order owed much to his willingness to make concessions to key groups, an aspect of his reign neglected or underrated in the standard heroic accounts, with their focus on the restoration of strong monarchy. The context in France was different from the Empire in 1555, but the reality of compromise was similarly apparent. The Pope, the major aristocrats of the Catholic League, led by the Duke of Mayenne, and the Huguenots each accepted Henry on terms. His famous renunciation of Protestantism in order to gain the throne – 'Paris is worth a mass' – was a testimony to the importance of affirming the attributes of Catholic kingship in order to secure his position. The major Catholic aristocrats were bought off with a recognition of their provincial power-bases. This was necessary in order to ensure their renunciation of the alliance of Philip II of Spain, as well as their abandonment of the more radical urban elements of the Catholic League. The resulting compromise both reflected the realities of power and also laid out the prospectus of Bourbon monarchy. This was not the case with the Huguenots. In 1598, by the Edict of Nantes, they were granted liberty of conscience, a measure of public worship, and the right to retain garrisons in about 200 towns, with the crown agreeing to pay the garrisons of about half the towns. These concessions were to be eroded in the 1620s and revoked in 1685.

Similarly, in Habsburg Hungary, the strength of the local nobles and the limitations of Habsburg power helped Calvinism and other Protestant sects (which flourished, more generally, in sixteenth-century Eastern Europe)[2] to survive and flourish. Lutheranism, Calvinism and Anti-Trinitarianism were, eventually, officially recognized.[3] However, these concessions, also, were subsequently put under pressure, especially in the late seventeenth century.

In the Low Countries the Dutch Revolt, which began in 1566, led to the overthrow of Philip II of Spain's rule in the northern provinces, but, in the south, it was possible for him to regain authority. This owed much to the successes of the Spanish Army of Flanders from 1579.[4] However, again, it was necessary to make concessions, and a series of agreements, such as the Perpetual Edict of 1577, marked the attempts to devise a settlement acceptable to Spanish Captain-Generals and the Walloon nobility. In a parallel fashion, the States General of the newly independent United Provinces had to negotiate for support rather than command it. As a reminder of the need not to consider countries or regions in isolation, the run of Spanish military success came to an end, in large part, because much of the Army of Flanders, under its brilliant commander Alexander Farnese, Duke of Parma, was committed by Philip II into an eventually unsuccessful attempt to prevent Henry IV from gaining control of France. The Spaniards relieved Rouen in 1590 and Paris in 1592.

After Henry was crowned, Spanish forces continued to intervene, particularly in north-eastern France, where they seized Calais and Amiens. There were also Spanish expeditions to Brittany and eastern France. Classically, these were seen as failures, but, by the Treaty of Vervins of 1598, Henry IV had to accept Spanish hegemony in Western Europe, with the highpoint of Spanish success, registered in the 1559 Peace of Cateau-Cambrécis, confirmed. Spanish hopes of putting a client on the throne of France had failed, but there had been no good candidate and, without one, the basis for any lasting success was limited. Furthermore, in 1598, it was unclear whether the compromises of authority and power that had characterised the establishment of Bourbon rule would not leave France lastingly weak.

Other rulers also faced serious challenges. In Scotland, Francis II of France's widow, Mary, Queen of Scots, faced opposition from a group of powerful Protestant aristocrats, the Lords of the Congregation. In 1567 she was forced to abdicate in favour of her infant son, James VI, after she married James, Earl of Bothwell, who had been responsible for the death of her second husband. Mary escaped in 1568, but was defeated at Langside and fled to England. Her son, James VI (r. 1567–1625) was subject to the control, and later influence, of the major Protestant nobles.

There was also no compromise in Sweden with the position of an unpopular ruler. The Catholic Sigismund Vasa (also Sigismund III of Poland, r. 1587–1632) became king of Sweden in 1592, but his Catholicism helped his Protestant uncle, Duke Charles of Södermanland, to incite and organise opposition to him. In 1597, civil war began, and, the following year, Sigismund arrived with troops. After indecisive campaigning, Sigismund returned to Poland in 1598, abandoning his supporters. He was deposed by the *Riksdag* in 1599, at the behest of Charles, who became Charles IX in 1604. Sigismund was also found wanting in Poland, leading, in 1606–09, to a noble rising, the Rokosz of Sandomierz.

If royal authority was successfully challenged in Sweden and Scotland, in both Portugal and Ireland it was imposed in accordance with royal wishes. In 1580, Philip II was able to enforce his claim to the Portuguese succession, employing both widespread bribery and a successful invasion. The process was eased by the willingness to maintain distinct institutions and separate practices and privileges. Philip II became Philip I of Portugal. No new state was created. This was not simply a prudential choice but also a reflection of the deep sense of legitimism that affected both rulers and élites and helped bind them together. Religious division, the factor that most challenged legitimism, was not at issue in Portugal, while there was no good rival candidate for the throne. Sebastian II, who had been killed in battle in 1578 during his disastrous invasion of Morocco, had left no children.

In Ireland and Russia, in contrast, religious divisions hindered the chance of settling issues by compromise. In Ireland, the Reformation encouraged attempts to impose authority. Anxious about the risk of papal or Spanish intervention, Henry VIII had himself proclaimed king of Ireland in 1541. With the Catholics increasingly treated under Elizabeth I (r. 1558–1603) as a potentially rebellious threat, there was pressure for the 'plantation' of areas with English settlers, a process that further exacerbated relations. From the late 1560s, in a process of government different to that across most of Europe, rule became increasingly military in character and intention, leading to fresh attempts to extend and enforce control.[5] Rebellions led the English to resort to the routine use of force and ensured that Catholic landowners increasingly lost their land. The imposition of English law and custom in Ulster after the suppression of the 1595–1603 rising led the leading Catholic landowners to flee to Italy in 1607. Indeed, the character of the conflict has led to the suggestion that monarchies in this period were, by their nature, centralising institutions, seeking administrative uniformity.[6] This is an exaggeration, and the union between Scotland and England in 1603 was only a personal one, but it is easy to see how research on such advancing frontiers of power as Ulster has led to such conclusions.

James I (VI of Scotland) then confiscated the lands of those who fled: 3,800,000 acres of Ulster were seized. Some of the less fertile portion was granted to the native Irish, but the rest was allocated to English and Scottish settlers, Crown officials, the established (Protestant) Church, and, in return for financial support for the plantation, the City of London. At the same time, large portions of Antrim and Down in Ulster were granted as private plantations, and also settled largely by Scots. By 1618, there were about 40,000 Scots in Ulster, a number that helped to ensure that few Scots were available to settle in the new British colonies in North America and the West Indies. Other plantations were established further south in Ireland, for example in Wexford, Leitrim, Westmeath and Longford. Across much of Ireland, the native Irish landowners had been dispossessed in favour of Protestants, and in Ulster the native population as a whole saw their position deteriorate as large numbers of Protestants were settled. Discontent over land, religion and political status was to explode in the rising of 1641, a rising that overthrew royal power across much of Ulster and was accompanied by the massacre of Protestants. The question of how best to organise and command forces to oppose this rising helped precipitate the crisis in England over Charles I's intentions and those of his parliamentary opponents.

The situation in Ireland is a reminder of the degree to which fault-lines of tension existed in Europe, with political division interacting with religious and/or ethnic differences. The latter were also important to the character of social control over serfs across much of Eastern Europe, for example of Ukrainians by Polish landlords. When religious and/or ethnic differences were combined with tenurial relations, the latter were generally harsher. This was true of Ukraine, and also of Valencia where Moriscos (ostensibly converted Muslims) formed much of the labour force in the sixteenth century before being expelled in 1609.

Religious tension was not only seen in tenurial relations. It was also a factor in social and political differences across much of Europe, helping structure communal identities, and providing a dynamic for developments. This was particularly true of cities, where trade and other opportunities brought people of different religions together. Such pluralism was often poorly accommodated by political authorities and popular attitudes.

Other instances of religious animosity included the revolt of the Moriscos in Granada in 1568–70. This was brutally suppressed, with large numbers of Moriscos slaughtered. Religious tension also played a large role in the rivalry between Catholic Poland and Orthodox Russia, not least with Polish intervention in the Russian Time of Troubles (1604–13). Sigismund III's eldest son, Wladyslaw, was acclaimed as Tsar after the Poles entered Moscow in 1610, but anti-Polish attitudes thwarted this attempt. The only way the Russians would have accepted Wladyslaw in the longer term would have been if he had converted to Orthodoxy and 'gone native'. In Ethiopia, the sole Christian state in Africa, there were serious rebellions when Susenyos (r. 1607–32) converted to Catholicism, and these helped lead to his abdication.

Religion was far from the sole issue at stake in political tension or strife in Europe, and any analysis of wars of religion, such as those in France and Ireland, reveals the importance of other factors in creating tensions and provoking political breakdown. The role of non-religious factors can also be seen in China, where, from 1582, there were weak emperors, increasingly arbitrary central government, oppressive taxation and growing financial problems. These encouraged both rebellions and a quest for power among ambitious leaders. Li Zicheng, a rebel who had become a powerful regional warlord, captured Beijing in 1644 and provoked the suicide of the last Ming emperor. Li proclaimed the Shun dynasty, but his army was poorly disciplined and he lacked the support of legitimacy, powerful allies and an effective administrative apparatus. The collapse of the Ming dynasty, and thus of the Chinese frontier defence system, gave the Manchu their opportunity to conquer China. This was a political shift that was at least as important as any in Europe, and it underlines the close relationship of domestic and international developments.

The fate of Ming China offers an interesting parallel with that of Christendom. Although the divisions of Christendom had helped the Ottomans conquer the Byzantine (Eastern Roman) Empire, the Balkans and Hungary, they were unable to repeat their success after the mid-sixteenth century. This was crucial to the history of Christendom. In part, it reflected the growing strength of Christian resistance in the central Mediterranean and the Danube valley, particularly the role of the Habsburgs, both Austrian and Spanish. This helped the mobilisation and transfer of resources to points of contact. German troops were deployed in Hungary, and Spanish troops and money stiffened resistance in Italy. A Spanish force from Sicily relieved Malta from Ottoman attack in 1565 and the Spaniards made a major contribution to the fleet that defeated the Ottomans at Lepanto in 1571.

Furthermore, the Ottomans did not benefit in their zone of contact with Christian Europe from an ability to win over many local interests, as they had done ealier in Wallachia and Moldavia, and, outside Christendom, in Egypt. In addition, the role of the Ottoman Empire's long-standing rivalry with the Safavid dynasty of Persia was important to the slackening in Ottoman pressure, as was over-extension and the functional problems of operating on distant frontiers.

In early modern Christian Europe, religious issues posed fundamental questions for the redefinition of nation and society. The more that loyalty was conceived in religious terms, the narrower and more exclusive these concepts risked becoming. As a consequence, in states riven by religious division, particularly France and Poland in the late sixteenth century, attempts were made to provide different definitions of loyalty and membership of the political community. That of the *politiques* in France looked towards modern concepts, as did the Warsaw Confederation of 1573, which allowed liberty of conscience to all nobles (although the equality that was offered was both qualified and conditional); but this development was cut short in both France and Poland by Counter-Reformation determination, intolerance and clarity in the seventeenth century. A religious definition of loyalty was enforced in both.

Instead, it was federal systems, particularly the Holy Roman Empire and the Swiss Confederation, that most successfully handled the tension between identity and religious diversity, as well as being able, thanks to their dispersal of the rights of sovereignty, to provide a theory and practice of self-defence that did not entail the dissolution of government.[7] This, however, was only after attempts at uniformity had been defeated in civil conflict: brief in the Swiss Confederation, but, thanks in part to external intervention, far more protracted in the Empire. A more conditional diversity was eventually accepted in Britain, and again only after civil conflict and (in 1688) external intervention. A separate religious settlement for Scotland was won by the Presbyterians, but the Catholics failed in Ireland, in part because political-religious identity in England, Scotland and, therefore, Britain owed much to anti-Catholicism, but largely due to military defeat.

It is necessary to complement the revisionist perspective outlined in Chapter 2 and its emphasis on cooperation, with an awareness of the extent to which force, including new military forms, was employed by rulers in order to advance their power and enforce their authority. Thus, Cosimo de' Medici, ruler of Tuscany from 1537 until 1574, built three citadels around Florence, each under the command of a non-Florentine. This overawing of the city was important to the consolidation of his power, and, in 1569, Cosimo became the first Grand Duke of Tuscany. Republicanism had been defeated in Florence, not just for one generation, but, thanks to the creation of a dynastic state, also thereafter.

Also in Italy, and again limiting urban autonomy and republican tendencies, after Pope Paul III had suppressed a salt tax revolt in Perugia in 1540, he had a citadel built there. Similarly, Pier Luigi, Duke of Parma (r. 1545–47) built a citadel at Piacenza as part of a campaign to establish his power that also saw moves against the castles of the aristocracy. This campaign was unwelcome, and he was assassinated. Having regained Amiens from Spanish forces in 1597, Henry IV of France ordered that a citadel be built there in order to establish royal power; earlier in the year, the city had refused to accept a royal garrison as they claimed the right of relying on their militia for their defence. This had helped the Spaniards seize the city.

The tension between urban demands for civic militias and royal pressure for royal garrisons was widespread. It reflected the importance of military force as an aspect of authority. A number of issues were related to this. Governments tried to keep artillery a monopoly, as, without cannon, it was difficult to seize fortresses. The building of the latter, particularly of the new-style *trace italienne* in fortifications constructed in order to lessen the impact of artillery, was another activity that governments sought to control. In addition, efforts were made to weaken or destroy fortifications that were not under governmental control or which there was no wish to garrison. Thus, in the English Civil Wars in the 1640s, Parliamentary forces slighted Royalist fortresses, once they had been taken, in order to remove their defensive capability, and, after 1660, the restored Royalist government took steps to end the defensive strength of what had been Parliamentary strongholds.

More generally, governments, such as that of Henry IV of France, sought to destroy the fortifications of domestic opponents, and the cumulative effect of rebellion and civil warfare in the century 1550–1650 led to a considerable limitation of aggregate non-royal defensive capability, in so far as the nature of the sources permits the use of such a clumsily phrased index. There were also important shifts in individual countries, including the enforced surrender by the Huguenots of their defensive positions in France.

Furthermore, central governments built and enhanced fortresses, both at home and in their colonies, in order to provide secure bases for authority that overawed potential opposition. Much of this construction was in frontier zones, and designed principally against foreign opponents, but, as an important side-effect, such fortresses helped to consolidate government authority in what were frequently newly conquered regions. Riga fulfilled this function for the Swedes in Livonia from 1621 until 1710, and other fortresses, such as Stettin and Stralsund, served a similar function for them elsewhere. The same was true of French conquests, with Dunkirk or Besançon helping strengthen control over French Flanders and Franche-Comté. In addition, fortresses played an important role away from sensitive frontiers. Having had Marseille occupied by royal troops in 1660, and a section of the city wall demolished, Louis XIV built a citadel there; while, after the rebellion of the Sicilian city of Messina was suppressed in 1678, its ruler, Charles II of Spain, imposed a substantial garrison in a new citadel.

It is also important to complement the limitations to governmental military capability mentioned earlier (see pp. 48–9) with reference to an increase in aggregate capability. The frequency of conflict in the sixteenth century in part reflected the extent to which the ability of European states to finance military activity increased in the late fifteenth and early sixteenth centuries, with their greater political consolidation, administrative development and economic growth, as populations recovered from the fourteenth-century epidemic of (probably) bubonic plague, the Black Death. Although this process of consolidation was to be challenged as the impact of the Reformation increased domestic divisions, the demographic growth of the sixteenth century helped ensure that more resources could be tapped, both manpower and finances.

Yet alongside these developments came a pressure on available resources that would have led most monarchs and ministers to smile at any suggestions that there were more resources to tap. The problems associated with raising sufficient funding to sustain high levels of operational warfare were faced by all the major European combatants, and were probably managed best by the Ottomans. Across Europe, desertion and mutinies were frequent responses from troops when pay was not forthcoming and credit with local communities was withdrawn.

Growing governmental strength and sophistication were most apparent at sea, where fleets far larger and more powerful than those of the fifteenth century were created and maintained. Maritime capability and warfare required detailed planning, logistical support, political commitment, administrative competence, leadership and training, as well as an ability to overcome the challenges posed by technological innovation. The maritime expeditionary warfare of the Mediterranean, Baltic and Atlantic was an important aspect of the warfare of the period. The availability of the resources that could be directed by governments was, also, obvious in the ambitious fortification programmes of the period. Furthermore, the new fortresses were defended by cannon, and states were willing and able to deploy large numbers of them.

Yet it is unclear that military revolution is an appropriate term for this process. The teleological language employed can be very misleading. Military adaptation, particularly to the opportunities and problems for co-ordination of individual arms, is a more appropriate term. In addition, far from war being won by planned action, it was frequently the side that was less handicapped by deficiencies that was successful: coping with problems was the major skill of command, both on campaign and on the battlefield.

Within states, the effectiveness of force, and thus of the extension of the power of the ruler, was partly dependent on the political context, especially the possibility of international intervention, but also on a range of other factors, including the nature of the dynastic succession. International intervention was crucial when Ferdinand of Bavaria, Prince-Bishop of Liège (r. 1612–50) clashed with the city of Liège over his attempts to control it. He turned to Austria and Spain for military assistance, only for their opponents, France and the Dutch, to provide counter-pressure. It was not until 1649 that Ferdinand was able to deploy about 3,000 troops in order to enforce his will. The Dutch had negotiated peace with Spain the previous year, France was convulsed by the *Fronde*, and the Wittelsbachs now enjoyed peace in the Empire and, in particular, a cessation of French and Swedish attacks on Bavaria. Aside from the international context, which reflected the bishopric's strategic position in the Meuse Valley bisecting the Spanish Netherlands, and the important role of Liège and Huy as bridging points over the river, the opposition to the bishop was also an aspect of the continued vitality of urban independence, or at least autonomy, in the politics of the period.

The positions of Emden in East Friesland, Königsberg in East Prussia, Hildesheim in the prince-bishopric of that name, and Erfurt in the prince-archbishopric of Mainz were all similar. It was no accident that there were crises involving the use of force over the position of all of these, with Erfurt and Königsberg being subjugated soon after Liège. While urban independence in states outside the Empire could be assailed outside a jurisdictional context, within the Empire it was also necessary to consider the role of the imperial constitution and the relevant institutions. Nevertheless, there was a parallel with the situation of cities outside the Empire. It is noteworthy that much of the mid-seventeenth-century crisis focused on the control of cities, including Amsterdam, Barcelona, Beijing, Constantinople, Lisbon, London, Moscow, Naples and Paris. As centres of government, they were lodestars of authority, control over which helped signify legitimacy. The failure of royal or princely forces to gain control of London in 1641–42 and of Amsterdam in 1650 was crucial to political developments, and also left a mark in the urban fabric of power, with no large citadel under royal/princely control built at, or near, either city.

The international context was also important in states larger than Liège. The ability of the Habsburgs to impose their views on Habsburg Hungary and Transylvania was greatly lessened by the prospect of Ottoman intervention. Victory in Spain for Philip V in the War of the Spanish Succession (1701–14) led to an imposition of central control, with the abolition of the provincial *fueros* in the Crown of Aragon and central control of finances, including, in 1718, the issue of a new coinage designed to circulate there and in Castile. The 'Nueva Planta' or 'new form' of government was imposed on Catalonia in 1716. As with changes in the Scottish Highlands after the defeat of the Jacobites by the forces of the Hanoverian dynasty at the battle of Culloden in 1746, this new regime rested on victory and was sustained by a military presence, with garrisons, fortifications and, in Scotland, roads. In Barcelona, a big citadel was built in 1715–18. In many areas, this was as much an aspect of government as the revisionist stress on consensus. Indeed, 'the presence of Castilian officials and troops gave the provinces of the Crown of Aragon the ineradicable feeling that they were an occupied people'.[8]

Despite the presence of military posts, frontier zones were a major sphere of lessened control for central governments, with control, instead, being exercised by local groups, particularly extended kinship networks. In the colonial sphere, frontier zones saw a marked dissipation of authority and power, with colonial governors finding, whatever their sovereign's claims, that they were dependent, outside the fortified posts, on often uncertain relations with native peoples and on the shifting world of settler–native links.

Again, international relations were important, both in Europe and in the colonies. James VI of Scotland's succession to the English throne in 1603 was followed by a firm campaign of repression against the border reivers or moss-troopers who dominated the Anglo-Scottish border lands. Many were killed, and one of the most persistently troublesome clans, the Grahams, were forcibly transplanted to Ireland in 1606. Conversely, a lack of co-operation between France and Spain helped keep their border zone along the Pyrenean chain lawless and made it difficult to counter the smugglers of the region, whose bands were often led by nobles.

A disputed succession was crucial to the exacerbation of accumulated tensions into violence, not only in Muscovy in the first two decades of the seventeenth century, but also in the lands of the Austrian Habsburgs. In 1608, disputes between the Emperor Rudolf II and his brother Matthias led to the invasion of Bohemia by the latter in a successful attempt to seize control of Austria, Moravia and Habsburg Hungary. The militarisation of politics in the region was further displayed with a high level of armed preparedness by the Estates. In 1611, the Estates of Bohemia clashed with Archduke Leopold, whom Rudolf wanted as his successor, and the determination of the Estates led Rudolf and Leopold to back down. In concert with the Estates, Matthias entered Prague with an army, Rudolf was intimidated into abdicating, and Matthias was crowned as King of Bohemia.

The crown–élite harmony discussed in Chapter 2 was scarcely compatible with such disruption, and religion provided an added volatility, helping to lead to an outbreak of full-scale conflict in Bohemia in the early stages of the Thirty Years' War. In Bohemia, and more generally, the war arose from the exacerbation of long-standing disputes: some had been shelved in the 1550s, but others, particularly over Habsburg power and authority in the *Erblande* (Habsburg hereditary lands), and widespread concern about Spanish ambitions, had become a serious problem in the 1600s and 1610s. The victory in Bohemia of Habsburg forces in 1620, a direct result of the battle of the White Mountain, led to Catholicisation, to the expropriation of Protestant landholdings, and to the creation of a new Catholic landed élite that had few, if any roots in local communities, and that looked to the Habsburgs.

The same was true of France where, in fresh civil wars, the Huguenots were defeated in 1622 and 1628–29. This was an aspect of the interrelated crises that faced rulers and ministers. The Huguenot challenge was intertwined with problems of foreign policy, just as aristocratic factionalism was to be linked to war with Spain later in the reign of Louis XIII (r. 1610–43). The defeat of the Protestants opened the way for a renewed integration of crown and élite in both France and the *Erblande*, although the example of Poland shows that this factor alone was insufficient to create harmony. There, instead, there was a very different political culture and institutional structure, with much greater suspicion of royal pretensions.

Alongside the role of force in France, there was also a longer-term attenuation of Protestantism, particularly among the nobility. This owed much to social pressures and political opportunities. In the former, intermarriage was important, with mixed marriages leading to the bringing up of children in the dominant Catholicism. In the latter, nobles and others found that opportunities for royal patronage were in large part dependent on religion. Similar pressures played a role in the Upper Palatinate, which was conquered from the Calvinist Elector Palatine by the army of the Catholic League in 1621, and, thereafter, ruled by the Bavarian Wittelsbachs and re-Catholicised.[9]

As far as French towns are concerned, Michael Wolfe observes that their relationship with the crown faced considerable strain during the Wars of Religion, but he puts the emphasis on a longer-term process of accommodation:

> The *bonnes villes* much preferred strong kings to weak ones, believing that their cherished liberties could only be secure if the monarchy was stable. Municipal fortifications, therefore, never represented a defiance of state authority, but rather a localised expression of it ... urban politics became increasingly subsumed under the complex, negotiated accommodations of the *système louisquatorzien*.

Linked to this was a decay in urban fortifications away from frontier regions. Town authorities and élites preferred to spend on other goals, and indeed to use the land hitherto occupied by defences for profit.[10] In contrast, in Safavid Persia, under Abbas I (r. 1587–1629), the destruction of many fortifications may have arisen from a desire to concentrate power, although other factors, including the nature of foreign threats, could also have been important.[11]

In the mid-seventeenth century, much of the world was involved in a series of economic and political crises. These are generally referred to, collectively, as the mid-seventeenth-century crisis and seen in European terms, although China was the part of the world most disrupted, while there were coups in Persia (1645) and the Ottoman Empire (1648), and civil war in Mughal India in 1657–60. To look just at Christian Europe, religion was not a key issue in most of the rebellions of the period, although it did play a major role in the British Civil Wars of 1638–52. The outbreak of the English Civil War was the result of a political crisis in 1640–42 that stemmed from risings in Scotland (1638) and Ireland (1641). In Scotland, the absentee Charles I's support for bishops and his autocratic handling of Scottish interests and patronage led to a Presbyterian and national response that Charles failed to suppress. Charles resorted to force, but lacked the necessary strength to do so successfully, and the two Bishops' Wars (1639–40) not only revealed his inability to subjugate Scotland, but also a failure to protect parts of northern England from invasion and occupation. The ability of the Scots to gain control of north-east England, whence London's coal supplies derived, was a biting demonstration of Charles's failure, a singular proof of the degree of integration of a national economy, and an indication of its vulnerability to disruption.

The way in which the Scots rapidly raised an effective army (albeit against less than impressive opposition) showed the continued possibilities for military strength enjoyed by non-sovereign bodies able to claim the authority of nationhood within composite states. The Portuguese and Catalan risings of 1640 demonstrated the same capability. Charles turned to England to raise the necessary resources to deal with the Scots, but the Long Parliament that was called in 1640 challenged his authority and power, a process accentuated in 1641 when a Catholic rebellion in Ireland made it necessary to consider how best to raise and command an armed response.

Britain in the 1640s and 1650s displayed the potential fragility of the established political order and the radicalism that could exist, especially in religious circles. Aside from executing the king in 1649, creating a republic, and abolishing both the House of Lords and the episcopacy, the Interregnum regimes in Britain pushed through a host of changes in political, social, economic and religious matters. These indicated the capacity for radicalism in seventeenth-century Europe, but it was one achieved only as a consequence of radicalisation at the close of a bitter civil war, and it was not to be repeated in British history. Instead, what were seen as the excesses of the Interregnum were subsequently held up as a warning against change, particularly during the Exclusion Crisis of 1678–81 and then again during the crisis caused by the unpopularity of James VII of Scotland and II of England (r. 1685–88).

Elsewhere in Europe, while a radical politico-religious agenda was in part offered by the rebels against Habsburg authority in Bohemia and Austria in the early stages of the Thirty Years' War, none the less an important aspect of the disorders of the 1640s and 1650s was that religion played little role in most of them. The Huguenots played no role in the *Fronde*, the serious challenge to the power of the regency government of Louis XIV in 1648–53. Unlike conditions in the earlier Dutch Revolt, religion was similarly absent from the mid-century crises in the Spanish Empire.

Instead, these crises reflected a combination of unease over the political complexion of regimes, especially the Mazarin ministry in France, the burdens arising from war, regional particularism, particularly in the Spanish monarchy, and the general atmosphere of strain derived from the demographic and economic crises of the period which, variously, included plague, falling agricultural production, and famine. Domestic tensions channelled and exacerbated the role of war in creating policy disputes and financial pressures, that both weakened crown–élite ties and challenged links within composite monarchies. Like the early stages of the British rebellions, the particularist rebellions in Catalonia and Portugal in 1640 were essentially reactive calls that responded to governmental actions or problems, rather than attempts to produce a new political order. In the Spanish Empire, the financial burdens of war with France and the Dutch interacted with strong regional antipathy to rule from Madrid and to its attempts to share the cost of the conflict, although there was no rising in the Milanese; or indeed in most of Italy.[12] In France, the crisis led to civil war as well as to constitutional moves, including an assembly of nobles in 1651, and to schemes to summon an Estates-General. In Poland, political and military collapse in the face of Russian and Swedish attack in the 1650s helped undermine the attempt to create an effective parliamentary monarchy, although the court's failure to win sufficient support and magnate rivalries were also crucial.[13]

The variegated character of politics in the mid-seventeenth century was also amply revealed by the crisis. A number of milieux of debate, dissension and conflict co-existed and, at times, interacted and even combined. These included court, ministry, aristocracy, towns, Church, regions, peasantry and the world of print. Interest in the nature and impact of political culture ensures that the latter has received particular attention. This has led to the application of the term public sphere to French political debate and contention in 1614–17, and to attention to the role of print in polarising public opinion in mid-seventeenth-century England.[14] Indeed, the development of a relatively unregulated press there after the lapsing of the Licensing Act in 1694 helped lead to a different form of political culture, one in which there was an expectation of news and thus of novelty, if not change; while, in turn, news and fact were increasingly differentiated from exemplary prose in which morality was seen as defining accuracy.[15]

In some respects, the results of the mid-seventeenth-century crises revealed the strengths of prevailing political systems. Despite severe economic conditions, population decline (which reduced society's ability to cope with the savage financial burdens of governmental tax demands), seemingly intractable conflicts, and unpopular governments, there was no sustained fundamental challenge outside Britain to the political, social and religious bases of society. A radical movement in Bordeaux, the *Ormée*, had very few members. The peasants' rising in central Switzerland in 1653 was a more serious rising, and, like that in Austria in 1626, indicated the ability of peasants to make a significant impact, but it was not sustained.

The movements in Catalonia, Portugal and Naples attracted far more support than the *Ormée*, and the first two were far more sustained than the peasants' risings of 1626 and 1653. Their essentially conservative aims were securely located in contemporary political culture. This helped ensure that Portuguese independence was regained with little disruption of traditional political and social patterns. The situation was less stable in Catalonia and Naples, in part because of the degree of urban radicalism in both.

In all three cases, French intervention played an important role. It helped block Spanish attempts to reconquer Catalonia until the *Fronde* intervened, while supporting Portugal until Spain granted independence in 1668. In contrast, the failure of the French to support Neapolitan opposition to Spain was important to the latter's ability to exploit social and political divisions in Naples in order to regain control. Fortunately for Philip IV (r. 1621–65), there was no crisis at the centre of the Spanish monarchy comparable to those in China, England, France, Russia and the Ottoman Empire. There was dissension and factionalism in Castile, but they did not coalesce.

Absolutism has been seen as a reaction to the mid-seventeenth-century crisis, as in Denmark in 1660 and Sweden in the 1670s,[16] although this was not invariably the case, for example not in Switzerland. Across Europe, the emphasis on social and political cohesion that characterised the century from the 1650s helped ensure that there were fewer serious rebellions in Western Europe than in the previous century, although other factors also played a role, including the international context. The series of risings in 1700–1715, including in France, Hungary, Moldavia, Scotland, Spain and Ukraine, did not see the same degree of sustained international intervention as those in 1638–52, although, in part, this was a matter of opportunity.

Furthermore, a greater emphasis on Eastern Europe might lead to a revised chronology that questions the extent to which the mid-seventeenth-century crisis led to a period of greater order. Looked at differently, it might be inappropriate to try to fit all of Europe into one general model. Instead, it is more useful to note variations and then consider their analytical value. At the simplest level, there was a major difference between Western and Eastern Europe. In the latter, social and ethnic tensions were greater, and the stability of the composite monarchies was less secure than in Western Europe, possibly because there was less emphasis on consensus. This argument has to be handled with care, particularly if the perspective is Catalonia, Ireland or the Scottish Highlands. Nevertheless, the major transfers of territory in Eastern Europe in the seventeenth century, as the Austrian, Ottoman, Russian and Swedish empires expanded and contracted, helped create an instability that led to rebellions as areas with a tradition of autonomy if not independence, such as Moldavia, Transylvania and Ukraine, sought to contest the process. As there were fewer states in the region, so rebellions were mostly against control as part of composite states, rather than risings at the centre of power.

When rebellions occurred in Europe after 1660, religion could, again, play a major role, as with the British civil war of 1688–91 and the Rakoczi rising in Hungary against Habsburg rule in 1703–11. In general, however, an implicit co-operation prevailed. It was made explicit when rulers promised to respect élite and other interests, as with Philip IV's declaration in 1652 that he would respect the privileges of the Catalans, part of the process by which the Catalan Revolt ended, and William III's acceptance of the Bill of Rights in England in 1689, a move designed to help legitimate the coup by which he had replaced his uncle and father-in-law James VII and II.

Each of these measures was designed to ensure consent to rulership re-established or established by force, and underlined the desire and need to win consent for such developments.[17] Rulers seeking to acquire territory generally sought to do so with the co-operation of the local élites. Louis XIV maintained the distinct identities of Artois and Franche-Comté when he acquired them through war (1659 and 1678), and Peter the Great guaranteed the privileges of the local German Protestant nobility when he overran Estonia and Livonia in 1710, although he adopted a harsher position in Ukraine. Earlier, there had been an opposition among the Livonian nobility against Swedish rule in the 1690s, but it did not become violent. Augustus of Poland tried to use the refugee Livonian noble Patkul as a leader of a rising against Sweden, but that failed to materialise.

Peter's father, Alexis, had shown, when he invaded White Russia (Belarus) in the 1650s, as part of a thirteen-year war with Poland (1654–67), that a harsh approach to acquiring control could play a major role in Eastern Europe. This campaign was presented as part of a wider struggle between Orthodoxy and Catholicism, and Russian troops were accordingly blessed by priests and marched under sacred banners. Catholic churches were seized and converted to Orthodox uses. Religious hostility played a less pronounced role in conflict between Lutheran Sweden and Russia, in part because there was no equivalent to the tension between Catholicism and Orthodoxy in Ukraine. There was no Lutheran equivalent to the Uniate Church, by which the Catholics also tried to win the Orthodox over to papal authority. Furthermore, the Catholic Poles had tried to seize the Russian throne, ensuring that the Romanov dynasty of Russia saw them as the leading threat, a view given added force by the severity of the shortlived conflict between the two powers in 1632–34. The contrasts between Russian policy towards Poland and Sweden are a reminder of the variety in political attitudes during the period.

Newly acquired territories could, in part, be incorporated by recruiting troops. This was true both of soldiers and of officers. The nobility officered the new standing armies that rulers instituted, and did so even if there had been initial concern about their creation. In addition, the range of activities, especially fencing and hunting, that had served to make nobles and gentlemen worthy of status[18] was more closely linked to a culture of military service. The nobles also served as commissioners on the bodies that organised society for war. Of the 499 nobles present at the Swedish *riksdag* of 1693, 248 held military appointments, and, in the Swedish and Russian Tables of Ranks, military service was highly esteemed. As many as 35 per cent of the old Danish nobility and 17 of the new were in military service in 1700, compared with only six and eight respectively in the civil service. Frederick II (r. 1740–86) reduced the percentage of commoner officers in the Prussian army. Aristocratic military service was proportionately less important in Western Europe, especially in Britain, Spain and Italy, other than Piedmont; but it was still of consequence. By the 1690s, over 20,000 French nobles were serving in the French army and navy, a bond that testified to aristocratic confidence in Louis XIV. Contemporaries stressed the pressure for war from the nobility at the time of France's entry into the Wars of the Polish (1733) and Austrian (1741) Successions.

The percentage of foreign officers in the armies of major powers declined as these armies were expanded, although such officership remained far more common than it was to be after 1815. This reflected the continued importance of the bond of personal service to a ruler in the ethos of the European nobility. Thus numerous Italian and German nobles served other rulers, especially the Austrian and Spanish Habsburgs. The Dutch, Russians, Swedes and Venetians also recruited large numbers of foreign officers. The French had less need to do so, although foreign regiments, particularly Swiss and German, played a major role in their army. Aside from military service, rulers could also recruit foreigners for responsible positions in other branches of service, such as diplomacy. This underlines the limited scope of nationalism or proto-nationalism at governmental level and, instead, the importance of a personal theme of service that was readily reconciled with that of dynastic policies.

It became increasingly common in the second half of the eighteenth century to wear military uniform. This was the clothing of order and obedient hierarchy, and it encapsulated the participation of nobles in the service state. This participation helped lessen the tensions created by financial pressures on the nobility, while the wearing of uniform and, more generally, Tables of Ranks underlined the ability of rulers to take the leading role in judging aristocratic conflicts over rank and precedence. The foundation of new honorific orders such as the Order of the Bath in England had the same effect. Élites are monoliths only to outsiders. Instead, noble society was riven by tensions, particularly over local predominance and status. In both functional and idealistic terms, rulers were necessary arbitrators.[19]

At the same time, the renewed emphasis on social order and decorum seen in the seventeenth century created problems for individual aristocrats. There are signs that some pursued new models of selfhood, that entailed a hostile response to dependency. The impact of familial and public authority, a combined ideology of lineage and hierarchical order, appears to have led to unwanted responses, such as the pursuit of friendship at the expense of family, the critique of religious tradition by libertines, and the aristocratic constitutionalism seen in France in the 1700s. Such tensions were not new, but it has been suggested that cultural contradictions became more acute in the seventeenth century because moral debate acquired a new centrality in polite society, while the growing coherence of official ideology allowed less room for the expression of contradictory values.[20]

Aside from providing nobles with employment, and satisfying their sense of mission, the armed forces that expanded in size in the late seventeenth century also strengthened the control of social élites over their regions and, particularly, labour force. French troops suppressed revolts, in the Boulogne region in 1662, the Vivarais in 1670, and Bordeaux and Brittany in 1675, more effectually than the forces used against the *Croquants* and the *Va-Nu-Pieds* in 1639.

Force, however, was not the major element in political control. Towns, where people were most concentrated and least under traditional patterns of social control, were, in large part through a process of accommodation, brought under a greater degree of central political authority, and what has been seen as a culture of retribution against those introducing unwelcome innovations was brought to an end, at least in so far as revolts were concerned.[21] This lessened the possibility that towns would encourage dissidence in surrounding rural areas. Paris had defied and expelled royal forces in 1588 and 1648, but, thereafter, did not do so again until 1789, although disturbances in Madrid in 1766 led to the fall of the chief minister.

The monarch who most clearly personified absolutism was Louis XIV of France (r. 1643–1715). Born in 1638, he came to the throne as a child and did not assume effective rule until the death, in 1661, of Mazarin, the Italian-born cardinal who had succeeded his patron Richelieu as first minister. Europe was awed by Louis's strength and frightened by his actual and supposed ambitions. He advanced France's boundaries, though at considerable cost. These costs attracted criticism within France in his latter years, as Louis became less successful, but, earlier, there had been widespread support for his dynastic and territorial aggrandisement. Indeed, Louis helped give France much of its modern shape. This was particularly so on the north-eastern, eastern and southern frontiers, although the south-eastern frontier with Italy was not fixed until Napoleon III gained Savoy and Nice in 1860. Thanks to gains during the reign of Louis XIV, cities such as Besançon, Dunkirk, Lille, Perpignan and Strasbourg became possessions of the French crown, even if the process of Frenchification was frequently long-drawn-out, and in some areas, such as Franche-Comté, Lille and, even more, Strasbourg, it encountered much opposition.

On the domestic scene, Louis renewed harmonious relations with the social élite. These had been lost during the period of the cardinal-ministers (Richelieu and Mazarin), because they had clearly based their position on the support of that section of the élite that was willing to back them, and had therefore compromised the inclusive theory of personal monarchy. The cardinal-ministers had also suffered from their inability to bring France's conflict with Spain (1628–31, 1635–59) either to a victorious close or to an end, and from the financial strains and sense of dissatisfaction that arose as a result. Nevertheless, the Decline of Spain thesis ensures that their period of prominence (1624–61) is generally discussed in terms of a series of French successes, with insufficient weight placed on both failures and costs.

The same is true of Louis XIV's years of personal monarchy prior to the growing difficulties that more obviously characterised his reign from the late 1680s and, in particular, from the mid-1690s. Earlier, Louis's skilful management of patronage helped win a degree of domestic support that minimised the political costs of war. Furthermore, the War of Devolution (1666–67) was shortlived as well as successful. Although the Dutch War (1672–78) did not lead to the crushing defeat of the Dutch that Louis had anticipated, while the coalition he had assembled to support his aggression rapidly disintegrated, there was enough success and glory to satisfy pride and to encourage the sense that, while he could not dictate events, Louis was, nevertheless, the leading ruler in Christian Europe.[22]

Louis XIV's broad-based co-operation with the nobility, rather than any supposed absolutist agenda of centralisation and bureaucratisation,[23] brought stability to France and represented a revival of the Renaissance monarchy of the early sixteenth century, albeit leading to a more powerful state than the earlier version, not least in its ability to tax and in the size of both army and navy. With the exception of the unsuccessful Huguenot Camisards in the 1700s, 1675 was the last year of large-scale revolts in France prior to the Revolution. Louis's reign did not see the precarious evasion of crisis that had characterised those of his grandfather, Henry IV (r. 1589–1610), his father Louis XIII (r. 1610–43), and his own minority. Thanks, instead, to the creation of an important measure of domestic stability under Louis XIV, the minority of his successor, his great-grandson Louis XV (r. 1715–74), was less disturbed than his own or that of Louis XIII had been. Louis XIV's successors were to squander an impressive political legacy.

The essential conservatism of Louis XIV can be grasped by contrasting him with Peter the Great of Russia, tsar from 1682, although he wielded complete power only in 1689–1725. Although his authority looked back to Byzantine models and Mongol influences, Peter sought to modernise his country to a degree that was alien to his royal predecessors and to his counterparts. Major administrative and economic reforms were pushed through, although many were only partly implemented. Drawing heavily on current Western models – Prussian and Swedish in government, British and Dutch in technology and trade – Peter helped to give Russian government and élite society a Western orientation, widening the gulf between them and the bulk of the population, among whom he was widely regarded as a diabolical changeling. The new capital he founded at St Petersburg on the river Neva symbolised the new Westward-looking attitude. The city was founded in 1703 and the court and government transferred in stages from 1709. Moscow, the epitome of old Russia, was no longer acceptable as the capital. With its determined emphasis on novelty and a breach with the past, Peter's reign marked a potentially radical departure in the use of state power, as well as in Russian history. Indeed, the 'Europeanisation of Russian culture' he encouraged (although, whatever the myth, did not begin) helped ensure that political ideas, both in favour of the authority of the tsar and in support of a powerful aristocracy, looked to European models.[24]

In practice, novelty and radicalism at the level of the state were tempered by the weakness of Russian administration, in particular the difficulty of creating new bureaucratic mechanisms, by the continued dominance of the government by the nobility, and by the apathy, if not resistance, of the bulk of the population towards Peter's policies: 'the problem of Peter's reign was that the informal structures of power were not in the tsar's favor, nor were they in favor of the process of reform'.[25] The myth of Peter was in some ways more important than the reality. His legacy was a troublesome one, both with respect to the long-term development of Russia and, in the short term, as far as his successors were concerned.

Nevertheless, Peter's aspirations looked forward to those of the Enlightened Despots such as Frederick the Great of Prussia (r. 1740–86), Catherine the Great of Russia (r. 1762–96), Joseph II of Austria (sole ruler 1780–90), and Charles III of Spain (r. 1759–88). As also with Frederick certainly and with earlier Russian rulers, however, Peter's major concern was supporting his military capability.[26] War continued to dominate the political agenda and governmental systems of European rulers. Alongside religion, it was the sphere in which state activity most affected the people of Europe.

With his stress on novelty and change, Peter was unusual. Furthermore, his policies were unpopular, not least with his son, Alexis, an opponent of Peter's strategy for modernisation, who died in 1718, probably as a result of excessive interrogation under torture: forty blows from the knout.[27] There were attempts after Peter's death, especially during the reign of his grandson

Peter II (r. 1727–30), to reverse his policies and attitudes, but they failed. Peter II died young of smallpox (whereas Louis XV survived his attack in 1728 and lived until 1774), the 1730 crisis over royal authority was resolved in favour of the new ruler, Tsarina Anna, and Westernisation was entrenched as government policy.

The tensions that such policies could give rise to were also seen in Ethiopia, another Christian imperial system, where the monarch's role was less constrained by an autonomous Church than anywhere in Europe west of Russia. Iyasu I (r. 1682–1706) made a major attempt to reverse the weakness of the Ethiopian monarchy and the growth in provincial independence that had become more apparent from 1642 when the army was destroyed by the nomadic Galla. Iyasu built up the royal bodyguard as a separate army supported by a treasury to prevent it from following the militia in becoming overly connected to particular areas. He also built up a new militia among loyal Galla tribes who converted to Christianity, but found it very difficult to gain lasting success, and was assassinated by domestic opponents.

The dominant theme in Europe in the early eighteenth century was continuity, not change. Continuity manifested itself not only in the persistence of markedly inegalitarian and conservative social, economic and political relationships, the continued centrality of religion and the Christian moral code, and the persistence of a predominantly low-efficiency agrarian economy, but also in a society and a political culture that continually referred back to the past. There was little sense of future progress or of the desirability of widespread change. Political systems that were subsequently to be dismissed as anachronistic, such as the Holy Roman Empire and the Habsburg monarchy, appeared vibrant.[28] Both, indeed, displayed considerable vitality from the 1680s to the 1720s, successfully responding to French and Ottoman challenges. The eighteenth century opened, in both the domestic and international spheres, with a traditional agenda of political concerns, objectives, ideals and methods.

Alongside a chronological presentation in terms of political programmes and stability, it is also appropriate to look at the question of 'indoctrination' raised in Chapter 2. This can be reconceptualised by asking how far cultural trends contributed to stability, and also how far they reflected political impulses and developments. The discussion focuses on the Baroque, the dominant artistic mood and language of the seventeenth and early eighteenth centuries. A recent study summarised the established view of the Baroque:

In art it begins in Rome with work which owes a lot to Michelangelo's impatient deformations of Renaissance prototypes and quickly progresses to something more extrovert and untrammelled on scales seldom seen before. In religion it is tied to Counter-Reformation reassertions of Catholic orthodoxy against Protestant incursions, but shows individualist traces suspiciously similar to Protestantism, at least to untrained eyes. In politics it corresponds to the increasing centralization of power in the monarch and the vigorous ritual displays which accompany it.[29]

In practice, the definition of styles for any particular art form is a matter of controversy, and this is even more the case if an attempt is made to fix ideological and political contexts. Stylistic pluralism was common in the work of individual artists or particular periods and countries. Traditional themes continued to be addressed, old genres survived, and old methods were used at the same time as new developments and insights advanced. Far from a simple definition being appropriate, the Baroque was a wide-ranging style and set of images and themes. These were not restricted to the world of Catholicism and royal authority. Baroque forms were also adopted in Protestant countries, for example the architecture and landscape work of Sir John Vanbrugh in England. The Baroque has been seen in terms of disorder mastered, a theme that apparently lent itself to absolutism, but the degree to which the Baroque could be seen not as a style of order and control could lead to the suggestion that it was morally and culturally subversive. In his *Vitruvius Britannicus* (1715), the influential Scottish Palladian architect Colen Campbell (who looked back to the work of the sixteenth-century Italian architect Andrea Palladio (*c*.1508–80), who, in turn, was inspired by Classical models) wrote:

> How affected and licentious are the works of Bernini and Fontana. How wildly extravagant are the designs of Borromini, who has endeavoured to debauch mankind with his old and chimerical beauties, where the parts are without proportion, solids without their true bearing, heaps of materials without strength, excessive ornaments without grace, and the whole without symmetry.[30]

Rather than take part in stylistic debate, it is instructive to discuss intentions, more particularly the use of culture in order to support authority. This was not a new theme, but it was one that was pushed hard in the early modern period. In part, this reflected the need of rulers to strengthen their authority as a result of the challenges posed by religious heterodoxy and conflict, and, in part, the extent to which court culture from the Renaissance gave a greater impetus to competition through image.[31] The extent to which this rivalry played a role is unclear, but there is evidence of rulers seeking information about the building plans of counterparts,[32] as well as other aspects of their courts. Rulers also sought to assert dynastic claims by using display and ceremony. This was particularly necessary because a number of dynasties were newly established. This number included the Tudors, the Romanovs and the Bourbons, successively, in France, Spain and Naples. Heraldry and other means proclaimed the inherited right of newly established dynasties.[33]

The role of building and ceremony in exalting royal glory was abundantly displayed under Louis XIV. This was particularly so at Versailles, the new palace that proclaimed his power. In the *Salon de la Guerre* at Versailles, finished and opened to the public in 1686, Antoine Coyseux presented Louis as a stuccoed Mars, the God of War. In addition, building in Paris during his reign – with its repertoire of royal column, triumphal arch and monumental avenue – was designed to enhance the splendour of the monarchy as well as the capital. In royal iconography, the monarchy symbolised France, a symbolisation and ideological centrality that was pushed hard during this reign, but became less credible thereafter.[34] Artifice played a major role in the creation of the image of Louis, a process facilitated by the absence of anything equivalent to subsequent cults of sincerity.[35] The monarch became the centre of a cult of ornamental heroism. Other rulers deliberately fostered the same process.[36]

An emphasis on culture as a form of indoctrination raises the question of its impact. This is unclear, but none the less important for that. In part, it is a question not of the influence alone of culture, in the shape of the creation of an artistic image and language of royal authority, glory and power, but rather of its position and process as part of a ideological and mental world that encompassed the role of rulers as war leaders, defenders of religion, supreme judges, and sacral figures with deeply symbolic powers, particularly that of touching for scrofula, 'the king's evil'. This sacralisation had been challenged by the Reformation, but it remained strong across much of Europe, including Russia. Indeed, although the explanation of royal power changed, the imperial cult under Napoleon indicated the extent to which such ideas remained potent.

An emphasis on royalty meant an emphasis on sovereign monarchies. By 1700 these were more clearly the established state form in Christian Europe than had been the case in 1500, and, even, 1550. In the earlier period, it had appeared possible that city states, city leagues and/or empires would be the dominant forms. In the case of the last, the rise of Habsburg power had brought the possibility of the overshadowing of the new states referred to subsequently as the new monarchies. The shift from this situation to that in 1700 was an important dynamic in European history. However, it was far from inevitable. Just as, in Chapter 3, it was suggested that composite states had considerable strength, so it can be argued that bodies other than sovereign monarchies were not without a future, and thus that the very form of the territorial state, whether composite or not, was not inevitably the most successful. Indeed, the structural advantages of sovereign, territorial authority are open to debate. It has been suggested that territorial states with such authority triumphed by providing a clear-cut final decision-making authority, which made it easier to overcome particularism.[37] This may underrate the consensual aspect of such states, and may also minimise the role of scale. Territorial states may well have been no more effective as decision-makers, but, instead, better able to deploy the forces needed to subjugate opposition when it occurred.

For example, there was no large urban polity able to offer the terms laid out in Ivan IV's Decree on Service (1556). This held all nobles liable for lifelong services, including the most powerful boyars and princes with allodial estates, and was part of a social politics that bent the nobility to military service while compensating them with the enserfment of their peasant tenants. Such a social politics would be a point of comparison with the Ottoman Empire and other Islamic territorial states. Like their Christian counterparts, these states faced opposition to their authority and power on both internal and external frontiers.

From another perspective, territorial states have also been seen as protection providers that won the support of mercantile élites that would otherwise have backed urban political forms. Thus, territorial states developed as combinations of the landed power of rulers and rural élites with the financial resources and mercantile interests of urban élites, creating 'a positive cycle of resource extraction, stability and an increasing resource base'.[38] This could also be seen in the range of systems for administering Europe's overseas activities. Alongside territorial control by officials, there were mercantile companies given extensive powers. The profits from shipping spices back to Europe led to the foundation of the (Dutch) United East India Company, which was granted a charter giving it political and military powers, including the right to make war, peace and treaties, and to construct fortresses.

Territorial states might appear to be more effective protection providers, such that cities did not require modern fortifications or large militias, but that does not mean that city states and leagues were necessarily redundant. Indeed, urban republics were widely applauded in the sixteenth and seventeenth centuries as models of good government and civic virtue. They could be seen to resonate with Classical values that were closely associated with republicanism. Public virtue was widely held to be a republican characteristic, the product of states with a 'balanced' constitution.

By the eighteenth century, the perception of such republics, particularly the most famous, Venice, was far less positive. Although the city had a strong appeal as a centre of culture and, even more, pleasure, the republic of Venice was seen as an increasingly inconsequential state, and as a model only of rigidity. Tyrannical aspects of its governmental system attracted criticism, and Venice was held up by outsiders as an example of the dangers of oligarchical government. In 1763, Francis, Marquess of Tavistock advised the Earl of Upper Ossory 'to study a little the constitution of the Republic of Venice, in order to inspire you with a proper dread of aristocracy'.[39] The following year, another British tourist, Henry, 2nd Viscount Palmerston, wrote 'under the form of an oligarchy it seems to be a perfect tyranny', but he added an observation that is worthy of note when considering the general issue of the redundancy of particular governmental systems:

These powers though enormously great yet often changing hands and those who exercise them one moment being subject to them the next are not often abused and they are agreeable to the common people who are in general below any apprehension of them for themselves and who find in them their best defence against the nobles whose tyranny would be very great over their inferiors were it not for this check. The people in general are attached to this government and live happy under it: the taxes are not heavy, they have generally plenty and it is the policy of the state to encourage every pursuit of pleasure in all ranks of people.[40]

The notion of territorial states as combinations of landed power and urban élites is a somewhat instrumental account but it helps explain the ability of states to derive strength from two different economic milieux. This entailed a process of negotiation and compromise, sometimes interspersed with episodes of violence. The political strategies involved played a role in the politics of the period, but dynastic and confessional issues and disputes were more important to their course and content.

It is also worth noting the extent to which processes of negotiation and compromise can be re-examined by looking at them as ways in which governance as a whole, and the tasks and powers that central government sought to convey in particular, provided opportunities to solve local problems, affirm local status, and participate in the wider community. Thus, the extent to which the early modern period saw the creation and/or development of a range of identities, including regional and local as well as national and state, did not necessarily circumscribe the role and powers of the latter. Instead, there was a positive interaction, with the state able to benefit from other forms of identity, although this was far from automatic. The judicial role of the state was particularly valuable in this respect, as it arbitrated between local jurisdictions, while the very practice of law enforcement offered a means for social peace and order.[41]

Participation in the wider community was a matter not simply of gaining benefits and status, important as both were, but also of responding to political and religious impulses. Yet this response could be directed against the demands of central government, and this underlined the conditional quality of the local reception of outside governance. Both reception and conditionality were a matter not only of protecting local interests, but also of responding to wider currents. A failure by rulers to win support in the latter respect could lead to the rapid collapse of the process of government, as local agencies, and the élites that controlled them, no longer felt that governance served reasonable purposes.

The Reformation touched off a serious crisis across much of Europe in the sixteenth and early seventeenth centuries, by raising fundamental issues of legitimacy, but, aside from this, there was the less prominent, but more insistent, process of reception – variously accommodation and evasion, the two often not separate – of government. Whether government was central or local, lay or ecclesiastical, there were tensions over social and religious behaviour, with communal forms of surveillance and discipline playing a major role. The availability of these alternatives can be seen as a defiance of agencies of central control, but, in practice, there was a more symbiotic relationship. The agencies were frequently unable alone to meet communal needs for surveillance and discipline that accorded with local sensitivities, and, instead, were more effective when they arbitrated in accordance with these assumptions and interests. The same was true of tensions between economic interests.[42] As with all systems of accommodation, however, access by the population to arbitration and support varied greatly in accordance with social power and norms.

The different ways of conceptualising early modern states underline the difficulty of assessing the capability of governmental systems. At the end of the seventeenth century, although the Bourbon monarchy of Louis XIV offered a model to several other rulers, there was still a considerable diversity in government and politics. This diversity had been emphasised when William III gained the British Isles and was to be taken further when the death of Charles XII in 1718 was followed by the beginning of the Swedish Age of Liberty.

Notes

1. S. Carroll, *Noble Power during the French Wars of Religion. The Guise Affinity and the Catholic Cause in Normandy* (Cambridge, 1998).

2. K. Maag (ed.), *The Reformation in Eastern and Central Europe* (Aldershot, 1997).

3. G. Murdock, *Calvinism on the Frontier, 1600–1660: International Calvinism and the Reformed Church in Hungary and Transylvania* (Oxford, 2000).

4. For a recent introduction, G. Darby (ed.), *The Origins and Development of the Dutch Revolt* (2001).

5. C. Brady, *The Chief Governors. The Rise and Fall of Reform Government in Tudor Ireland, 1536–1588* (Cambridge, 1994); N. Canny, *Making Ireland British, 1580–1650* (Oxford, 2001).

6. H. Morgan, *Tyrone's Rebellion* (Woodbridge, 1993).

7. R. von Friedeburg, *Self-Defence and Religious Strife in Early-Modern Europe. England and Germany, 1530–1680* (Aldershot, 2002), p. 7.

8. H. Kamen, *Philip V of Spain* (New Haven, CT, 2001), p. 116.

9. T. Johnson, 'The Upper-Palatinate nobility and the Counter Reformation', in B. Kümin (ed.), *Reformations Old and New: Essays on the Socio-Economic Impact of Religious Change, c. 1470–1630* (Aldershot, 1996), pp. 147–68.

10. M. Wolfe, 'Walled towns during the French Wars of Religion, 1560–1630', in J. D. Tracy (ed.), *City Walls. The Urban Enceinte in Global Perspective* (Cambridge, 2000), pp. 347–8. More generally, see D. Parker, *The Making of French Absolutism* (1983).

11. R. Mathee, 'Unwalled cities and restless nomads: firearms and artillery in Safavid

Iran', in C. Melville (ed.), *Safavid Persia. The History and Politics of an Islamic Society* (1996), pp. 409–10.

12. D. Sella, *Italy in the Seventeenth Century* (Harlow, 1997).

13. R. Frost, *After the Deluge. Poland-Lithuania and the Second Northern War 1655–1660* (Cambridge, 1993).

14. J. Sawyer, *Printed Poison: Pamphlet Propaganda, Faction Politics and the Public Sphere in Seventeenth-Century France* (Berkeley, CA, 1990); B. Dooley and S. Baron (eds), *The Politics of Information in Early Modern Europe* (2001).

15. C. J. Sommerville, *The News Revolution in England. Cultural Dynamics of Daily Information* (Oxford, 1996); M. McKeon, *The Origins of the English Novel 1600–1740* (Baltimore, MD, 1987).

16. K. J. V. Jespersen, 'Absolute monarchy in Denmark: change and continuity', *Scandinavian Journal of History*, 12 (1987), pp. 307–16. For Germany, R. G. Asch, 'Estates and princes after 1648: the consequences of the Thirty Years War', *German History*, 6 (1988), pp. 113–32; W. W. Hagen, 'Seventeenth-century crisis in Brandenburg. The Thirty Years War, the destabilization of serfdom and the rise of absolutism', *American Historical Review*, 94 (1989), pp. 302–35; and J. A. Mears, 'The Thirty Years' War, the "General Crisis", and the origins of a standing professional army in the Habsburg monarchy', *Central European History*, 21 (1988), pp. 122–41.

17. M. J. Braddick, *State Formation in Early Modern England, c.1550–1700* (Cambridge, 2000).

18. H. Berry (ed.), *The Noble Science: A Study and Transcription of Sloane MS. 2530, Papers of the Masters of Defence of London, Temp. Henry VIII to 1590* (1991).

19. D. Bohanan, *Crown and Nobility in Early Modern France* (Basingstoke, 2001).

20. J. Dewald, *Aristocratic Experience and the Origins of Modern Culture. France, 1570–1715* (Berkeley, CA, 1992); O. Ranum, 'Courtesy, absolutism and the rise of the French state 1630–60', *Journal of Modern History*, 52 (1980), pp. 426–51.

21. W. Beik, *Urban Protest in Seventeenth-Century France. The Culture of Retribution* (Cambridge, 1997).

22. A. Lossky, *Louis XIV and the French Monarchy* (New Brunswick, NJ, 1994).

23. R. Mettam, *Power and Faction in Louis XIV's France* (Oxford, 1988); J. Collins, *The State in Early Modern France* (Cambridge, 1995); S. Kettering, *Patrons, Brokers, and Clients in Seventeenth-Century France* (New York, 1986); A. Hamscher, *The Conseil Privé and the Parlements in the Age of Louis XIV: A Study in French Absolutism* (Philadelphia, PA, 1987).

24. P. Bushkovitch, *Peter the Great: The Struggle for Power 1671–1725* (Cambridge, 2001), pp. 434–44.

25. P. Bushkovitch, *Peter the Great* (Lanham, MD, 2001), p. 171.

26. S. Dixon, *The Modernisation of Russia 1676–1825* (Cambridge, 1999).

27. L. Hughes, *Peter the Great. A Biography* (New Haven, CT, 2002), pp. 128–9.

28. M. Hughes, *Early Modern Germany, 1477–1806* (Basingstoke, 1992).

29. R. Harbison, *Reflections on Baroque* (2000), p. viii. For the Baroque as a cosmopolitan style in an area where it made a major impact, T. D. Kaufmann, *Court, Cloister and City. The Art and Culture of Central Europe, 1450–1800* (1995) and, on the governmental dimension, H. Lorenz, 'The imperial Hofburg. The theory and practice of architectural representation in Baroque Vienna', in C. Ingrao (ed.), *The State and Society in Early Modern Austria* (West Lafayette, IN, 1994), pp. 93–109. See also G. L. Buelow (ed.), *The Late Baroque Era from the 1680s to 1740* (Basingstoke, 1993).

30. J. Lees-Milne, *English Country Houses: Baroque, 1685–1715* (1970); K. Downes, *Sir John Vanbrugh* (1987); C. Ridgway and R. Williams (eds), *Sir John Vanbrugh and Landscape Architecture in Baroque England 1690–1730* (Stroud, 2000); S. Parissien, *Palladian Style* (1994), p. 79.

31. J. Dunindam, *Myths of Power. Norbert Elias and the Early Modern European Court* (Amsterdam, 1995); J. Adamson (ed.), *The Princely Courts of Europe. Ritual, Politics and Culture under the Ancien Régime 1500–1750* (1999); V. Press, 'The imperial court of the Habsburgs from Maximilian I to Ferdinand III, 1493–1657', in R. G. Asch and A. M. Birke (eds), *Princes, Patronage and the Nobility* (Oxford, 1991), pp. 289–312; J. P. Spielman, *The City and the Crown. Vienna and the Imperial Court 1600–1740* (West Lafayette, IN, 1993).

32. P. S. Fichtner, *Emperor Maximilian II* (New Haven, CT, 2001), p. 99.

33. S. Anglo, *Images of Tudor Kingship* (1992).

34. R. W. Berger, *A Royal Passion. Louis XIV as Patron of Architecture* (Cambridge, 1994); C. Mukerji, *Territorial Ambitions and the Gardens of Versailles* (Cambridge, 1997).

35. P. Burke, *The Fabrication of Louis XIV* (New Haven, CT, 1992).

36. S. J. Klingensmith, *The Utility of Splendor. Ceremony, Social Life, and Architecture at the Court of Bavaria 1600–1800* (Chicago, IL, 1993); M. Tanner, *The Last Descendant of Aeneas. The Hapsburgs and the Mythic Image of the Emperor* (New Haven, CT, 1993).

37. H. Spruyt, *The Sovereign State and Its Competitors* (Princeton, NJ, 1994).

38. J. Glete, *War and the State in Early Modern Europe. Spain, the Dutch Republic and Sweden as Fiscal-Military States, 1500–1600* (2002), p. 7. For a similar emphasis, S. Ogilvie, 'The state in Germany. A non-Prussian view', in J. Brewer and E. Hellmuth (eds), *Rethinking Leviathan. The Eighteenth-Century State in Britain and Germany* (Oxford, 1999), pp. 167–202.

39. Tavistock to Upper Ossory, 12 September 1763, London, Bedford Estate Office, Russell Letters.

40. Southampton, University Library, Broadlands Archive 11/3.

41. S. Hindle, *The State and Social Change in Early Modern England, c. 1550–1640* (Basingstoke, 2000).

42. C. R. Phillips and W. D. Phillips, *Spain's Golden Fleece: Wool Production and the Wool Trade from the Middle Ages to the Nineteenth Century* (Baltimore, MD, 1997).

CHAPTER 6

Eighteenth-century Consequences

§ IF every century displays both change and continuity, the eighteenth was no exception. In some respects, this may seem a surprising verdict, as the century appears to mark a major discontinuity. The combination of the American and French revolutions with the onset of the Industrial Revolution brings in the modern world, and also the habit of thinking in terms of utopian, or at least dramatically improved, future scenarios, a practice that encourages a belief in the value of change and of a process of continual change.

Although the American, French and Industrial revolutions were all dramatic, there were also the less violent transformations in thought and expression variously summarised as the Scientific Revolution, the Enlightenment, and the rise of the public sphere. The last, a development largely of print culture and urban spaces, has attracted considerable attention in recent decades and has been seen as creating a new political culture. This posed both an opportunity and a challenge for existing systems, particularly that of France. The failure of the French crown to respond has been seen as creating a crisis of legitimisation in France, although such an approach risks minimising the importance of specific political developments there. Defeat by Britain in the Seven Years' War (1756–63), in which the French navy was destroyed and most of the colonies lost, has been seen as leading to a crisis in French political culture that resolved itself into a shift in the relationship between state and people, specifically a move from being subjects of the monarch to becoming citizens. This has been presented as a crucial linguistic prelude to the revolution.

Governments had for decades sought to influence public opinion through printed propaganda and to gain an insight into the public mood through systematic police reporting. However, although the public mood within France was seen as important, it was not until the second half of the century that it was regarded as a source of political legitimacy. The notion of honour and *gloire*, generally presented, in the seventeenth century, in personal (the monarch) and dynastic terms, was instead increasingly seen in terms of the nation and country. This is a reminder of the limitations of a top-down approach to the issues of authority and government in the eighteenth century. Far from solely being driven by such problems as the costs of warfare and the contentious policies of the Enlightened Despots, there was also a dynamic set of changing notions of nation, public, society, civilisation and country. Monarchical authority, it is claimed, ceased to be the appropriate definition of public allegiance and patriotic enthusiasm, although the extent to which these can be recovered for analysis should not be exaggerated. Indeed, a major problem with the discourse analysis is that it reifies concepts, making them causal forces of great potency. Furthermore, there is a tendency, common among intellectuals, to assume, if not exaggerate, a role for ideas that rests on an act of faith.

Distinguishing between monarch and people / country was scarcely new. Indeed, it was a standard trophe of political contention. If it was necessary or convenient frequently to stress the role of evil ministers, this was known to be a political fiction. The extent to which monarch and people / country could be differentiated was indicated in the first four decades of the century in, for example, criticism of new dynasties and their policies (Bourbon in Spain, Hanover in Britain, Hesse-Cassel in Sweden), as well as in opposition to Westernisation policies in Russia. In France, various strands of criticism interacted to decry the policies of Louis XIV's last years, of the succeeding Regency government, of the ministry of the Duke of Bourbon (1723–26), and of that of Cardinal Fleury, particularly the clash with the *Parlement* of Paris in 1732. Thus the degree to which it is appropriate to emphasise a new political configuration in France, stemming from the Seven Years' War, or the mid-century clashes over Jansenism, or the Maupeou Revolution of the early 1770s, is open to question. As so often in work on the eighteenth century, it reflects a failure to give due weight to earlier circumstances.[1]

New ideas could be exploited in radical directions, but this was far from a necessary end-product. Indeed, it was government ministers in France who planned a large public art museum, a project eventually brought to fruition in the Louvre of 1793.[2] Far from being the monopoly of one particular group or tendency, ideas and discourse enjoyed a more diffuse currency. Visiting Milan in 1771, William, 2nd Earl of Shelburne wrote of 'the Literati, by all accounts new in Italy – at present you may be recommended from town to town from one set of literati to the other, as formerly from convent to convent'.[3]

Most of the scholarship on radical tendencies and revolutionary movements is inclined to emphasise their range and impact, but this risks underrating, even ignoring, the strength of contrary tendencies.[4] This is part of a more general failure to consider the contours and vitality of conservatism. In simplistic terms, conservatism is misunderstood in two major respects. First, the inherent strength of conservative positions is underrated by those who take a teleological position and regard them as bound to fail. Second, the capacity of conservative systems to generate their own strategies for change is neglected by those who prefer to focus on liberal strategies and / or think of change, in Hegelian terms, as a product of the clash between reactionary conservatism and progressive radicalism.

Both these flaws affect the assessment of the eighteenth century. For example, the stress on radical Enlightenment thought[5] fails adequately to consider the limited impact of such arguments on the mass of religious believers. The continued importance of religious identities and conflict can be seen across Europe and throughout the century. It was particularly important in Germany and the Habsburg lands in the first half of the century. Protestant vitality and revival were seen in developments such as the Pietist movement and the Moravian Brethren, while, in Catholic Europe, the first half of the century has been presented as a golden age of rural preaching missions, as religious orders developed their earlier work against heresy, ignorance or indifference. Each of these orders in turn drew on networks of support.[6]

Counter-Reformation zeal led to pressure on Protestants, especially, but not only, in the *Erblande* and the Archbishopric of Salzburg: the Protestants in the latter were forced to emigrate in 1731.[7] Although toleration was advocated by some writers, and there were improvements in the treatment of those outside established Churches, the extent of toleration was limited in many states.[8] The penal restrictions on the Huguenots in France were not relaxed until the 1780s and their harsh treatment helped account for the unsuccessful rising in the Cevennes in the 1700s.

Protestant persecution of Catholics was, in turn, at issue in Ireland, and the argument that the penal statutes constituted little more than an intolerable system of petty oppression has been questioned, although it is generally agreed that the situation improved from mid-century.[9] This was helped by the death, in 1766, of 'James III', the Jacobite claimant, who had taken his nominating role to bishoprics seriously, and had helped mould a hierarchy opposed to any accommodation with the Hanoverians.[10] Similarly, religion played a major role in the breakdown of the Anglo-American world.

The continued ideological and practical vitality of the nexus of faith and privilege was to be amply demonstrated during the response to the French Revolution and Napoleon, and any reading of earlier decades that is not through the blinkers of fashionable *philosophe* thought helps account for this vitality.[11] Yet there has been insufficient effort in general works to consider political and cultural developments in light of this perspective.[12] Furthermore, in Catholic Europe, an area in which religious pluralism was rare, the French Revolution acted to reintroduce sectarian politics. The novelty of this, and the long-established hostility to the heterodox, lent force to the hostile response.[13]

Religion also played a major role in the culture of the period, although it is one that has received insufficient scholarly attention. For example, the powerful and popular hymns of the period have been marginalised in the formation of the conventional literary canon.[14] Similarly, the role of devotional themes in painting and sculpture has received too little consideration, as indeed have the churches as patrons of the arts. Devotional themes and images were important to piety, providing ways in which life could be understood and hope grasped. Churches were the physical embodiments of many communities, and it is easy to understand the shock created by the destruction of the fabric of faith by the French revolutionaries in the 1790s.

These religious currents were also of political importance. Thus Pietism played a major role in Prussian political culture and was an important factor behind the traditional institutional, political and military accounts of state development and aggrandisement. The Pietist work ethic was crucial to the vocational focus that played a major role in the creation of a service state and nobility. Frederick William I (r. 1713–40) demanded more from his troops than a subconscious affirmation of, or resigned acquiescence to, their fate. He wanted them to share his belief that to endure suffering in this world was the duty of the God-fearing individual. The army chaplain's job consisted of inculcating in the troops the concept of a moral order. This policy was effective and reflected the capacity of an eighteenth-century state to respond to cultural shifts and, in turn, to employ them in shaping society.[15]

While allowing for the strength of what were to be termed conservative tendencies, it is also important to consider the degree to which the stress on the value of change was not only different to the position in the sixteenth and seventeenth centuries, but also an aspect of a new relationship between government and society, in so far as the two can be separated. Issues of chronological demarcation are important, in particular the viablity of the compartmentalisation of the eighteenth century and the creation of a chronology that treats its early years as the concluding period of the era of Louis XIV, and then, after a period much of which is in shadow, focuses on Maria Theresa, George III and the Enlightened Despots.[16] The nature of this chronology, and the extent of this period of shadow, varies by country and subject; but it is certainly true that we know less of the Portugal of John V (r. 1706–50) than that of Joseph I (r. 1750–77) and Pombal, less of the Spain of Philip V (r. 1700–46) and Ferdinand VI (r. 1746–59), than that of Charles III (r. 1759–88), less of the Russia of Catherine I (r. 1725–27), Peter II (r. 1727–30), Anna (r. 1730–40), Ivan VI (r. 1740–41) and Elizabeth (r. 1741–62) than of that of Peter the Great (r. 1689–1725) and Catherine the Great (r. 1762–96), and so on.

There have been improvements, not least the appearance of recent scholarly work on Philip V and on the Fleury ministry,[17] but the weight of research and publication continues to fall on the second half of the century. This is true of Austria, Britain, France, Prussia, Russia, Spain and Sweden. Furthermore, work on the first half of the century does not play a major role in accounts of the eighteenth century as a whole. While this remains the case, it is difficult to establish what was novel about the Enlightened Despots, and how their aspirations and achievements should be assessed.

This is part of a larger problem of deciding how best to relate the two halves of the century. There are essentially two approaches. The first treats the entire century as a unit. In this perspective, the greater clarity permitted by work on the second half largely illuminates a longer-term situation. Alternatively, it can be argued that there was significant change during the century, with the later decades being very different to the earlier. This approach is taken in a variety of subjects, including demographics, economic history, and that of imperial regulation, and can also be seen in work on British and French history and on Enlightened Despotism. In each case, however, the detailed chronology of change is different, and the weight placed upon a 'tipping point' or period of transition varies.

If century-long units are to be adopted, then the first half of the eighteenth century in many respects sits more comfortably with the second half of the seventeenth. Thus, whereas in an impressive recent collection on the eighteenth century, the editor, T. C. W. Blanning, argued that 'If no single concept or metaphor can summarise adequately an epoch lasting a century, the one word that best bridges all aspects of the eighteenth century is "expansion"', conversely, Derek Beales divided his fine discussion of religion and culture at mid-century, and aimed 'to show how different were the tendencies of the first half of the century from those of the second half'.[18]

In addition, it is unclear, in many cases, how far changes in the second half of the eighteenth century were prefigured earlier. In particular, it is unclear how far the policies of the Enlightened Despots differed from those of the 1690s–1710s when the pressures of war appear to have combined in, for example, Austria in the early years of Charles VI (r. 1711–40), Regency France, the Prussia of Frederick William I (r. 1713–40), the Russia of Peter the Great, England in the 1690s, Spain in the 1700s and 1710s, and the Savoy-Piedmont of Victor Amadeus II (r. 1675–1730), with reform impulses drawing, variously, on cameralism, Pietism, 'political arithmetic', mercantilism and early Enlightenment thought: all of these have been seen as influential in the period.[19]

There were also shifts in the style of power. Louis XIV's image changed in his later years with a new reliance not on allegorical themes, but on a closer engagement with issues of policy.[20] Similarly, the ethos of the government and style of the court of Brandenburg-Prussia under Elector Frederick III (r. 1688–1713; from 1701 King Frederick I)[21] was very different from that under his son, Frederick William I. More generally, there was less stress on the themes and idioms of sacral monarchy.[22] This can be linked to a longer-term shift in sensibility from the attitudes, themes and trophes inaccurately, but helpfully, summarised as Baroque to those summarised as Classical, although the latter did not gather pace until the second third of the eighteenth century.[23]

Enlightened Despotism, the term used to describe the governance of several of the leading European states in the period 1740–90, especially Austria, Prussia and Russia, encompasses two separate emphases on aims and policies. One stresses the influence of new ideas on the purpose of society – the Enlightenment – and concentrates on a relatively idealistic approach to domestic reform. The second approach emphasises the role of war, not least the need to maximise state resources in order to prepare for it. Peter the Great's reform programme was in part a consequence of the demands posed by the lengthy struggle with Sweden in the Great Northern War (1700–21), while, in Spain, the fiscal and governmental reforms introduced under Philip V (r. 1700–46) and his successor, Ferdinand VI (r. 1746–59), were, in large part, intended to ensure that Spain was able to develop as a major military power. The army was strengthened and a substantial navy, supported by effective dockyards, was created, and Spain was able to take an assertive role in Italy in 1717–20, 1733–35, and 1741–48.

Austrian policies in the early 1750s were a consequence of the loss of Silesia to Prussia and a prelude to an attempt to regain it in the Seven Years' War (1756–63).[24] That war was followed across Europe by a widespread attempt to tackle the financial burdens arising from the conflict and to prepare for what appeared to be another inevitable round of warfare, an attempt that taxed political assumptions and governmental capability. In France, where the government's debt had risen to about 2,350 million livres at the close of the conflict, the burden of servicing the loan by the payment of interest was over half of the total government expenditure by the end of the decade.[25] Such figures challenged the domestic and international position of the ministry in France, Britain and other states. Debt and credit played a major role in both the details of politics and in the relationship between constituent parts of the government system, such as the crown and the Estates in France.

In Russia, war can also be linked to reform. Catherine the Great's governmental reforms of 1775 stemmed from the problems of resource mobilisation and control revealed in the Russo-Ottoman War of 1768–74 and the Pugachev rebellion, as well as reflecting the interplay of ministerial factions,[26] although Catherine herself was a keen legislator and an ardent sponsor of reform and change.[27] Defeat by Russia led to attempts, under Abdülhamid I (r. 1774–89) and, even more, Selim III (r. 1789–1807), to improve the army and to reform related institutions and practices in the Ottoman Empire.[28]

Across much of Europe, renewed attempts to tackle financial burdens followed the period 1778–83, years in which Britain, France, Spain, the United Provinces, Austria and Prussia were all involved in either the War of American Independence or the War of the Bavarian Succession. Indeed, the need to respond to the specific problems these wars had revealed or accentuated, and to prepare for the renewed bouts of conflict believed imminent between Britain and France, and Austria and Prussia, were to play an important role in the revolutionary crisis of the 1780s, alongside the popular radicalism that attracts more attention.

To return, first, to the governmental systems of the pre-revolutionary period, larger armies and aristocratic officership[29] ensured that eighteenth-century states were militarised (and with a matching social structure), and therefore responsive to changes in military circumstances. This process was adapted to traditional state structures by continuing the practice whereby monarchs, and members of royal families, held command positions.

This was challenged by the frequency of female rulers, including, in the eighteenth century, Anne of Britain (r. 1702–14), Maria Theresa of Austria (r. 1740–80), and Catherine I (r. 1725–27), Anna (r. 1730–40), Elizabeth (r. 1741–62) and Catherine the Great of Russia (r. 1762–96). The combined reigns of the four female Russian rulers ensured that female rule was more frequent there than male in the eighteenth century. The difficulty posed by female succession varied. As with other monarchs, there was the reversionary interest, for example the future Peter III under Elizabeth, the future Paul I under Catherine II, Joseph II under Maria Theresa, and, first, the Electress Sophia of Hanover and, then, the future George I of Britain and Hanover under Anne. In addition, the role of marital choice and of spouses was more important for female than for male rulers. This was particularly the case with Charles XII's successor, Ulrika Eleonora (r. 1718–20), who swiftly abdicated the Swedish throne in favour of her Hessian husband Frederick I (r. 1720–51). Similarly, Maria Theresa's marriage to Francis of Lorraine, the Emperor Francis I, brought particular commitments to Austrian policy. Not all female rulers were so affected by spouses. Catherine I, Anna and Catherine II of Russia were widows, and Elizabeth did not marry, while Prince George of Denmark, the husband of Anne of Britain, had little impact on policy. Female rulers, anyway, took pains to underline the link of monarchy and officership. Under Maria Theresa, a military order was established, many officers were ennobled, and uniforms were more commonly worn at court.[30]

As in the sixteenth and seventeenth centuries (see Chapter 2), more than is generally appreciated, most eighteenth-century rulers sought both to co-operate with the socially powerful and to pursue what was practical, and, therefore, in the formulation and execution of their policies, respected privilege and precedent. Given that, at Catherine the Great's accession in 1762, the Russian government suffered from a lack of information, with no figures for the annual revenue of the imperial government and no list of towns,[31] it is not surprising that, however much government policies did have a general impact on society, individual initiatives frequently had few results. However, it is far from easy to decide how best to evaluate contemporary standards of effectiveness, while evidence and scholarship that might form the basis of modern assessment are frequently lacking.

The ideal of informed and enlightened statesmanship was clear. In 1779, Thomas Erskine, an opposition British MP and a meritocrat, urged Parliament to reject a bill to vest the sole right of printing almanacs in the universities of Oxford and Cambridge. Alluding to the possibility that parliamentarians might be affected by their place of education, and thus support the bill, Erskine added:

Yet I persuade myself that these learned bodies have effectually defeated their own interests, by the sentiments which their liberal sciences have disseminated amongst you; – their wise and learned institutions have erected in your minds the august image of an enlightened statesman, which, trampling down all personal interests and affections, looks steadily forward to the great ends of public and private justice, unawed by authority, and unbiased by favour.[32]

Reality was otherwise. Informed opinion was generally divided over the desirability of government policies. Abstractions, such as Enlightenment, Enlightened Despotism, Enlightened Absolutism and Enlightened Government, dissolve under scrutiny to reveal a world in which issues were far from clear.

Furthermore, aside from disagreements over goals, there were problems over implementation. Compromise was common and rulers were often, primarily, trying desperately to cope with their immediate problems, or, if they were planning for the future, were more interested in war and international relations than in domestic reform. At the same time, however, that it is unclear how far the shift from a Baroque to an Enlightened sensibility transformed social attitudes, it was, nevertheless, the case that there were changes in governmental aspirations, not least in supporting education. Social policies in education, poor relief and health extended the scope of government.[33] Prince Kaunitz, chancellor and the leading Austrian minister from 1753 until 1792, has been presented in terms not only of foreign policy but also of genuine humanitarian impulses, not least a sincere concern for popular welfare. Franz Szabo has argued that Kaunitz was 'patently affected by the novel ideas of the Western Enlightenment with its stress on secularism, cultural and intellectual growth, individual merit, human dignity and the liberation of individuals from traditional bonds'.[34] This set of ideas was different to those linked to economic development in preceding centuries.

A more obscure figure, but one who might have been a long-reigning monarch, Catherine II, the Great's, murdered husband and briefly-reigning predecessor, Peter III of Russia (r. 1762), has also been presented as an Enlightenment ruler, who sought to use his power to define the expectations of the élite and to reject an earlier, more conservative, generation's political position. Peter's withdrawal from conflict with his idol Frederick II of Prussia in the Seven Years' War has been praised for creating a political climate advantageous to his domestic programme, and the secularisation of Church lands helped with resources; but the ambiguous relationship of reform and authority is captured with the argument that the autocratic methods of both Peter and Catherine II (r. 1762–96) created rigidity in the application of reform and stifled political dialogue.[35] Government attitudes helped politicise the issue of reform in Russia, and a similar process occurred elsewhere.

If reform was the expression of an entire European political culture that rose to prominence in mid-century, as has been argued, then the different political courses that followed arose in part from the response to the degree of authoritarianism shown by rulers. Discussion of the role of Peter III is a reminder that monarchical authority continued to have a personal quality. It is no accident that the governmental movement in Europe is referred to in terms of Enlightened Despots, with the emphasis on individuals. This was appropriate, although ministers could also be crucial, as was seen with Kaunitz (Austria), Pombal (Portugal), Struensee (Denmark), Campomanes (Spain), and Tanucci (Naples). It has been argued that sovereigns were delegating more of the detailed tasks of government to ministers in the mid-century,[36] although there are plenty of earlier signs of such delegation.

The attitudes of individual British and French ministers were also important. Thus, Walpole and North, the dominant British ministers in 1720–42 and 1770–82 respectively, were not committed to reform, although, even so, Walpole sought to change the tax system with a shift to excises, while North's efforts to regulate imperial finance and, more particularly, the East India Company, helped precipitate the crisis in relations with Britain's North American colonies. Other leading ministers, including Henry Pelham in 1748–54, George Grenville in 1763–65, and William Pitt the Younger in 1783–1801, were more eager reformers and, in the last two cases, self-proclaimed reformers. As was so frequently the case during the century, British reform focused heavily on fiscal matters, although other issues were also important. Thus Henry Pelham's ministry saw attempts at social reform, including measures aimed against lawlessness, as well as Jewish naturalisation and reform of the calendar.[37]

Despite the differences in the political system, it was no accident that the names of French ministers, such as Calonne, Maupeou and Vergennes, rather than the monarchs, also play a major role in discussion of governmental action and of politics. In part, this was a product of the character and attitudes of Louis XV, and Louis XVI, but an emphasis on ministers also reflected the development of government functions.[38] It is also pertinent to note the continuing role of ministerial politics which joined the need to develop hierarchies of policy-making and administration, and clashes over policy, to more traditional issues of patronage. This was true not only of France but also of other states. Thus, in Spain, the Count of Aranda, president of the Council of Castile from 1766 to 1773, was regarded as the head of what was called the Aragonese Party, a group of prominent individuals who were hostile to what were seen as overly autocratic tendencies within the government. Ministerial politics were also very much in evidence in states where the ruler appeared autocratic: both Russia and the Ottoman Empire.[39]

In practice, across Europe, whether the motivation behind policy was primarily linked to international relations or to humanitarian domestic goals, or to both, in the shape of reforming, and thus strengthening, society, the net effect was pressure on relations between crown and social élite, now seen in terms of established interests. The texture of the resulting politics varied, in large part as a consequence of differences between the states in question and between the determination, ability and sensitivity of their rulers. Thus, the Habsburg monarchy under Joseph II (r. 1780–90) faced a more serious challenge than its Russian counterpart under Catherine the Great (r. 1762–96), although, had the Pugachev rising in Russia been more sustained, the comparison might be less apparent. Yet the Habsburg system was to show more resilience than the Bourbon monarchy in France, in part because of the accession of a new ruler, Leopold II (r. 1790–92), who proved more adroit than his brother Joseph. Similarly, the British crisis of 1775–83 was, in the event, less serious for the politics and society of Britain than the revolution was to be for France, but, at the time, the loss of much of the empire, as well as widespread discontent in Britain and Ireland, seemed to presage a total collapse. Commentators in the early 1780s thought of Britain as in crisis and regarded it as a minor factor in international relations.

After about 1750, European monarchs were more prepared than hitherto to risk abandoning traditional norms, a shift due to a different ideology, and a response to the particular need to improve governmental capability after the War of Austrian Succession (1740–48). A lessened emphasis on the sacral aspect of kingship encouraged a stress on the monarch as the first servant of the state, and was an aspect both of a spread of reform Catholicism that owed much to Jansenism,[40] and of a more general process of social and cultural transformation of established hierarchies that was particularly evident in government aspirations[41] and in major cities such as Paris.[42] Monarchs wore military uniform, demonstrating their role as servants of the state.[43] In England, there was no particular public enthusiasm for statues and other monuments for the royal family.[44]

The dialectic of war and reform, however, also created tensions that could lead to political crisis and military weakness. Joseph II's attempts to reform Austria in the 1780s and French attempts in the same period to strengthen the state, through the process and contents of reform, can both be seen in this light, as can the attempts to widen the tax-base of the British imperial system after the Seven Years' War. The last led, particularly in the Stamp Act crisis of 1765–66, to a marked deterioration in relations with many of the American colonists.

At the same time, there is room for considerable differences of opinion over the extent to which the Enlightened Despots threatened to cause political breakdown. One recent stimulating, albeit Whiggish, approach sees the Habsburg inheritance and Joseph II as an incompatible pair:

> out of the various crises of the seventeenth century came a Habsburg
> Monarchy which had a distinctive identity ... As the casualties had included

Protestantism, the bourgeoisie, the towns and urban culture, it was a Monarchy which was essentially static, conservative and defensive. Its future was seen to lie in regaining the past ... The Monarchy always seemed to be a generation or so behind the rest of Europe ... Geography and history thus conspired to create for Joseph II an inheritance for which such adjectives as 'different' or even 'unique' seem unusually inadequate.[45]

Josephine modernization thus appears to have threatened the very strength of the Habsburg state, not least by failing to accept 'the wonderful diversity of the Monarchy',[46] and by protecting the peasantry, but, in a social politics very different from that of the Prussians, being unwilling to favour the land-owners. In contrast, it has also been argued that the Habsburg state was not backward, but, instead, characterised by growing population and territory, an improving economy and better public finances. By the end of the century, regional and ethnic particularism was, it is claimed, increasingly transcended by a common identity.[47]

Consideration of Austria underlines the difficulty of assuming that state success can be readily assessed and thus that a typology of state forms, to explain different capabilities and, for example, account for the fate of Poland, can be devised. The Austrian Habsburg inheritance lacked powerful representative systems comparable to Poland, and the Habsburg position in the *Erblande* was not elective. Yet the reform initiative of the 1710s was not maintained, and, in 1740–41, the Habsburg polity faced a terrible crisis comparable in some respects to that of Poland in the 1650s and the 1700s. The death, without male heirs, of Charles VI in 1740 was followed by a contested imperial succession (won by Charles Albert, Elector of Bavaria, an opponent of the Habsburgs, who became Charles VII), by foreign invasion (by Bavaria, France, Prussia, Sardinia, Saxony and Spain), and by a serious lack of unity among the socio-political élite in the Habsburg lands. In Bohemia, there was considerable support for the Bavarian claimant in 1741.

The Habsburgs survived the crisis, albeit with the permanent loss of Silesia and parts of Lombardy, but it was far from inevitable that they would do so. The same was true of the serious crisis of 1787–90 provoked by the policies of Joseph II. This crisis saw a serious degree of violence and political breakdown in the Austrian Netherlands, and a breakdown in royal authority in Hungary where many of the supporters of Josephine Enlightenment came from the Protestant minority.[48]

A more lasting Habsburg failure might have led to a different analysis of success in the eighteenth-century states system. A similar point might be made for Russia which, in 1727–30 and 1740–41, faced dynastic uncertainty, political crisis, and, in the first, pressure for constitutional change and, in the second, foreign invasion, with the Swedes hopeful of exploiting domestic divisions. Similarly, Jacobite victory in Britain in 1745–46 might have led to a different hierarchy of achievement, more particularly if the new Jacobite order had altered, as seems likely, the relationship between England and Scotland and/or the position of Parliament. The extent to which Jacobite success was possible was a matter for controversy for contemporaries, and this has not changed subsequently. Whereas most English scholarship until the late 1970s assumed the Jacobite cause to be doomed, this appeared less obviously the case to scholars of international relations, and since the late 1970s there has been a reinterpretation of the stability of the Hanoverian regime that contests in particular J. H. Plumb's assertion that political stability had been created by the mid-1720s.[49] Even if the latter is assumed, it is important to consider the 1678–1722 period on its own merits and not as a prelude to what came later. Such an approach avoids the danger of reading back from the peaceful accessions of George II and George III in 1727 and 1760 respectively.

At the same time, it is important not to exaggerate the degree of stability in Britain that had been created by the mid-1720s. Instead, much was due to the absence of war in the 1720s and 1730s. This minimised fiscal strains and opportunities for opposition politicians, and also ensured that the dangerous combination of international and domestic crises was avoided. The hazards presented by such a combination were to be made readily apparent in the mid-1740s, and it is easy to underestimate the crisis then by treating it simply as a matter of the Jacobite rising in 1745. The threat to British stability in the mid- and late 1750s is less apparent, but, aside from the French invasion plan of 1759, the political instability of 1754–57 revealed ministerial vulnerability, particularly to military defeat, especially Admiral Byng's failure to win a naval triumph over the French in 1756 and the subsequent loss of Minorca. Had the Seven Years' War continued to go badly, then the political situation would have been more serious, and this indeed appeared likely. Allied to Prussia, which was at war with Austria, France, Russia and Sweden, Britain was part of the weaker international bloc. Unlike in previous wars dating back to 1635, and then again in the sixteenth century, France now did not have to consider the enmity of Austria. Its forces could not campaign in the Low Countries, Italy or Spain. Britain therefore was more exposed to French attack. This underlines the role of contingency.[50] More generally, the demands of war helped affect domestic stability and drive the process of governmental change in Europe.

However much the threat to the continuity of the *ancien régime* from Enlightened Despotism can be questioned, there is a clear need to consider the challenge posed by the French Revolutionary and Napoleonic period. It was then, for example, that Spain was plunged into a civil chaos far more disruptive than the civil war that had been an aspect of the War of the Spanish Succession. In the Habsburg lands, Enlightenment values were discarded during the Revolutionary/Napoleonic period, although the extent to which this undermined a development that might otherwise have been strong is open to debate.[51]

The treatment of the revolution throws considerable light on the question of eighteenth-century stabilities. Any emphasis on it as arising from contradictions within French political culture point in a different direction to an analysis that sees the revolution as stemming from a political crisis that got out of control. Both approaches have been emphasised in recent scholarship. In the latter account, the revolution, in its early stages, could be accommodated to traditional political assumptions, and be seen not as a new development, a product of spreading radicalism, but rather as a conventional political crisis in which a ruler faced serious domestic problems, primarily aristocratic factionalism and serious financial difficulties. These appeared to affect France's international capability, specifically its ability to wage war or sustain a military confrontation, but they were not novel in type, and did not therefore necessarily appear insuperable, or likely to provoke a fundamental change in the French political system.

It was indeed possible to envisage a revival of French strength. This was in fact to come, eventually, through revolutionary change, but it is inaccurate to assume that that was the only way in which such a revival could occur. Furthermore, it is all too easy to see revolutionary change as necessarily stemming from structural features in the French system.

The latter approach is frequently emphasised. Thus Joel Félix argues that 'any large-scale attempt at permanent reform in a traditional and only partly unified economy risked provoking fratricidal debates between the supporters of a "moral economy" in which market forces remained under strict state control, and advocates of economic liberalism who aimed at breaking the old-established structures of privilege which benefited the privileged and stifled growth', while Gail Bossenga claims that 'the dilemma of the old regime was that its legal system was so favourable to the commercialisation of privilege' and that this led to a 'monetization of social relationships' that left élite claims to legitimacy based in honour and service weak, and Munro Price suggests that the prime cause of the fall of the absolute monarchy was its failure to break free from the bonds of the social hierarchy and transform its basis of support.[52]

However, these suggestions raise the question of why the same was not true elsewhere. A monarchy that was intellectually and imaginatively bankrupt is one possible conclusion, but a wider comparison would help. The strengths of the British system could not prevent revolution in America in 1775, widespread agitation in England in 1780, and rebellion in Ireland in 1798. Joseph II's pressure for change did not win the Habsburgs stability. A valuable discussion of the important reforms in French military administration in the 1760s has pointed out that they increased costs and thus heightened the government's damaging reliance on venality and corporate credit.[53] Yet, at the same time, post-war reforms in the British Empire helped precipitate the crisis of the American Revolution.

In 1788 and early 1789, when Austria seemed to face a far greater domestic crisis, it appeared, instead, that a revival in France, producing a more effective monarchy, would come either through a solution to the political crisis achieved by traditional means, or by means of institutional reform and constitutional revival that focused on a new partnership between crown and nation. Such a partnership was a crucial issue in the most prominent public political sphere earlier in the century, the *Parlement* of Paris. It had been disrupted by legal–ecclesiastical disputes over Jansenists and Jesuits, leading to a serious political breakdown in the 1760s and early 1770s. This posed the question whether consensus could be restored as a working system in the *Parlement*,[54] but it is difficult to see the situation as initially more serious than that in Britain on a number of occasions earlier in the century, and particularly than in 1688–89. George I, George II and George III had been unable to sustain favoured ministers in office. The legislative programme of the Stanhope–Sunderland ministry had been defeated in 1719 and Walpole had been taken back into office in 1720. Despite the wishes of George II, the excise legislation had been defeated in 1733, Walpole had fallen in 1742 and Carteret in 1744, Carteret had been unable to create a stable ministry in 1746, and Pitt had gained office in 1756. George III had had to put up with the fall of Bute in 1763 and North in 1782, and with the creation of a series of unwelcome ministries, culminating in the Fox–North administration in 1783, a measure that led him to contemplate abdication.

It is unclear why the strains in the French political system should be regarded as radically more serious than these occasions, although possibly the most difficult problem was that of a cumulative lack of experience in France with a political process focused on public, adversarial politics and seeking stable compromises that would establish how far change was viable without breakdown. This can be presented in part as a matter of discourse, with, in particular, a lack of agreed concepts about loyal dissension, but consideration of international comparisons encourages instead an emphasis on political problems.

Even in states with a public institutional politics, it proved difficult to maintain agreement about basic parameters, and a politics of conspiracy flourished, as Sweden during the Age of Liberty showed.[55] There, and elsewhere, the difficulty of securing agreement was exacerbated by the rise in the belief that sovereignty lay with the people. In newly independent America, it was to be difficult to establish political conventions and a practice of peaceful settlement of differences. The first quarter-century of the new republic witnessed risings in Massachusetts and Pennsylvania, separatism in Vermont, secret negotiations with both Britain and France, conspiracies by politicians and generals, and suspicions about the intentions of opponents and the reasons why the army was being built up. Given these tensions, the importance of George Washington's willingness to give up power and not to seek a presidency for life was apparent. There was to be no Bonapartism in the USA, or, to underline the danger of ignoring earlier parallels, no equivalent to the Cromwellian Protectorate. Each of these examples serves as a reminder of the difficulty of creating new political systems that did not revert to monarchy. This appeared the obvious form of government to most commentators, certainly for large states.

Within individual states, however, the nature of monarchy was far from constant. In France, it was seen less and less in the eighteenth century as rooted in the Divine Right of Kings (an ideology that precluded much criticism of the crown), and, increasingly, in secular, 'contractual' terms, which left it exposed to criticism on secular grounds. This decline in the 'sacral' qualities attaching to French monarchy was also more generally the case across Europe.

Although the relative weakness of the French monarchy appears clear in hindsight, it is worth noting that some of the subjects of Louis XV and Louis XVI had opposed reform attempts because they feared that their government might become a despotism. By 1789, this problem appeared soluble. The attempted transition to a newly revived representative character in French constitutional monarchy was difficult, in part because of Louis XVI's unwillingness to be flexible, but the failure was far from inevitable. The revolution was far from a homogeneous and unilinear process but, instead, developed in fits and starts.

A lack of respect for the monarch was important in the developing crisis, and it took pornographic form, especially in accounts of the loves of Louis XV and the life of Louis XVI's wife, Marie Antoinette. Both lessened respect for the monarch. Controversies over pre-revolutionary scandals helped to politicise important sections of the population. Scandals relating to the royal family and aristocracy became public topics. Tales of marital betrayal and breakdown became infused with political meaning.[56] This lack of respect was to culminate in the decapitation of Louis XVI in 1793: monarchy apparently was invalid because the monarch lacked the attributes of leadership.

This scholarly approach represents a way to assess royal authority that gives due weight to cultural rather than functional factors: 'Few states were as body centered as seventeenth- and eighteenth-century France. The rhetoric, rites, and rhythm of political life derived from bodies. Political discourse abounded in body metaphors,'[57] as indeed was also the case elsewhere.[58] The notion of disease in the body of the state was a potent one in societies that had a strongly organic concept of political entities, however much that might be covered by mechanistic ideas relating to constitutional questions. The mechanistic approach to statehood and statecraft was attractive to some sections of enlightened opinion, but organic notions appear to have continued to enjoy sway. This focused attention on the ruler, as the organic approach presupposed a directing head, as well as using the royal body as a metaphor of more general health. Debates about body metaphors provide a way to explore beliefs and tensions in *ancien régime* France and to understand problems in the image of Bourbon monarchy. The image of the royal body was employed to criticize as well as to support the monarchy.

Again, however, there is need to avoid a simple theme of rising crisis. Indeed, if Louis XIV was determined to stress his potency and other aspects of manliness that, in part, was a response to earlier questions of respect for the body of French kings. Questions of homosexuality and/or effeminacy gravely affected the reputation of Henry III of France and James I of England, while there was a more general lack of manliness in French kingship between 1559 and the 1650s, with the conspicuously priapic exception of Henry IV, a monarch who linked manliness and potency with his prestige and success as a ruler.[59]

Manliness was particularly pressing as an issue in two respects: military leadership and personal relations with the élite, including the choice of favourites. It was possible for a monarch whose personal preferences led to suggestions of homosexuality to act as a warrior leader, most obviously with William III.[60] It was certainly important for all monarchs to try to associate themselves with success in war. Any claims to do so were trumpeted in the iconography of kingship. Martial poses enabled rulers to strike echoes with both medieval forebears and Classical models. Far from this being redundant in the eighteenth century, the Enlightened Despots gave new force to the linkage. This was particularly apparent with Frederick II of Prussia, but other rulers, including Joseph II, Peter III and Frederick II of Hesse-Cassel, sought to emulate at least aspects of Frederick's martial reputation.

This espousal of a particular type of manliness was also seen in personal relations with the élite. To be associated with martial types helped communicate a sense of reliability and purpose, and at least offered an emphasis on duty that met current suppositions.

Earlier French anticipations of unimpressive kingship did not lessen the problems created in an age of personal monarchy by Louis XV's failure, in his last two decades, to maintain royal *gloire* and by Louis XVI's pedestrian lack of appeal. Although he played an active role in the formulation of foreign policy, Louis XVI failed to win personal glory on the battlefield, or indeed to associate the monarchy with military success, seriously lacked charisma, and was unable either to control the tempo of domestic affairs or to exert positive influence.[61] This was serious. Monarchy was still personal, and the image of the monarch a crucial aspect of governmental strength. Frederick II had thought it appropriate to build a large, imposing palace, the New Palace, at Potsdam in the 1760s.

Louis XVI, however, was insufficiently royal for contemporary tastes. This was despite the possibilities laid out by his office: Louis's court was larger than the central government. There were about 2,500 people in the

King's household in 1789, leaving aside the twelve other independent royal households, but there were only about 660 officials in the ministries. Yet, possibly because he was more pious than his grandfather, Louis XV, Louis was indifferent to his court, failed to employ vanity as a weapon, and was unable to use the court to develop his *gloire* and to strengthen his relations with the aristocracy.[62]

This was an important instance of the weakness that characterised the royal position. This weakness, rather than any strength of opposition, was the crucial factor during the 1780s, both prior to the meeting of the Estates General in 1789 and once that body had met and been found wanting for its task. In 1789, although a few of the future deputies, such as the Abbé Sieyès and the Marquis of Volney, were greatly influenced by radical political ideas, the impact of the radical Enlightenment on the working assumptions of the majority seems to have been 'practically nil'.[63] Instead, there was an emphasis on continuity as well as discontinuity in 1789, and *ancien régime* thinking played an important role in the ideas expressed that year, as well as in seminal documents such as the Declaration of Rights of 1789.[64]

Rather than causing the crisis, radical ideas spread as a consequence of the revolution. This spread owed something to the pressure of events and something to the extent to which there was a clear social character to many of the factional alignments. The conservative groups were dominated by the privileged, and socio-cultural divisions among the deputies helped to focus and sustain political perceptions. Issues were also important, not least the need to solve problems of state finance and church reform, although there was nothing akin to the crisis in England created by the rebellion in Ireland in 1641, nor to that in Russia posed by continued German military success in 1917, to force the pace of change and engender a sense of immediate calamity. Indeed, the relatively limited degree of violence in the early stages of the French Revolution is instructive. The storming of the Bastille was symbolic but also unusual. The early revolutionary authorities treated their political opponents of both right and left with a degree of restraint and indulgence that was remarkably consistent with the liberal and humanitarian ideals of the pre-revolutionary judicial reform movement, although it also resulted from strategic decisions to seek support from anti-revolutionary authorities, as well as from a hesitation in embracing radical solutions.[65] A constitutional monarchy presiding over a successful reform programme, the goal sought by Montesquieu,[66] might well have been viable had Louis XVI been willing to support it.

As a reminder of the role of chance at the level of the monarch, the political histories of Austria, Britain and Sweden would have been different had Joseph II not died in 1790, and his brother Leopold II not done the same in 1792, had George III failed to recover from his apparent madness in 1788–89, ensuring that his eldest son, George (later George IV), become regent and replaced the ministry of William Pitt the Younger, and had Gustavus III not been assassinated in 1792.

An emphasis on the viability of constitutional monarchy can clearly be seen as a revisionist view on the revolution, although the state of the historiography is so complex that several revisionisms are on offer.[67] This historiography, alas, is frequently arcane and self-regarding. Furthermore, the important advance towards comparative consideration of the revolution seen with the work of R. R. Palmer and Jacques Godechot[68] has not been adequately pursued.[69] There is, indeed, a disjunction between scholarship stressing the importance of international relations in the causes and course of the revolution and work on the comparative dimension. The first looks at the role of failure in war and foreign policy, especially defeat by the Prussians at Rossbach in 1757 and the humiliating climbdown in the Dutch Crisis of 1787, in sapping the prestige of the French monarchy,[70] and also at how international ambitions and rivalries, particularly over Poland, lessened the commitment of other states to fighting the revolutionaries, particularly after the latter were victorious in 1794 and 1795.[71]

This dimension is important, not least because it underlines the role of contingency. Radical movements in the Austrian Netherlands, the United Provinces, Geneva and Liège were suppressed by external force. That this course failed in France was due not to any special characteristics of the revolution – a unique social structure or discourse of revolution – but, rather, to particular political circumstances, both domestic and international, and ultimately, to the military campaigns and political resolve of 1792–94. To try to demonstrate that this account is wrong requires a more determined engagement with the comparative context than that seen at present. The latter would suggest that by the 1780s France was less effective than Prussia and Austria, let alone Britain, in rationalising reform and maximising the state's resources, but that does not imply that the situation was irretrievable in 1789.

There are points of more widespread value in the historiography of the revolution. In general, the traditional account of the revolution, with its emphasis on the motivation and conflict of social groups, has been displaced in favour of an emphasis on the need to focus on the contours and consequences of political disagreement and ideological debate,[72] although important work continues to appear on the social dimension.[73] This emphasis on political culture parallels the general reconsideration of early modern European society. The extent to which such parallels should be seen as validating each other is unclear, but they certainly argue to widespread shifts in the interpretation of the entire period. Both the sociological and the ideological account of the causes of the revolution suffer from an emphasis on structure, rather than agency, more specifically on the weakness of the *ancien régime*, rather than on its fall.

As a separate issue, another course for the French revolution would have led to different retrospective judgements about the relative strength of states and political systems in the eighteenth century. Indeed, the Revolution helped to compromise constitutional reform, encouraging other monarchs to rely on more authoritarian solutions, although these solutions can also be seen as stemming from the character of the political systems of Central and Eastern Europe: Austria, Prussia and, even more, Russia were unlikely to follow the French route.

Different retrospective judgements arising from a successful programme of reform introduced by a constitutional monarchy in France underline the role of contingency, particularly when creating explanatory models. Consideration of other states is, again, instructive. Bitterly divided in the 1640s and 1680s, England, for example, still successfully acted like a major power in the 1650s and 1690s. George I's accession in Britain in 1714 was followed by a civil war in 1715–16, as those of James VII and II (1685), William III (1689) and, in Poland, Augustus II (1697) and, far more, Augustus III (1733) also were. However, the civil wars in Britain after 1637–51 were swiftly over, especially in England.

There was an elective character to the Williamite position and the Act of Settlement (1701), as there was to Polish kingship, although the elective character of the latter was normative and long-established. Possibly the important difference was that in Britain the Jacobites were not able to prevent William III and the Hanoverians from winning parliamentary support, whereas, in Poland, the political and constitutional system did not work to the benefit of the Saxon kings, Augustus II and III of Poland. Indeed, Jacobitism helped to preserve a measure both of Whig unity and of Whig–royal cohesion.

This provides a context within which to consider the case for English or British exceptionalism, which is an important theme for work on the eighteenth century. Here again there is the problem of assessing the role of political contingencies alongside that of particular characteristics of British society. The argument that eighteenth-century England was a commercial society takes note of the importance of the 'middling order' and of the politics and 'discourse' of trade, especially the value of individual effort.[74] Yet it is unclear that this approach, or indeed an emphasis on London, on popular politics, or on the culture of print, can be readily accommodated to the high politics of the period. Not only was there a different social and cultural background to politics focused on élite influence,[75] but, in addition, there was a narrative to British politics that was not readily explained in terms of social background. Instead, dynasticism, international relations, and the role of contingencies highlighted by counterfactualism,[76] appear more pertinent.

If Polish political culture 'moved significantly in an English direction' between 1790 and 1792, the international context was such that the new constitution of 1791 was not given the chance to prove itself.[77] Swedish developments also indicated the role of contingency. The 'Age of Liberty' that followed the death of Charles XII in 1718 was brought to a close by Gustavus III in 1772, and his system, in turn, collapsed when his son, Gustavus IV, was deposed in 1809 after the Russian victory over the Swedes in Finland. Similarly, the regency government in Sweden that followed Gustavus Adolphus's battlefield death in 1632 at Lützen had led to a shift towards aristocratic conciliar government. It is far from clear that a general model of state development can be built on such a basis, although much of the strong royal power established by Gustavus III in 1772 and 1789 survived until the mid-nineteenth century, albeit in a more constitutional form and with increasing control from the *Riksdag* (Parliament).[78]

The French Revolution was to pose a challenge to states and societies in some degree comparable to that of the Reformation, although an easy comparison has to be resisted because the Reformation operated both on a different timescale and, across much of Europe, was better able to win widespread popular support. Both episodes saw universalist, Utopian and sometimes millenarian aims, a paranoid style, fanaticism, a degree of popular participation and mobilisation, and a rejection of limited means and goals and of traditional social and ideological conventions and legal and institutional frameworks. These features strengthened each other. Thus the overthrow of social and cultural bonds led to an increasing fluidity of identity that led to an exacerbation of distrust.[79]

There was also a parallel in both the Reformation and the revolutionary crises between the interaction, tension and clash of the universalist message of individual creeds or of revolutionary programmes, widely seen as subversive of all order, and the specific, generally more local and localised, requirements and policies of particular groups in both contexts.[80]

The tendency to see modern revolutions in secular terms has led to an underrating of their shared structural characteristics with confessional violence, not least such violence aimed at overthrowing established structures, and attacking either the established faith or the faith of an important section of the community. Thus the radical ideas and institutions of the Catholic League in France in the 1590s[81] prefigured those of the revolution and the counter-revolution. Similarly, the unpopularity of the illegitimate revolutionary regime within France repeated that of the Cromwellian Protectorate in England, although the revolutionary regime was far more unpopular, and, indeed, caused a civil war because it pushed change far harder. The attempt to enforce the conscription stemming from its engagement in a major war was also a cause of resistance.

Such comparisons serve to challenge the use of a linear model when assessing European developments. Instead, they introduce an episodic theme of serious, but unpredictable, crisis. This model made more sense to contemporaries. The strength of cyclical imagery in theories of history was readily apparent throughout the period. It remained pertinent in the eighteenth century, and was greatly influenced by the respect for the Classical world expressed by influential writers, such as Montesquieu, author of *L'Esprit des Lois* (1748).

The long-standing debate between the ancients and the moderns had resolved, for many commentators, into a stress on the novelties of the modern world, especially the expansion of European control into areas unknown to the Classical world and, as a consequence of the Scientific Revolution, the availability of new intellectual solutions. Thus, in his *Decline and Fall of the Roman Empire* (1776–88), a very successful book in its day, Edward Gibbon had argued that, even if Europe succumbed anew to barbarian invasion from Asia, a course he thought European advances in firepower and fortification made unlikely, this was of less consequence than at the time of the fall of the Roman Empire, because European civilisation had been reborn in the New World.[82]

Nevertheless, an emphasis on improvement and improvability, which was an important part of the Enlightenment mentality, was overshadowed by a more pessimistic strain that stressed the fragility of achievements. This drew on cyclical theories of growth and decline, and also on the diffuse but powerful impact of Christian themes of sin and fall. Indeed the 1790s were to see a powerful expression of millenarian and apocalyptic thought. This again was a parallel to the Reformation.

In both cases, the disruption of customary ideas encouraged a resort to established idioms and interpretations that revealed what seems to us to be a darker side of a collective imagination.[83] This appears particularly out of keeping with an Enlightenment that prided itself on reason, but, as the writings of enlightened intellectuals make clear, this cult was, in part, expressed in defiance of what was seen as a wider popular superstition. Furthermore, to restrict attention simply to the fashionable world, it displayed interest in a wide range of activities, phenomena and beliefs, such as Freemasonry, monsters, the occult and Mesmerism,[84] that cannot be easily reconciled with a secular, rational account of the eighteenth century. Far from presenting a unitary conception of the Enlightenment, it is necessary to underline the greatly differing and frequently contradictory tendencies that it encompassed.[85]

The period 1550–1800 closed, as it began, with international rivalry linked to domestic subversion, and the two, combined, challenging, and, in part, overturning, established systems of authority and practices of power. It also ended, as it had begun, with contemporaries feeling that they lived in an age of uncertainty and doubt, and anxious about the probable course of developments. This is a more impressive conclusion than the schematic theories beloved by so many subsequent commentators.

Notes

1. Focusing on recent works in a massive literature, T. C. W. Blanning, *The Culture of Power and the Power of Culture. Old Regime Europe 1660–1789* (Oxford, 2001); A. Farge, *Subversive Worlds: Public Opinion in Eighteenth-Century France* (Cambridge, 1994); D. K. Van Kley, 'In search of eighteenth-century Parisian public opinion', *French Historical Studies*, 19 (1995), pp. 215–26; E. Dziembowski, *Un nouveau patriotisme français, 1750–1770. La France face à la puissance anglaise à l'époque de la guerre de Sept Ans* (Oxford, 1998); D. A. Bell, *The Cult of the Nation in France. Inventing Nationalism, 1680–1800* (Cambridge, MA, 2001).

2. A. McClellan, *Inventing the Louvre: Art, Politics, and the Origins of the Modern Museum in Eighteenth-Century Paris* (Cambridge, 1994).

3. Shelburne, journal, BL Bowood Mss. vol. 104 fol. 10.

4. W. R. Everdell, *Christian Apologetics in France, 1730–1790: The Roots of Romantic Religion* (Lewiston, NY, 1987); D. M. McMahon, 'The Counter-Enlightenment and the low-life of literature in pre-Revolutionary France', *Past and Present*, 159 (1998), pp. 77–112.

5. J. I. Israel, *Radical Enlightenment. Philosophy and the Making of Modernity 1650–1750* (Oxford, 2001). For the social context as well as an emphasis on change, T. Munck, *The Enlightenment. A Comparative Social History 1721–1794* (2000).

6. T. Johnson, 'Blood, tears and Xavier-water: Jesuit missionaries and popular religion in the eighteenth-century Upper Palatinate', in B. Scribner and Johnson (eds), *Popular Religion in Germany and Central Europe, 1400–1800* (Basingstoke, 1996), pp. 183–202.

7. W. R. Ward, *The Protestant Evangelical Awakening* (Cambridge, 1992); D. Hempton and M. Hill, *Evangelical Protestantism in Ulster Society 1740–1890* (1992); L. Châtellier, *The Religion of the Poor. Rural Missions in Europe and the Formation of Modern Catholicism, c.1500–c.1800* (Cambridge, 1997).

8. O. P. Grell and R. Porter (eds), *Toleration in Enlightenment Europe* (Cambridge, 2000).

9. I. Murphy, *The Diocese of Killaloe in the Eighteenth Century* (Blackrock, Co. Dublin, 1991).

10. P. Fagan (ed.), *Ireland in the Stuart Papers 1719–65* (Blackrock, Co. Dublin, 1996).

11. D. Bell, 'Culture and religion', in W. Doyle (ed.), *Old Regime France 1648–1788* (Oxford, 2001), p. 79.

12. N. Aston, 'The golden autumn of Gallicanism? Religious history and its place in current writing on eighteenth-century France', *French History*, 13 (1999), p. 221.

13. H. Mitchell, 'Resistance to the revolution in western France', *Past and Present*, 63 (1974), pp. 94–131.

14. D. Davie, *The Eighteenth-Century Hymn in England* (Cambridge, 1993).

15. R. L. Gawthrop, *Pietism and the Making of Eighteenth-Century Prussia* (Cambridge, 1993). See also M. Fulbrook, *Piety and Politics. Religion and the Rise of Absolutism in England, Württenberg and Prussia* (Cambridge, 1983).

16. An effective introduction to the last is offered by H. M. Scott (ed.), *Enlightened Absolutism. Reform and Reformers in Later Eighteenth Century Europe* (1990).

17. H. Kamen, *Philip V of Spain* (New Haven, CT, 2001); P. R. Campbell, *Power and Politics in Old Regime France, 1720–1745* (1996).

18. T. C. W. Blanning (ed.), *The Eighteenth Century* (Oxford, 2000), pp. 1, 133.

19. R. A. Dorwart, *The Administrative Reforms of Frederick William I of Prussia* (Westport, CT, 1953) and *The Prussian Welfare State before 1740* (Cambridge, MA, 1971); J. W. Stoye, 'Emperor Charles VI: the early years of the reign', *Transactions of the Royal Historical Society*, 5th series, 12 (1962), pp. 63–84.

20. P. Burke, *The Fabrication of Louis XIV* (New Haven, CT, 1992).

21. L. Frey and M. Frey, *Frederick I. The Man and His Times* (New York, 1984).

22. P. K. Monod, *The Power of Kings: Monarchy and Religion in Europe, 1589–1715* (New Haven, CT, 1999), pp. 273–315.

23. N. Zaslaw (ed.), *The Classical Era from the 1740s to the End of the 18th Century* (1989).

24. P. G. M. Dickson, *Finance and Government under Maria Theresa 1740–1780* (2 vols, Oxford, 1987).

25. H. M. Scott, *The Emergence of the Eastern Powers, 1756–1775* (Cambridge, 2001), pp. 68–72; J. C. Riley, *The Seven Years War and the Old Regime in France: The Economic and Financial Toll* (Princeton, NJ, 1986).

26. J. T. Alexander, *Catherine the Great: Life and Legend* (Oxford, 1989).

27. J. T. Alexander, *Autocratic Politics in a National Crisis. The Imperial Russian Government and Pugachev's Revolt, 1773–1775* (Bloomington, IN, 1969).

28. S. Shaw, *Between Old and New: The Ottoman Empire under Sultan Selim III, 1789–1807* (Cambridge, MA, 1971).

29. J. M. Smith, 'Honour, royal service and the cultural origins of the French Revolution: interpreting the language of army reform, 1750–1788', *French History*, 9 (1995), pp. 294–314.

30. M. Hochedlinger, 'Mars ennobled: the ascent of the military and the creation of a military nobility in mid-eighteenth-century Austria', *German History*, 17 (1999), pp. 141–76.

31. R. Jones, *Provincial Development in Russia. Catherine II and Jakob Sievers* (Cambridge, MA, 1984), p. 37.

32. W. Cobbett (ed.), *The Parliamentary History of England from the Earliest Period to the Year 1803* (36 vols, 1806–20), vol. 20, col. 621.

33. J. Van Horn Melton, *Absolutism and the Eighteenth-Century Origins of Compulsory Schooling in Prussia and Austria* (Cambridge, 1988); K. Keller, 'Saxony: *Rétablissement* and enlightened absolutism', *German History*, 20 (2002), p. 331; C. Ingrao, *The Hessian Mercenary State. Ideas, Institutions and Reform under Frederick II 1760–1785* (Cambridge, 1987).

34. F. Szabo, *Kaunitz and Enlightened Absolutism 1753–1780* (Cambridge, 1994), p. 351.

35. C. S. Leonard, *Reform and Regicide. The Reign of Peter III of Russia* (Bloomington, IN, 1993).

36. H. M. Scott, 'Prussia's royal foreign minister: Frederick the Great and the administration of Prussian diplomacy', in R. Oresko, G. C. Gibbs and Scott (eds), *Royal and Republican Sovereignty in Early Modern Europe* (Cambridge, 1997), p. 500.

37. R.T. Connors, 'Pelham, Parliament and public policy, 1746–1754' (Ph.D. thesis, Cambridge, 1993)

38. M. Price, *Preserving the Monarchy: The Comte de Vergennes, 1774–87* (Cambridge, 1995).

39. D. L. Ransel, *The Politics of Catherinian Russia: The Panin Party* (New Haven, CT, 1975); P. LeDonne, *Ruling Russia: Politics and Administration in the Age of Absolutism, 1762–1796* (Princeton, NJ, 1984).

40. T. C. W. Blanning, 'Comment', *Austrian History Yearbook*, 30 (1999), pp. 223–4.

41. M. Antoine, 'La monarchie absolue', in K. M. Baker (ed.), *The Political Culture of the Old Regime* (New York, 1987), pp. 3–24; M. Kwass, 'A kingdom of taxpayers: state formation, privilege, and political culture in eighteenth-century France', *Journal of Modern History*, 70 (1998), pp. 295–339.

42. D. Garrioch, *The Making of Revolutionary Paris* (Berkeley, CA, 2002), pp. 283–90.

43. P. Mansel, 'Monarchy, uniform and the rise of the frac', *Past and Present*, 96 (1982), pp. 103–32.

44. N. Smith, *The Royal Image and the English* People (Aldershot, 2001), p. 165.

45. T. C. W. Blanning, *Joseph II* (Harlow, 1994), p. 17. On Joseph, see also D. Beales, *Joseph II, Vol. I. In the Shadow of Maria Theresa, 1741–1780* (Cambridge, 1987), and 'Was Joseph II an Enlightened Despot?', in R. Robertson and E. Timms (eds), *The Austrian Enlightenment and Its Aftermath* (Edinburgh, 1991), pp. 1–21.

46. Blanning, *Joseph II*, p. 205.

47. C. W. Ingrao, *The Habsburg Monarchy 1618–1815* (Cambridge, 1994). See also, G. Klingenstein, 'Revisions of enlightened absolutism: the "Austrian monarchy is like no other"', *Historical Journal*, 33 (1990), pp. 155–67.

48. E. H. Balázs, *Hungary and the Habsburgs, 1765–1800. An Experiment in Enlightened Absolutism* (Budapest, 1997).

49. J. H. Plumb, *The Growth of Political Stability in England, 1675–1725* (1967).

50. J. M. Black, *America or Europe? British Foreign Policy, 1739–1763* (1988).

51. P. P. Bernard, *Jesuits and Jacobins: Enlightenment and Enlightened Despotism in Austria* (Urbana, IL, 1971) and *The Limits of Enlightenment: Joseph II and the Law* (Urbana, IL, 1979).

52. J. Félix, 'Economy', G. Bossenga 'Society', and M. Price, 'Politics: Louis XVI', in W. Doyle (ed.), *Old Regime France 1648–1788* (Oxford, 2001), pp. 41, 76, 248.

53. R. Blaufarb, 'Noble privilege and absolutist state building: French military administration after the Seven Years' War', *French Historical Studies*, 24 (2001), pp. 245–6. See also D. D. Bien, 'Offices, corps, and a system of state credit: the uses of privilege under the ancien régime', in Baker (ed.), *Political Culture of the Old Regime*, pp. 89–114, and G. Bossenga, *The Politics of Privilege: Old Regime and Revolution in Lille* (Cambridge, 1991).

54. B. Stone, *The French Parlements and the Crisis of the Old Regime* (Chapel Hill, NC, 1986); J. Swann, *Politics and the Parlement of Paris under Louis XV, 1754–1774* (Cambridge, 1995).

55. M. Roberts, *The Age of Liberty: Sweden 1719–1772* (Cambridge, 1986).

56. J. W. Merrick, *The Desacralization of the French Monarchy in the Eighteenth Century* (Baton Rouge, LA, 1990); V. Cameron, 'Political exposures: sexuality and caricature in the French Revolution', in L. Hunt (ed.), *Eroticism and the Body Politic* (Baltimore, MD, 1991), pp. 90–107; L. Hunt, *The Family Romance of the French Revolution* (Berkeley, CA, 1992), pp. 108–30; S. Maza, *Private Lives and Public Affairs. The Causes Célèbres of Prerevolutionary France* (Berkeley, CA, 1994).

57. S. Melzer and K. Norberg (eds), *From the Royal to the Republican Body. Incorporating the Political in Seventeenth- and Eighteenth-Century France* (Berkeley, CA, 1998), p. 1.

58. R. Braverman, *Plots and Counterplots. Sexual Politics and the Body Politic in English Literature, 1660–1730* (Cambridge, 1993).

59. E. H. Dickerman, 'Henry IV and the Juliers-Cleves crisis: the psychohistorical aspects', *French Historical Studies*, 8 (1974), pp. 626–53; Dickerman and A. M. Walker, 'The choice of Hercules: Henry IV as hero', *Historical Journal*, 39 (1996), pp. 315–37.

60. T. Claydon, *William III and the Godly Reformation* (Cambridge, 1996).

61. J. Hardman, *Louis XVI* (New Haven, CT, 1993); Hardman and M. Price, *Louis XVI and the Comte de Vergennes: Correspondence, 1774–1787* (Oxford, 1998); Price, *The Fall of the French Monarchy. Louis XVI, Marie Antoinette and the Baron de Breteuil* (2002).

62. P. Mansel, *The Court of France 1789–1830* (Cambridge, 1988).

63. T. Tackett, *Becoming a Revolutionary: The Deputies of the French National Assembly and the Emergence of a Revolutionary Culture, 1789–1790* (Princeton, NJ, 1996), p. 304.

64. D. Van Kley (ed.), *The French Idea of Freedom: The Old Regime and the Declaration of Rights of 1789* (Stanford, CA, 1995).

65. N. Aston, 'Patriotism, pressmen and political culture in the French Revolution', *Historical Journal*, 33 (1990), p. 1007.

66. B. M. Shapiro, *Revolutionary Justice in Paris 1789–1790* (Cambridge, 1993); H. B. Applewhite, *Political Alignment in the French National Assembly 1789–1791* (Baton Rouge, LA, 1993); E. H. Lemay and A. Patrick, *Revolutionaries at Work: the Constituent Assembly 1789–1791* (Oxford, 1996).

67. See, for example, S. Maza, 'Politics, culture and the origins of the French Revolution', *Journal of Modern History*, 61 (1989), pp. 704–23; V. R. Gruder, 'Whither revisionism? Political perspectives on the ancien régime', *French Historical Studies*, 20 (1997), pp. 245–85; G. Kates, 'Introduction', to G. Kates (ed.), *The French Revolution: Recent Debates and New Controversies* (New York, 1998), p. 11; H. Chisick, 'Public opinion and political culture in France during the second half of the eighteenth century', *English Historical Review*, 117 (2002), pp. 48–9, 76.

68. R. R. Palmer, *The Age of the Democratic Revolution* (1961); J. Godechot, *France and the Atlantic Revolution of the Eighteenth Century* (1965).

69. Though see T. Skocpol, *States and Social Revolutions: A Comparative Analysis of France, Russia, and China* (Cambridge, 1979); J. Pelenski (ed.), *The American and European Revolutions, 1776–1848: Sociopolitical and Ideological Aspects* (Iowa City, 1980); H. A. Barton, 'Scandinavia and the Atlantic Revolution, 1760–1815', *Proceedings of the Twelfth Consortium on Revolutionary Europe, 1750–1850* (1983), pp. 145–58; J. Kaits and M. H. Haltzel (eds), *The Global Ramifications of the French Revolution* (Cambridge, 1994).

70. M. Price, 'The Dutch affair and the fall of the *Ancien Régime*, 1784–1787', *Historical Journal*, 38 (1995), pp. 875–905; O. T. Murphy, *The Diplomatic Retreat of France and Public Opinion on the Eve of the French Revolution, 1783–1789* (Washington, 1998); B. Stone, *The Genesis of the French Revolution: A Global Historical Interpretation* (Cambridge, 1994).

71. P. W. Schroeder, *The Transformation of European Politics 1763–1848* (Oxford, 1994), pp. 74–150; Blanning, *The French Revolutionary Wars, 1787–1802* (1996).

72. Blanning, *The French Revolution: Class War or Culture Clash?* (2nd edn, Basingstoke, 1998). For recent studies of the politics, J. Hardman, *French Politics 1774–1789: From the Accession of Louis XVI to the Fall of the Bastille* (1995) and P. M. Jones, *Reform and Revolution in France. The Politics of Transition 1774–1791* (Cambridge, 1995).

73. For an attempt to join the two, J. Markoff, *The Abolition of Feudalism: Peasants, Lords, and Legislators in the French Revolution* (Pennsylvania, PA, 1996).

74. P. Langford, *A Polite and Commercial People: England 1727–1783* (Oxford, 1989); J. Barry and C. Brooks (eds), *The Middling Sort of People: Culture, Society and Politics in England, 1550–1800* (Basingstoke, 1994); R. Porter, 'The new eighteenth-century social history', in Black (ed.), *Culture and Society in Britain 1660–1800* (Manchester, 1997), pp. 29–50; B. Harris, 'Praising the middling sort? Social identity in eighteenth-century British newspapers', in A. Kidd and D. Nicholls (eds), *The Making of the British Middle Class? Studies of Regional and Cultural Diversity* (Stroud, 1998), pp. 1–18.

75. H. Wellenreuther, 'The political role of the nobility in eighteenth-century England', in J. Canning and Wellenreuther (eds), *Britain and Germany Compared: Nationality, Society and Nobility in the Eighteenth Century* (Göttingen, 2001), pp. 99–139; J. C. D. Clark, *English Society 1660–1832* (Cambridge, 2000).

76. J. Black, 'A different West? Counterfactualism and the rise of Britain to great power status', *Francia*, 28 (2002), pp. 129–45.

77. H. A. Barton, *Scandinavia in the Revolutionary Era, 1760–1815* (Minneapolis, MN, 1986).

78. R. Butterwick, *Poland's Last King and English Culture. Stanislaw August Poniatowski 1732–1798* (Oxford, 1998), pp. 317–18.

79. H. G. Koenigsberger, 'The organisation of revolutionary parties in France and the Netherlands during the sixteenth century', *Journal of Modern History*, 27 (1955), pp. 335–51; D. N. Hood, 'Protestant–Catholic relations and the roots of the first popular counterrevolutionary movement in France', *Journal of Modern History*, 43 (1971), pp. 245–75.

80. J. H. M. Salmon, 'The Paris sixteen, 1584–94: the social analysis of a revolutionary movement', *Journal of Modern History*, 44 (1972), pp. 540–76; M. Greengrass, 'The sixteen; radical politics in Paris during the League', *History*, 69 (1984), pp. 432–9.

81. T. Tackett, 'Conspiracy obsession in a time of revolution: French elites and the origins of the Terror, 1789–1792', *American Historical Review*, 105 (2000), p. 713. See also D. Andress, 'Social prejudice and political fears in the policing of Paris, January–June 1791', *French History*, 9 (1995), pp. 202–26.

82. For a later parallel, M. Mazower, *Dark Continent: Europe's Twentieth Century* (1998).

83. E. Gibbon, *The History of the Decline and Fall of the Roman Empire*, ed. J. B. Bury (7 vols, 1896–1900), IV, 166. For Gibbon's thought, see R. McKitterick and R. Quinault (eds), *Edward Gibbon and Empire* (Cambridge, 1997) and J. G. A. Pocock, *Barbarism and Religion* (2 vols, Cambridge, 1999). For praise of Gibbon's knowledge of and judgements on 'the East', D. O. Morgan, 'Edward Gibbon and the East', *Iran*, 33 (1995), pp. 85–92.

84. R. Darnton, *Mesmerism and the End of the Enlightenment in France* (Cambridge, MA, 1968).

85. D. Outram, *The Enlightenment* (Cambridge, 1995).

CHAPTER 7

The Global Dimension

§ TWO issues have to be addressed: the importance of extra-European activities and expansion to developments within Europe, and the extent to which these developments can profitably be compared and contrasted with those elsewhere. Both issues concerned informed contemporaries. The first appeared to provide a vital adjunct of strength to the Atlantic states, as well as a testing ground for their competition, while the latter posed a basis for comparative judgement. In one case, with the Ottoman Empire, this comparison was apparently of direct importance to the ability of European states to protect their position. Elsewhere, European trans-oceanic expansion opened up possibilities for instructive contrasts, at least for contemporary commentators, although European rulers and ministers tended to look to each other for ideas about how best to devise improvements, and not, for example, to China.

From the outset, trans-oceanic voyages had sparked curiosity about the outside world. In Shakespeare's *King Henry VIII* (1613), the porter at the Palace-Yard wonders why there is so much noise: 'have we some strange Indian with the great tool come to court, the women so besiege us?'[1] Such curiosity was maintained throughout the sixteenth and seventeenth centuries, but there was a fresh upsurge of interest in the eighteenth as the Pacific was explored, and as 'discoveries' there were widely reported in an exploration literature that attracted purchasers and printer-entrepreneurs. Thus Captain James Cook became one of the European heroes of the age, his career widely reported in European publications. This contributed to the knowledge that was to help foster support for European expansion and also to further its pursuit.[2]

Colonial systems increased the extent to which the major European states (including Russia and, to a certain extent, Austria) were composite monarchies. By 1700, England, France, Portugal, Spain and the United Provinces all had far-flung imperial systems. The first four were characterised by crown colonies, although there was also a use, as there was more clearly with the United Provinces, of chartered trading companies that had sovereign powers, such as making treaties and controlling forces, while the Jesuit position in parts of Brazil and Paraguay indicated the autonomy of an ecclesiastical corporation.[3] The range of colonial experience was enormous, encompassing, as it did, very varied proportions of native peoples and European settlers, different relationships with local powers, and contrasting imperial institutions and projects. This range posed differing problems for imperial oversight and for theories of imperial purpose, government and landownership;[4] and also lessened the appropriateness of comparisons between colonies.

Salutary neglect by government, and delegation to local agents or chartered trading companies, were natural consequences of the dissipation of authority over distance and the range of other government commitments. However, the strategic, financial and commercial issues and opportunities involved ensured that governments often put more effort into overcoming the effects of colonial distance than they did with many regions in their European dominions.

Governmental intervention was facilitated and made more apparent by the preponderantly urban nature of colonial settlement. This owed much to the importance of overseas trade to the colonial economies, and to the use of natives or slaves as the agricultural workforce in many areas. Thus, the key points in the colonial empires were port-capitals such as Québec, New Orleans, Halifax, Boston, New York, Williamsburg, Savannah, Charleston, Kingston, Havana, Lima, Recife, Buenos Aires, Cape Town, Bombay, Madras, Calcutta, Pondicherry, Batavia and Manila. These cities contained the bulk of the politically active settler populations.

Governmental intervention was strongest in the fields of military capability and commerce: regulation was used to further strategic and mercantilist ends. Imperial systems obliged colonies to supply home countries with goods they could not produce themselves, and that could also be profitably re-exported, such as coffee, rice, sugar and tobacco, and they were obliged to use the system's ships, while, in return, colonies gained rights within particular systems. In many respects, this was a part of the mercantilism seen in home countries, but attempts could be made to push the process further because of the lesser degree of corporate privilege and political power in colonies and, also, the need there to devise new systems.[5]

The process was not without its tensions where settler populations were numerous and had a sense of continuity, coherence and rights. Thus in 1676 there was a serious rising among the British population in Virginia, Bacon's Rebellion, while in the 1680s James II's attempt to impose autocracy clashed with colonial notions of corporate government. The English found Massachusetts a particularly troublesome colony.[6]

More generally, aside from difficulties in urban centres of colonial life, particularly Boston, there was a separate focus of opposition in more marginal economic zones, especially on or close to the frontier of settlement. These areas could reject aspects of the governmental authority of the centres of power, not least their control over networks of trade, credit and debt. This led to opposition, not least in the form of refusals to pay debt, and in some instances, such as North Carolina in the early 1770s, to violence. This was to be a continuing tradition, leading, after British authority was rejected, to Shays' Rebellion in Massachusetts in 1786–87 and the Whiskey Rebellion in

Pennsylvania in 1794.[7] For the imperial government, such risings were less troublesome than defiance in the port cities, not least because the latter resonated, through the culture of print, more clearly with domestic concerns and criticisms. Thus Massachusetts was of greater concern to the British government than North Carolina.

As with the French Revolution, there is the question of how far it is appropriate to read from crises in order to argue the strength or weakness of particular systems. Thus the extent to which the failure of the British imperial system in North America in the 1770s and early 1780s should be seen both as inevitable and as indicative of structural weakness is unclear. The same point could be made with reference to the Latin American Wars of Independence that followed in the 1810s and 1820s. Most of the British Empire, including the West Indian colonies, Nova Scotia, Newfoundland and East and West Florida, did not rebel,[8] while government-sponsored anglicization did not lead to rebellion in conquered Québec, where, indeed, it was tempered by concern for the position of the Catholic Church.[9]

Local opposition within imperial systems, however, became more apparent in the eighteenth century. In part, this reflected more insistent attempts to regulate imperial systems as governments sought to strengthen them after the conflicts of 1739–63. These efforts were both part of a more general response to the weaknesses and needs revealed by war (see Chapter 6) and an anticipation of the imperial expansion of the late nineteenth century. The resulting fault-line, however, indicated the extent to which settler coherence posed new problems of politics and government, and did so without the rulers being able to rely on established patterns of authority and power, particularly patronage, as they did in Europe. Thus in Spanish America, there was a clash between *peninsulares* (natives of Spain) and *criollos* (creoles, American-born descendants of Spanish settlers), that matched comparable tensions in Portuguese Angola, in the British colonies in North America and the West Indies, and, to a lesser extent, in the French colonies. The policies of Charles III of Spain (r. 1759–88) generally ignored creole aspirations. This was true both of economic regulation and of political power. The role of creoles in government was restricted, and administrative reorganisation was pressed forward in order to increase central control. Similarly, Pombal, chief minister of Portugal in 1750–77, sought to alter the relationship between the mother-country and its principal colony, Brazil, co-opting Brazilians into the mechanisms of government, but on Portuguese terms.[10]

These and other systems encountered resistance, both from colonists and from European traders excluded from their privileges. The British, who had gained a dominant position in the Portuguese imperial economy in the first half of the eighteenth century,[11] were particularly concerned about Pombal's policies. They were also anxious to limit or subvert attempts to make the Spanish imperial economy a system closed to outsiders. This issue dominated

Anglo-Spanish relations for much of the century and helped to structure the maritime politics of the New World, and, increasingly, the Pacific. Although there was illicit trade with Spanish America, the British were unable to make it part of their informal empire comparable to the position of Brazil in the first half of the eighteenth century and of Latin America in the nineteenth century. Instead, the Spanish government, like the British for its own colonies, sought, particularly in the late eighteenth century, to direct its empire to economic and thus, it was thought, strategic advantage.

Not all colonists, however, opposed the process of enhanced control. Just as in Europe, there was also a measure of co-operation with central government, and even support for it. Rather than suggesting any inevitable clash, it is necessary to explain why the process of reaching and endlessly refining a consensus that underlay and often constituted government in this period broke down in some areas. In part, this reflected the extent to which the complex relationship of centre and periphery helped lead to the development of a sense of separateness in the colonies.

American independence was the first major political consequence of this. The rejection of the authority of a monarch by a part of his dominions, and the willingness to defend such a rejection with the use of force, were scarcely unprecedented when hostilities broke out in New England in 1775. The history of Catalonia or Hungary over the previous 150 years was ample demonstration of the precarious nature of authority. In the British world, there had been major rebellions as recently as 1715 and 1745 in Scotland. The American Revolution was significant not because it was a rebellion but because, very unusually, it was successful, and led to a new state; because it challenged the logic of colonialism; and because of the future importance of the United States. As such, it helped define and delimit the modern world.

In contrast, the overthrow of Safavid Persia by Afghan invasion in 1721–22, or the collapse of Mughal power in India in the first half of the century, particularly as a consequence of Maratha opposition, while regionally very important, lacked any comparable global impact. This is not a matter of Eurocentrism, but a comment on the links between different parts of the world. The fate of Safavid Persia was important in the Persian Gulf, to Oman, Afghanistan, northern India, Central Asia, the Caucasus and to the Ottoman Empire, all of which experienced the campaigning of Nadir Shah of Persia in the 1730s and 1740s, but it is difficult to see this as playing a formative role in the nineteenth- or twentieth-century world, not least because neither the Afghan control that had briefly followed the Safavids, nor the empire of Nadir Shah proved lasting. Just as the 1750s marked the fall of the empire of the Dzhungars of Xiankiang before the expansion of Manchu China, so the states of the region between the Ottoman Empire and Hindustan were unable to coalesce lastingly to provide a strength able to thwart the growing regional power of Britain and Russia.

The American Declaration of Independence of 1776 represented a modification, if not rejection, of much of the *ancien régime*. Slavery and an inegalitarian socio-economic structure were, of course, accepted in the new state, and the first was to cause a lasting political and cultural problem for the new state ultimately leading, in 1861, to its dissolution and to a bitter civil war (1861–65) in order to re-create it. The initial acceptance of slavery, nevertheless, was a necessary product of the federal character of the new state, and of the role of slave-holding and trading, not only in the economies of the southern states but also to their sense of identity and distinctiveness. In contrast, the abolition of, first, slave trading and, then, slavery in the British Empire reflected the limited extent of élite consensus in the early nineteenth century: the slave economies of the West Indies and Mauritius were largely ignored.[12]

Nevertheless, the political institutions and practices that characterized the newly independent society, ranging from republicanism to relative freedom of religion and speech, reflected the political vitality of aspirations within the European world that were not restricted to America. Combined with the economic and military strength of the USA, these institutions and practices proved important in moulding the world that was created from the successive declines of European power in the twentieth century.

As with other crises of authority, it is important not to overstate support, inevitability and novelty. The American Revolution, like other political movements in the late eighteenth century, arose as a result of political contingencies, and its aspirations and demands were rejected by many. Indeed, the strength and variety of Loyalist opinion in British North America are more than a footnote to eighteenth-century history. It is impossible to measure accurately the numerical strength of Loyalism, not least because, as with the rival Patriotism, issues of opportunity, as well as the shifting contrasts between support, commitment and activism played an important role. Nevertheless, between one-fifth and one-third of the population of European descent in the Thirteen Colonies can be seen as Loyalist in sympathy, with the same percentage Patriot, and the remainder neutral to one degree or another.

The causes of the American Revolution can be found more in an unwilling and largely hesitant response to the confused tergiversations of British policy, as remedies for the fiscal burden of imperial defence were sought in the context of heavy national indebtedness after the Seven Years' War, than in any general desire for liberty. The particular structural problems of colonial governance – distance and a lack of understanding of colonial society and aspirations – played major roles in the developing crisis, but did not cause it.

The American Revolution also looked back to seventeenth-century British traditions of resistance to unreasonable royal demands as much as to contemporary European intellectual debates. In some respects, it was a second version of the British Civil War, one in which the principal source of support for royal authority (from within the colonies) again came from Anglican loyalists. However, in contrast to England, this group was less numerous in percentage terms. Religion shaped the way in which British and colonial legal and political thinking developed and came to define particular issues as matters of principle and certain problems as non-negotiable. Whereas fewer than 10 per cent of the English population in 1776 were Dissenters, the proportion (among those of European descent) in the Thirteen Colonies that rebelled was over three-quarters. The rebellion of Dissent against what, to many Americans, seemed an assertive Anglicanism was a rebellion against the power of a polity of crown and Parliament claiming absolute power by the common law and dignified with divine authority by the Church. By pressing the case for a denominational reading of the revolution, the role of agents of modernisation, such as individualism, radicalism and liberalism, are downplayed.[13]

There was also novelty in the Thirteen Colonies, not least the disruptive consequences of rapid population growth and of the Protestant Great Awakening in religious consciousness, and challenges to established patterns and practices of authority and social influence. The British attempt after the Seven Years' War to project government and Parliament's sovereign authority across the Atlantic led to demands for the limitation of state power rather than encouraging dissension about the colonial bond.[14] This cut to the core of the nature of the empire, which was that of a reciprocal profitability controlled by the state, as expressed through the sovereignty of Parliament. Emphasising, instead, the specific interests and identity of the parts of the system threatened the integrity of the empire. In large part, this was a reflection of the failure to create powerful representative assemblies under the crown in the individual colonies, or, at least, in those with substantial settler populations. This was to be the course followed in the nineteenth century, and provided a managed path to partnership in the case of Australia, Canada, New Zealand and, eventually less successfully, South Africa.

However, such a course, although demanded by influential colonists, had not been followed in the eighteenth century. In large part, this reflected concern among Westminster parliamentarians that such a policy would increase the power of the crown, as it would have an independent relationship with each assembly. This attitude looked back to seventeenth-century suspicions that the crown would benefit from its separate position in England (and Wales), Scotland and Ireland, especially the last, as well as to eighteenth-century concern about the extent to which, from 1714, the position of the monarch as Elector of Hanover might affect British interests and policy. It is possible that a different political course within Britain, for example a Stuart restoration in 1745–46, followed by the re-establishment of the Edinburgh Parliament, would have made it easier to accept imperial parliaments, but this is unlikely, first, because such a restoration might well have provoked a rebellion in North America and, second, because of the authoritarian character of Stuart attitudes.

With its independence acknowledged by Britain in 1783, the United States was eventually to transform the European world. This newly independent state also offered a frame of reference for comparisons with Europe from within the European or Western world. It had a particular impact in fashionable French circles in the 1780s, but was also important elsewhere, including in Germany, the United Provinces, and Ireland.[15] It was possible to make direct comparisons between European states and the United States, not least about constitutional arrangements; and the role of language and distance, which made the Orient so obscure, were not at issue in the case of America. Trade with Europe rapidly revived after the war, and diplomatic and other links were established. As a result, the importance of using non-European peoples as the basis for comparison in Europe, whether long-established states like China, or those seen as noble savages, for example the Tahitians, diminished.

The most immediate point of reference for Christian Europe was the Ottoman Empire,[16] which indeed encompassed a sizeable part of Europe throughout the period, but this comparison was generally conditioned by the centuries of conflict with Islam. Although the decline of the Ottoman Empire from the 1680s reduced the threat, there was still a widespread tendency to see Islamic culture as anti-Christian and dangerous. This was particularly the case in the Mediterranean. Concern about Ottoman naval power and plans led to Christian maritime responses into the early eighteenth century, while Barbary corsairs remained a problem into the nineteenth century, helping lead the French to justify their annexation of Algiers in 1830. These corsairs attacked shipping and raided coasts, acquiring numerous slaves. A serious problem in their own right, which led, in the eighteenth century, to naval action against both the corsairs and their bases by a number of powers, including France, Spain and the Dutch, the corsairs also played a major role in keeping the idea of Islam as hostile alive in the European consciousness. They played a role in fiction and in the activities of religious fraternities.[17]

The serious defeats suffered by the Ottomans in 1683–97 led to a geopolitical shift in Christian attitudes towards the Islamic world. Earlier there had been much interest in winning the alliance of Persia against the Ottomans,[18] but this became less important, although it still played a role for the Russians in the 1720s–1730s.

The continued vitality of the Ottoman Empire was demonstrated in the eighteenth century with the defeat of Peter the Great of Russia at the River Pruth in 1711, the rapid conquest of the Morea from Venice in 1715, and the defeat of the Austrians, leading to the surrender of Belgrade, in 1739. The latter two were reversals of recent Ottoman losses of territory, and this encouraged a view that other such losses might not be permanent. Although the Ottomans suffered serious defeats at the hands of Russia later in the century, in the wars of 1768–74 and 1787–92, the Austrians were unable to continue their advance at Ottoman expense that had characterised the years

1683–1718. This did not mean that the Ottomans resumed the threatening posture in the Austrian and German mind they had adopted prior to 1683, but it did ensure a continuation of earlier themes of religious confrontation.

The monotheistic character of Islam helped attract some favourable comment, but the political character of the Ottoman Empire was associated with tyranny and arbitrary rule, and the harsh treatment of Christians who rebelled, particularly Greeks in 1770–71, attracted serious criticism.

China, in contrast, offered a more acceptable and readily apparent perspective from which European practices could be seen as deficient, at any rate prior to the second half of the eighteenth century. Jesuit and other intellectuals showed great interest in seventeenth-century China and were willing to make comparisons that were not always to the benefit of Christian Europe. China became the 'Great Other, showing possibilities of ways of thinking and organising society radically different from their own'.[19] The Chinese were associated with wisdom, and there was considerable interest in Chinese religion, although the political model was not applicable to Europe.

From the late eighteenth century, however, China, like other Oriental cultures, was increasingly seen as weak, and regarded as especially stagnant domestically, and as unable to offer the intellectual dynamism and respect for the individual sought by European commentators.[20] The accuracy of this assessment is open to question. While it was true that, by the late 1830s and, even more, 1860, China was clearly less successful militarily than the European powers, this was not necessarily a pertinent view in the late eighteenth century. Nevertheless, there was no apparent political and governmental progress in China, and nothing equivalent to the American Revolution or to Enlightened Despotism.

Less was known about Japan, or, even more, Korea, than about the Ottoman Empire, India or China, but, had more been known, it would not have provided a frame of reference within which Europe would have been found wanting. During the seventeenth century, there were growing economic problems in Japan, and, by its end, the government was faced with serious financial difficulties and there were major differences over policy. Alongside growing pessimism about the future in the writing of social commentators, there were more pressing demands and proposals for reform; as in France in the 1700s. Social tension increased in eighteenth-century Japan as an aspect of the central problem for government of allocating resources when production could not meet the demands of a rapidly rising population; although this helped to forward the integration of domestic markets. As a sign of widespread conservatism, most political, economic, cultural and intellectual efforts were directed at the preservation and strengthening of established arrangements, but, by the end of the century, there was greater interest in new political, economic and cultural forms.[21]

Alongside European judgements, by contrast, there were also interactions with non-Christian societies by people and institutions (trading companies) that were transcultural. These are of particular interest to scholars today,[22] although the extent of their contemporary impact was probably far greater for frontier zones than elsewhere. The respective roles, in Christian Europe, of new information (from zones of interaction), and of inherited opinion varied: it was difficult to discuss and conceptualise what was poorly, if at all, understood outside these zones.

In addition, there was a habit of conceiving of the distant world principally as an extension of the nearby, especially of its problems, configurations and patterns of causality. Thus, in England, West Africa and the Indian Ocean were seen in the seventeenth century principally in terms of English relations with other European powers, particularly the Dutch, while, in the seventeenth and eighteenth centuries, the Ottoman Empire tended to be seen by the English foremost as a sphere for commercial competition with France.[23] As such, it was perceived and used to register particular interpretations of English and French economic strength and commercial politics, rather than to forward any understanding of Ottoman society and culture.

Indeed, European powers competed with each other overseas, both militarily and economically, more than they competed with non-European powers. With the latter, there was more of a search for common advantage in commerce. This was certainly true of China and, less successfully due to its self-imposed isolation, Japan. More generally, a modern concentration on the zone of interaction can serve to distract attention from the processes, and purposes, by, and for, which images of abroad were constructed.

Aside from the value of comparisons for contemporaries, it is appropriate to ask whether there are many for modern scholars. In chronological terms, there is a rough congruence, with China and the Ottoman Empire, in particular, also badly affected in the mid-seventeenth-century crisis, although, in the case of China, the most serious challenge was external attack – by the Manchu. Without that, the internal rebellions in China would have posed less of a threat. In addition, the reality of compromise with local interests discussed in Chapter 2 was abundantly demonstrated in the Ottoman Empire, for example in Egypt.

In the late seventeenth century, there was a process of domestic consolidation and, at least attempted, external expansion by a number of states, including China, the Ottomans, Mughal India, Austria, Russia, France and Britain. These can be seen as aspects of an *ancien régime* spanning the Eurasian world. Nevertheless, there were important variations. China operated as a great power in a world without comparable rivals, a very different international context to the multipolar European system, and one that led to mutual incomprehension. Furthermore, although the Manchu–Han Chinese–Mongol combination that gave Manchu China its particular character, and its military effectiveness, made it a form of composite state, clearly represented in the army's banner system, it was a very different composite state to those in Europe. There, the interests of the constituent parts were expressed in, and protected by, constitutional and other privileges, particularly Estates and different tax arrangements. The best point of comparison with China within Europe was Russia, both because of factors of scale and due to the lack of intermediate institutions. There was also a measure of comparison between China's conquest of Xinkiang and Tibet in 1695–1760 and Russia's attempts at Asian expansion, which, in that period, were more successful against the Bashkirs east of the Caspian Sea than against the Ottomans and their Crimean Tatar allies or in Persia.

Thanks to a different strategic culture, which owed much to the earlier lack of contiguous comparable rivals, China was more ready to accept an international relations based on Chinese hegemony and the offer of tributes by neighbours than were European powers, which tended to want to consolidate control. This did not prevent Chinese attempts to enforce control in frontier zones, such as the war against Yang Yinlong in Southwest China from 1587–1600, which entailed the ending of the autonomy of a family that had long controlled part of the region, but these conflicts, at once wars of expansion as much as consolidation, were more common in Europe. Indeed, that leads to an underrating of Chinese vitality in the late eighteenth century, because there is an assumption among European commentators that dynamic states should expand. China did not do so after the defeat of the Dzhungars and the occupation of Kashgar in the 1750s. Instead, there were two frontier struggles, one, unsuccessful, in 1788–89, with Tongking (northern Vietnam), the other, successful, in 1792, when a Chinese force from Tibet invaded the expansionist Gurkha kingdom of Nepal and obliged it to accept the Chinese interpretation of the relationship between Tibet and Nepal. These were not impressive sequels to the conquests of the 1750s, but the Manchu Chinese state was, also, no successor to the medieval steppe empires of the Mongols and Timur. There was no drive to conquer Japan, as the Mongols had sought to do in the thirteenth century, and the frontier with Russia fixed in 1685 and 1729, which excluded Russia from the Amur valley, was seen as acceptable. Failure in Indo-China was a blow, but it was distant from the centre of Chinese concern, which was the Beijing–Xinkiang axis.

In Europe, the multipolarity of the states system, the anarchic nature of power politics, and the kaleidoscopic character of alliances, all helped to account for the development of 'realist' paradigms of international behaviour, and thus of judging other states. This contrasted with the imperial psyche of China in which geopolitical dominance and a sense that invulnerability was normal were linked to assumptions about the proper operation of international relations. The multipolarity also served as a comment on long-standing contemporary concern and speculation about the idea of a 'universal' monarchy in Europe; in other words a dominant state similar to China.[24]

There was no comparison between the trans-oceanic colonialisation and power projection of the Atlantic European powers and the more land-based character of non-European powers including those, such as China and the Ottoman Empire, with a lengthy coastline. In the late seventeenth century, the Emirate of Oman made raids on the coast of India and established a territorial presence on the Swahili coast of Africa, driving the Portuguese from Mombasa, where Fort Jesus fell after a long siege in 1698, but this activity was not matched by other powers. The Mughals, the Marathas and other Indian powers, such as Mysore, developed naval power but it was not central to their military activity or self-image, and this power was not sustained in the face of hostile European action. The Marathas came closest to posing a serious naval challenge, but their bases were finally subjugated by the British. Manchu China conquered Taiwan, but that was the extent of its amphibious operations. Neither China nor Japan intervened in the Philippines, and, although both considered doing so, their failure to do so says more about their attitudes. In addition, neither power made an impact further into the Pacific. What did not happen tends to be ignored, but, in light, in particular, of their current links with Australasia, it is worth underlining that neither China nor Japan launched voyages of exploration or created settlement colonies across the Pacific or around its rim.

However, in the late seventeenth century, the Ottoman, Mughal and Manchu empires each ruled populations that were larger than any European state. The Chinese population may have risen from 150 million in 1650 to 300 million in 1800, both figures greater than the population of European Christendom. In addition, each had been able to cope with serious problems in the mid-seventeenth century, and then to revive in strength. It is too easy to treat these states as failures and to minimise the strengths, even dynamism, of systems categorised as conservative.

In practice, there is insufficient comparative work, and less study of these states than those of Western Europe. Without systematic study of the early modern period, the assessment of nineteenth-century change outside Europe, and of the reasons for eventual failure at the hands of Western imperialism, will remain precarious. In approaching these countries, and this failure, it is important to dispense with any emphasis on the nation state as a pinnacle of their development.[25] Instead, it is important to underline the continued vitality of states that were empires, not colonial empires directed by the government of a nation state, but states that were imperial in their entire structure and governmental system. This was true not only of prominent instances such as China, but also of states that experienced considerable vitality and territorial expansion in the eighteenth century under the rule of dynamic monarchs, for example Burma and Siam, as well as newly created states such as Nepal, Vietnam, and the Sikh state in the Punjab.

Alongside this vitality, it is pertinent to note the continued importance of

Asian merchants in long-distance trade. The extent of European participation in, and control over, European–Asian trade links has been exaggerated. This was the case with maritime trade, but, in addition, overland links remained important and were dominated by Asians. This was true of the trade from India to the west via Kandahar in the seventeenth century, helping to account for the struggle between Mughals and Safavids for control of the city.[26] Such trade helped produce revenues and bullion flows that both assisted state-building and encouraged attacks by other states and by nomadic forces.

In terms of stability, the central issue in this study, it is worth noting that the Manchu in China, like the Mughals in India, faced serious risings, that unrest led to the dethroning of Ottoman sultans in 1703 and 1730, that the Safavids of Persia were overthrown by Afghan invaders in 1721–22, and that, in the late eighteenth century, there was a considerable shift in power from the centre to the peripheral Maratha states. The Maratha polity was greatly weakened by periods of civil war that, in general, reflected disputed successions. This helped the British in their Maratha Wars, as it lessened the cohesion of their opponents, playing a major role in the crucial campaign by Arthur Wellesley, later Duke of Wellington, in 1803. In Manchu China, risings included the huge millenarian White Lotus rebellion of 1796–1805 in Shaanxi, and risings by non-Chinese subjects, such as Miao revolts in Hunan and Guizhou in 1735–36 and 1795–1805, and the Jinchuan tribal rising in Sichuan in 1746–49.

The multi-ethnic character of empire posed a challenge that in some empires encouraged rule through the co-option of their élites, as well as a measure of religious toleration, as in Ottoman Europe. The Ottomans looked to the most tolerant of the schools of Muslim law. Conversion to Islam during the Ottoman period was important in some parts of the Empire, particularly Albania and Bosnia, and this has greatly affected the recent history of the Balkans, but the bulk of the Christian (and Jewish) subjects of the Ottoman Empire did not convert, and this posed few problems for the Ottomans prior to the rise of nationalism in the nineteenth century. In Hungary, there was neither forced Islamisation nor mass conversions to Islam.[27]

The Manchu were less willing than the Ottomans to accommodate subject peoples, although they were cautious in their management of Tibet and the Mongols. At the same time, they did not have to face settler revolts comparable to those that were to affect the Europeans in the New World, nor religious division comparable to that in Christian Europe.

Close attention reveals that, whatever the political and governmental system outside Europe, there was generally more accommodation, compromise and pressures from short-term exigencies than concern with formal structures might suggest. To take an example that has benefited from recent study, the Ottomans had conquered Egypt in 1517, but, in the seventeenth century, the Constantinople-based central government 'lost its ability to direct affairs ... Its remaining representatives ... could do little to halt the continuing penetration of the local households into the administration and garrison corps, nor could they halt the redirection of Egypt's extensive revenues from imperial to local objectives'. In addition, although the role of Mosul as a key military base on the most sensitive Ottoman frontier, that with Persia, ensured a greater role there for the army, and thus the central government, again, the theme is of accommodation with the local élite. Just as the expansion of Christian European armies created opportunities for mutual profit, so the supply of the Ottoman army led to the same benefits. More generally, provincial notables holding public office acted in an autonomous fashion. Looked at differently, this was an aspect of the flexibility of provincial administration.[28]

Nevertheless, there were also important differences between states. The formidable bureaucratic culture that was a legacy of the Chinese past maintained by the Manchu was not matched in Europe,[29] or, indeed, elsewhere. Nor in Christian Europe, with the possible exception of the Russia of Ivan the Terrible and Peter the Great, were attempts made to transform a state comparable to those seen in late-sixteenth-century Japan: 'The state created by Oda Nobunaga and Toyotomi Hideyoshi was basically a military hegemony imposed on the heads of all warrior bands of daimyo who had staked out their own territorial claims ... it was imposed *from above* by Nobunaga and Hideyoshi.'[30] Burma and Siam in the eighteenth century experienced the same process, at the hands of ruler-generals who were far more authoritarian and brutal than Peter the Great or Frederick the Great. The same was attempted in Persia by Nadir Shah, and helps explain his assassination in 1747. Similarly, Tashsin of Siam, who also showed signs of megalomania and paranoia, was overthrown by another general, Chakri, in 1782.

The Europeans might have possessed a system comparable to that in China, had the fusion of Church and state developed differently, but a widespread disengagement of the Church and clergy from state government took place in the early modern period, although Church-government remained an important aspect of administration. By fostering the impact of ideological goals on commercial practices and aspirations, such a fusion of Church and state might well have limited economic growth in Europe. In their stead, European states had not yet developed the large, self-consciously meritocratic bureaucracies produced by public institutions that were to provide the manpower for the expansion of government, and its information support systems, in the nineteenth century, and to help direct public culture and social policy towards government-based solutions. Dependent earlier, instead, on relations with the landed orders, rulers delegated out many of the functions of government and had only a limited ability to execute policies for change.

The term early modern is an unfortunate one if it is intended to imply comparisons with modern government. This is inappropriate for both the intentions and the scale of government. Differences in the latter are easier to note, but those in the former are more important, not least because they interacted with political culture and ideological norms. Modernity, in the sense of an explicit, or at least instinctive, preference for the new and a quest for the novel, was not yet central to government or politics. There was interest in new developments, but these were seen largely in terms of strengthening existing structures and of securing resources for the pursuit of competitive international relations. The same was true of spheres of activity generally presented in teleological terms. For example, each steam engine represented a determination to benefit from change, but it is also striking how few were in use in Europe in 1800, and how the main usage – for pumping water from mines – was essentially an improvement rather than a revolutionary leap forward.

Aside from the difference in governmental objectives and cultures, it is far from clear that Chinese government should be seen as able to escape the problems that affected European administration. Instead, there are signs that, alongside such impressive feats as the supply of the large forces that conquered Xiankiang in the 1750s, which has justifiably excited recent attention and praise,[31] there were serious problems including widespread corruption, losses of tax revenue, and a deleterious role for tax-farmers. As a result, from the 1720s, provincial officials were permitted to retain a percentage of taxes in order to support local administration. By providing reasonable salaries, this cut corruption.[32] It can also be seen as another aspect of the process revealed in studies of European government, such as that of Waquet (see Chapter 2). The use of tax farming in China, as in much of Europe, is a valuable indication of the deficiencies of public administration and of the openness of government to different systems of control, regulation and revenue-raising.

Looked at differently, comparisons of Chinese and Christian European government encourage the conclusion that it is unclear to what extent a particular type of state structure was necessary, for example, to the large-scale coal mining that China did not pursue,[33] or, more generally, to the modernisation seen as crucial in the West's ability to become central to global economic links, and thus to the process and profits of globalisation. This ability transformed the New World and created links across the Pacific. Andean and Mesoamerican (Central American) societies 'had virtually no knowledge of each other' before the Spaniards arrived.[34] The Spaniards not only led the way to such knowledge, but also created links across both the Atlantic and the Pacific.

The deleterious character of such links has attracted attention, particularly the spread of epidemic disease and the enforced and brutal movement of large numbers of slaves from Africa. What is equally clear is that the links reflected the operation of a developed maritime system able to respond to demands and to minimise the risks of travel by improved knowledge of navigation, including, eventually, the discovery of an accurate way to measure longitude at sea, by advances in ship construction and rigging, and by devices such as insurance. Globalisation also brought profit to societies with which the Europeans traded and there was a strong degree of mutual dependence,[35] but it was the Europeans (or, from American independence, Westerners) who organised the new systems.

Given the important roles of naval power and commercial regulation, it would be going too far to say that an absence of state structures, with their costs and limitations, was the most useful governmental context for European economic and maritime expansion, although the value of these roles should not be exaggerated. Navies were primarily used against European competitors, and not against non-Europeans. The low incidence of battles with the latter outside the Mediterranean and Black Sea in the period 1550–1800 is a matter of note, although the value of this measure is lessened by the extent to which the presence of naval strength acted as a deterrent.

Equally, European state navies, certainly in the sixteenth century, depended heavily on winning the support of groups that controlled and could finance warships. This was true, for example, of English and Spanish naval forces, not least when they clashed in the Armada campaign of 1588. This co-operation was less the case from the mid-seventeenth century, as the specialisation of warships (so that large merchantmen no longer joined the line of battles) interacted with the pressure for larger and permanent fleets derived from international competition.[36]

It was not until the Europeans attempted large-scale territorial conquest in the face of serious organised opposition that the scale and regularity of government-deployed resources became a crucial measure of European power in other continents. At that stage, it seemed apparent that the relationship between structures of command and longer-term developments affecting resource mobilisation were no longer favourable to non-European societies.[37] Yet this situation did not largely arise, certainly in Africa and East Asia, until the nineteenth century, and then, in many cases, until the last quarter of the century. Prior to the nineteenth century, the European impact on land in Africa and East Asia was limited, and David Quinn has suggested that 'if the springs of European enterprise had dried up ... only in the Americas, and there only where urban institutions were well grounded, had communities with the capacity for survival and possible growth come into being'.[38]

In the late nineteenth century, the crucial element in clashes between Europeans and non-Europeans may well have been differences in military capability, rather than in structures of command, although a number of non-European societies were more vulnerable because their style of government was still patrimonial autocracy. It is also appropriate to stress the extent to which the Europeans benefited in their imperial conquest and rule, across its span, from their ability to elicit – by coercion or more willingly – local support. This arose largely from the divisions within non-European polities, which in part reflected the fact that many were composite states, although the Europeans (and other expanding powers) also benefited from the multipolar character of power in many areas, such as the Caucasus, Central Asia and West Africa, and their consequent ability to tackle them in a sequential fashion, rather than to have to face a powerful united opposition.

In the early modern period, this had been more generally true of areas in which the Europeans made major conquests, such as Brazil, Siberia and nearby steppe regions, and North America. Other factors played an important role, not least the impact of new strains of disease, brought by the Europeans, such as smallpox, in particular in areas such as North America and North Asia where the population density was low. Nevertheless, the lack of large-scale state forms in all these areas, where the basic form of social organisation was tribal, affected their ability to mobilise resistance. It also helped the Europeans gain allies, as existing tribal rivalries were exploited. This helps account for the remarkable speed of Russian expansion across Siberia to the Pacific, as well as their success in the steppe regions.[39] The Russians had earlier benefited from divisions among the khanates that represented the Tatar heritage.[40]

It would be misleading to suggest that developments affecting resource mobilisation were limited to Christian Europe. Aside from greater Chinese capability in the logistics of steppe warfare, in India, from the mid-eighteenth century, in response to the new weaponry and tactics introduced by the British and French, Maratha armies became bigger and more professional, so that the policy of living off the land was no longer possible. This forced the development of revenue administration, banking and credit.[41]

To return to Europe in 1550–1800, commercial regulation by government was also not as necessary to encouraging investment as might be imagined. In the major contact zone between Western and non-Western trade, the Indian Ocean and the Western Pacific, European power was represented by private and corporate traders, rather than by the state. The Dutch and English East India Companies, and the private traders who enjoyed a frequently close but ambivalent relation with them (and were more important in the case of the English), were more dynamic and active than the Spaniards based in the Philippines, who were more under royal authority. Private trading was also central to Portuguese activity in Asia, and the Portuguese presence was correspondingly weakened by mercantile factors, especially a lack of capital, with all its consequences, including insufficient ships.[42] Although, in late-seventeenth-century Portugal, there was interest in reforms, not least in borrowing models from England, France and the Dutch, a state overly dependent on links with the nobility and a society 'still wedded to medieval and feudal legacies' could not carry through the changes necessary to mount a major challenge to the Dutch and English positions in Asian trade.[43]

In production terms, the crucial sources of internationally traded goods originating in the European world included the slave plantations created in the New World and, from the late eighteenth century, the new world of coal and iron being developed in particular areas of Europe and, then, the USA. Neither was under state control (unlike the gold and silver workings with their coerced labour forces in Latin America), although regulation did play an important role in trade. There were no vast forces of slaves at the disposal of European governments, while the respective strength and functions of imperial governments and mercantile groups were shown by the rapidity with which bullion brought from the New World was transferred from state control.

Similarly, the grain and naval stores (iron, timber, hemp, flax) exported from the Baltic to markets elsewhere in Europe were handled not by state trading companies but by independent merchants. The largest group was Dutch,[44] although English and other merchants were also important. These merchants acted as middlemen, underlining the creative role of commercial entrepreneurs in developing both markets and sources. This was seen, for example, in the role of Dutch finance and expertise in building up Swedish production and exports. Similarly, the availability of investment capital provided by middlemen was important to the spatial pattern of industrialisation in Europe.

An emphasis on the role of mercantile groups encourages a different approach to modernity, one in which government plays a secondary role to attitudes to, and practices of, capital use that, eventually, fostered a Western-dominated globalisation. In the sixteenth century, the English state had only a 'modest involvement with overseas ventures'.[45] More generally, government emerges as a protection cost as well as a format for arranging compromises between different interests, and a means to combat piracy. European 'trading states' have been seen as 'political units controlled by commercial interests',[46] a claim that pushes the case too far, but that directs attention to the relationship. This emphasis can be seen to parallel the emphasis on co-operation with the landed orders seen in other chapters. It is more helpful than the argument that élite conflict helped determine developments, particularly the spread of capitalism.[47]

Furthermore, such co-operation could be extended to enable negotiations with non-European mercantile and territorial interests as Europe's range increased.[48] These negotiations, which were an important aspect of the degree to which empires were transnational organisations drawing on broad networks of connections,[49] were central to much that is seen as distinctly European, ranging from the Atlantic slave trade to the trade between Western Europe and South Asia. Recent work on warfare in Atlantic Africa has focused on the military strength of African polities, not least their successful adoption of flintlock firearms in the eighteenth century, and has emphasised the lack of a European advantage in military capability on land, as opposed to offshore waters, where deep-draught European vessels did enjoy an advantage in fire-power. The lack of such a gap on land ensured that the Europeans had to trade for slaves on terms they could influence but not control.[50]

This is an uncomfortable point for some modern writers who are keen to ascribe guilt, and happiest to place all responsibility on the heads of Europeans, but, paradoxically, this approach minimises the capacity for independent decisions enjoyed by Africans. Indeed, in so far as comparisons can be made, European slave traders did not enjoy coercive advantages greater than those of Arab counterparts on the Indian Ocean coast of Africa, while those of Moroccan and other slave raiders operating across the Sahara and from the *sahel* belt into the forested regions further south were probably greater. The major European advantage rested on purchasing power, and this was derived from the prosperity of plantation economies in North and South America and the West Indies.[51]

Mention of slavery serves to underline the point that the compromises of negotiated shared interests, and of the relations summarised as globalisation, were made at the expense of others. It is important to see both. To treat the subject in terms only of compromise or simply of coercion is naïve and limited.

Notes

1. *Henry VIII*, V, iv.

2. D. Mackay, *In the Wake of Cook: Exploration, Science and Empire, 1780–1801* (1985); R. Drayton, *Nature's Government: Science, Imperial Britain, and the 'Improvement' of the World* (New Haven, CT, 2000).

3. P. Caraman, *The Lost Paradise: An Account of the Jesuits in Paraguay 1607–1768* (1975); D. Alden, *The Making of an Enterprise. The Society of Jesus in Portugal, Its Empire and Beyond, 1540–1750* (Stanford, CA, 1996).

4. R. A. Williams, *The American Indian in Western Legal Thought: The Discourses of Conquest* (New York, 1990); A. Pagden, *Lords of All the World. Ideologies of Empire in Spain, Britain and France, c. 1500–c. 1800* (New Haven, CT, 1995); D. Armitage (ed.), *An Expanding World. The European Impact on World History 1450–1800. Vol. XX: Theories of Empire, 1450–1800* (Aldershot, 1998).

5. G. J. Walker, *Spanish Politics and Imperial Trade 1700–1789* (1979); J. J. McCusker and R. R. Menard, *The Economy of British America 1607–1789* (Chapel Hill, NC, 1991).

6. S. S. Webb, *1676: The End of American Independence* (New York, 1984); R. Bliss, *Revolution and Empire. English Politics and the American Colonies in the Seventeenth Century* (Manchester, 1993).

7. D. P. Szatmary, *Shays' Rebellion: The Making of an Agrarian Insurrection* (Amherst, MA, 1980); T. P. Slaughter, *The Whiskey Rebellion, Frontier Epilogue to the American Revolution* (1986).

8. A. J. O'Shaughnessy, *An Empire Divided. The American Revolution and the British Caribbean* (Philadelphia, PA, 2000).

9. P. Lawson, *The Imperial Challenge: Quebec and Britain in the Age of the American Revolution* (Montreal, 1989); F. M. Greenwood, *Legacies of Fear. Law and Politics in Quebec in the Era of the French Revolution* (Toronto, 1994).

10. K. Maxwell, *Pombal. Paradox of the Enlightenment* (Cambridge, 1995).

11. H. E. S. Fisher, *The Portugal Trade: A Study of Anglo-Portuguese Commerce 1700–1770* (1971).

12. S. Drescher, *From Slavery to Freedom: Comparative Studies in the Rise and Fall of Atlantic Slavery* (New York, 1999).

13. J. C. D. Clark, *The Language of Liberty 1660–1832. Political Discourse and Social Dynamics in the Anglo-American World* (Cambridge, 1993).

14. B. Bailyn, *The Ideological Origins of the American Revolution* (Cambridge, MA, 1967).

15. H. Dippel, *Germany and the American Revolution, 1770–1800: A Sociohistorical Investigation of Late Eighteenth-Century Political Thinking* (Chapel Hill, NC, 1977).

16. C. Rouillard, *The Turk in French History, Thought and Literature, 1520–1660* (Paris, 1938); A. Çirakman, 'From tyranny to despotism: the Enlightenment's unenlightened image of the Turks', *International Journal of Middle East Studies*, 33 (2000), pp. 49–68; D. Goffman, *The Ottoman Empire and Early Modern Europe* (Cambridge, 2002).

17. A. Williams, 'Crusaders as frontiersmen: the case of the Order of St. John in the Mediterranean', in D. Power and N. Standen (eds), *Frontiers in Question. Eurasian Borderlands, 700–1700* (Basingstoke, 1999), pp. 217–25; A. Thomson, *Barbary and Enlightenment. European Attitudes towards the Maghreb in the Eighteenth Century* (Leiden, 1987).

18. R. Matthee, 'Iran's Ottoman diplomacy during the reign of Shah Sulayman I (1077–1105/1666–94)', in K. Eslami (ed.), *Iran and Iranian Studies. Papers in Honor of Iraj Afshar* (Princeton, NJ, 1998), pp. 152–9.

19. J. E. Wills, *1688. A Global History* (2001), p. 94.

20. H. Cohen, 'Diderot and China', *Studies on Voltaire and the Eighteenth Century*, 242 (1986), pp. 219–32; J. J. Clarke, *Oriental Enlightenment: The Encounter between Asian and Western Thought* (1997).

21. C. Totman, *Early Modern Japan* (Berkeley, CA, 1994).

22. See, for example, K. O. Kupperman, *Settling with the Indians: The Meeting of English and Indian Cultures in America, 1580–1640* (Totowa, NJ, 1980); R. White, *The Middle Ground: Indians, Empires and Republics in the Great Lakes Region, 1651–1815* (Cambridge, 1991); D. Goffman, *Britons in the Ottoman Empire, 1642–1660* (Seattle, WA, 1998); N. Matar, *Turks, Moors, and Englishmen in the Age of Discovery* (New York, 1999); L. Colley, *Captives. Britain, Empire and the World 1600–1850* (2002).

23. D. Goffman, *Britons in the Ottoman Empire, 1642–1660* (1998).

24. L. Kirk, 'The matter of Enlightenment', *Historical Journal*, 43 (2000), p. 1140.

25. R. A. Abou-El-Haj, *Formation of the Modern State. The Ottoman Empire, Sixteenth to Eighteenth Centuries* (Albany, NY, 1992).

26. S. Chaudhury and M. Morineau (eds), *Merchants, Companies and Trade: Europe and Asia in the Early Modern Era* (Cambridge, 1999).

27. G. Agoston, 'Muslim–Christian acculturation: Ottomans and Hungarians from the fifteenth to the seventeenth centuries', in B. Bennassar and R. Sauzet (eds), *Chrétiens et Musulmans à la Renaissance* (Paris, 1998), pp. 294–5.

28. D. Crecelius, 'Egypt in the eighteenth century', in M. W. Daly (ed.), *The Cambridge History of Egypt. II. Modern Egypt* (Cambridge, 1998), p. 60; J. Hathaway, *The Politics of Households in Ottoman Egypt: The Rise of the Qazdaglis* (Cambridge, 1997); D. Khoury, *State and Provincial Society in the Ottoman Empire: Mosul, 1540–1834* (Cambridge, 1997); E. L. Rogan, *Frontiers of the State in the Late Ottoman Empire. Transjordan, 1850–1921* (Cambridge, 1999), pp. 2–4.

29. R. Bin Wong, *China Transformed: Historical Change and the Limits of European Experience* (Ithaca, NY, 1997); K. Pomeranz, *The Great Divergence: China, Europe and the Making of the Modern World Economy* (Berkeley, CA, 1999).

30. A. Naohiro, 'The sixteenth-century unification', in J.W. Hall (ed.), *The Cambridge History of Japan. IV. Early Modern Japan* (Cambridge, 1991), p. 78.

31. P. C. Perdue, 'Culture, history and imperial Chinese strategy: legacies of the Qing conquests', in H. van de Ven (ed.), *Warfare in Chinese History* (Leiden, 2000), p. 277.

32. M. Zelin, *The Magistrate's Tael: Rationalising Fiscal Reform in Eighteenth Century Ch'ing China* (Berkeley, CA, 1992).

33. P. O'Brien, 'Making the modern world economy', *History*, 87 (2002), p. 552.

34. F. Fernández-Armesto, *Continuity and Discontinuity in the Sixteenth-Century New World* (Minneapolis, MN, 2001), p. 19.

35. R. J. Barendse, *The Arabian Seas. The Indian Ocean World of the Seventeenth Century* (Armonk, NY, 2002), p. 454.

36. J. Glete, *Warfare at Sea, 1500–1650. Maritime Conflicts and the Transformation of Europe* (2000); R. Harding, *Seapower and Naval Warfare 1650–1830* (1999).

37. C. A. Bayly, '"Archaic" and "modern" globalization in the Eurasian and African arena, *c.* 1750–1850', in A. G. Hopkins (ed.), *Globalization in World History* (2002), p. 68. For a different approach, focusing on Kondratieff waves and the ability to profit from leading sectors in the global economy, G. Modelski and W. R. Thompson, *Leading Sectors and World Powers. The Coevolution of Global Economics and Politics* (Columbia, SC, 1996).

38. D. B. Quinn, *European Approaches to North America, 1450–1640* (Aldershot, 1998), p. 331.

39. M. Khodarkovsky, *Where Two Worlds Met: The Russian State and the Kalmyk Nomads, 1660–1771* (Ithaca, NY).

40. H. R. Huttenbach, 'Muscovy's conquest of Muslim Kazan and Astrakhan, 1552–56. The conquest of the Volga: prelude to empire', in M. Rywkin (ed.), *Russian Colonial Expansion* (1988), pp. 45–69.

41. S. Gordon, *The Marathas 1600–1818* (Cambridge, 1993).

42. E. Van Veen, *Decay or Defeat? An Enquiry into the Portuguese Decline in Asia, 1580–1645* (Leiden, 2000).

43. G. J. Ames, 'Pedro II and the Estado da India: Braganzan absolutism and overseas empire, 1668–1683', *Luso-Brazilian Review*, 34 (1997), pp. 9–10.

44. J. de Vries, *The First Modern Economy: Success, Failure and Perseverance of the Dutch Economy, 1500–1815* (Cambridge, 1997).

45. N. Canny, 'The origins of empire', in N. Canny (ed.), *The Oxford History of the British Empire I. The Origins of Empire. British Overseas Enterprise to the Close of the Seventeenth Century* (Oxford, 1998), p. 3.

46. W. R. Thompson, *The Emergence of the Global Political Economy* (2000), p. 66.

47. For this argument, R. Lachmann, *Capitalists in Spite of Themselves: Elite Conflict and Economic Transitions in Early Modern Europe* (Oxford, 2000). For a different approach, C. Mooers, *The Making of Bourgeois Europe. Absolutism, Revolution and the Rise of Capitalism in England, France and Germany* (1991).

48. For East Africa, M. Pearson, *Port Cities and Intruders. The Swahili Coast, India, and Portugal in the Early Modern Era* (Baltimore, MD, 1998).

49. H. Kamen, *Spain's Road to Empire. The Making of a World Power* (2002), p. 491.

50. J. Thornton, *Africa and Africans in the Making of the Atlantic World, 1400–1800* (2nd edn, Cambridge, 1998), pp. 98–125, and *Warfare in Atlantic Africa 1500–1800* (1999), esp. pp. 127–39.

51. Among the mass of work on this subject, J. C. Miller, *The Way of Death: Merchant Capitalism and the Angolan Slave Trade, 1730–1830* (Madison, WI, 1988) and D. Eltis, *The Rise of African Slavery in the Americas* (Cambridge, 2000). A more emotive account is offered by R. Blackburn, *The Making of New World Slavery: From the Baroque to the Modern, 1492–1800* (1997).

CHAPTER 8

Conclusions

§ A consideration of power and authority in the quarter-millennium under review, 1550–1800, suggests that the revisionist case still holds up well. As with other overarching interpretations, it has to be seen not as an abstraction, divorced from society and from the pressures and products of crises, but as the summary of a constantly shifting process of adjustment. Yet, the key argument – that adjustment took place in terms of a relationship between rulers and élites defined by compromise, rather than by the workings of an authoritarian will – remains pertinent.

How then will the revisionist approach be in turn revised? Possibly the most productive developments will come as a consequence of the integration of further research, especially on Eastern Europe. The coverage of the period there is less good than that of Western Europe, in large part because of the preference for doctrinaire theory over empirical research that characterised the communist years, although other factors are also of importance. There was widespread wartime and subsequent destruction and disruption of records,[1] particularly those of landowning families. In the case of the élite, the political agenda combined with the destruction of records to make the details of their role obscure. In the communist years, there was also a shutting out of most Western scholarship, whereas in Western Europe detailed archival research by, in particular, American scholars made a major contribution, not least to encouraging debate within national scholarly traditions. This can be seen especially clearly in work on British and French history. In addition, the lower prosperity of Eastern Europe helped ensure a smaller scholarly community and one with fewer resources for archival research.

These circumstances will not change at once, and the potential impact of American and Western European scholarship will be constrained by language problems, while declining American interest in European history will also be a factor. Nevertheless, an increase in knowledge about Eastern Europe can be anticipated. This will bring with it a breakdown in simple theories that treat this area as a largely undifferentiated whole. In addition, general theories of European development will need to respond to this knowledge. This will further challenge the habit of treating France as a paradigm; an issue for research and a problem of analysis that has had an unfortunate consequence for our understanding of the period. A greater consideration of Eastern Europe, not least its variety, alongside recent work on German and Italian history, will underline the variety of the period. This may diminish emphasis on English/British exceptionalism, which tends to echo off the French paradigm as a benchmark for comparison without adequate consideration of the situation elsewhere.

It will also be appropriate to include discussion both of European empires and of the comparative dimension offered by work on states elsewhere in the world. The latter is far from easy, and it is necessary to appreciate the specific characteristics of particular states, but it would be unfortunate to neglect the excellent work being produced on states such as China, as well as the opportunities for comparative consideration of European developments.

Throughout the period, the clash between aspiration and reality characterised government, although its form varied. The contrast with the reality of limited power behind the official rhetoric of authority and triumph that characterised Baroque monarchy was less serious for the latter, because it sought to change relatively little, than was the comparable situation during the Enlightenment. Then, the potential of government, especially as a means to mobilise the resources of society in order to maximise the public welfare, however defined, was increasingly grasped. Thomas Pelham noted when he visited Lyons in 1777 that:

> there is a plan in agitation and indeed began for turning the course of the [river] Rhone so as to prevent the junction of the [river] Soane till at a league below the town: to make several additional streets with a large square; and a channel to run between the two rivers and supplied by them both, on which they propose making corn mills in order to avoid the present incommodious method of having mills on boats in the river.[2]

Such schemes were often fruitless, for example the attempt in the 1780s to develop a large artificial harbour at Cherbourg, but they provide an instance of the sense of capacity for change.

Many intellectuals and some rulers and ministers indeed hoped that by using government they would be able to reform society. The French economist Jean-Claude Vincent de Gournay coined the term 'bureaucracy'. Demands for more, and more readily accessible and useable information, drove what has been seen as an information revolution from the eighteenth century.[3] In France in 1716, Philip, Duke of Orléans, as regent, ordered a national enquiry to identify and assess the mineral resources of France. Instructions were sent to the *intendants* to undertake the enquiry, but their reports were to be sent to the Academy of Sciences, which was responsible for collating and analysing them.[4] In 1771, Shelburne reported from Milan, 'a most excellent work has been finished within these few years ... It resembles our Domesday Book and well deserves attention.'[5]

The call for stronger and more centralised administration had general implications that clashed with traditional conceptions of government as mediated through a 'system' reflecting privileges and rights that were heavily influenced both by the social structure and by the habit of conceiving of administration primarily in terms of legal precedent. Rulers, however, varied in their willingness to exchange the traditional foundations of royal absolutism in legal precedent and a particularist social order, for a new conception of government; and many of the reforms can best be understood in habitual terms, both as the response to established problems and also as the attempt to make existing practices work better.

There was no equivalent among Christian rulers, other than those of Russia, to Abbas I of Persia (r. 1587–1629), who developed a strong centrally controlled force based on Caucasian military slaves (*ghulams*). By increasing the land under his control, Abbas was able to fund this system which contributed to a string of successes, particularly against the Ottomans and the Uzbeks, that in turn strengthened his domestic position. Another instance of centrally controlled force was the corps of black slaves, personally attached to the Sultan by religious ties, created in Morocco by Malay Isma'il (r. 1672–1727), who wanted to be free from local political pressure. Slave children were trained as soldiers and then married to slave girls to produce more slaves, while, in addition, slave raids were mounted south into the Sahara. However, under his successors, the slave corps became a force for chaos, trying, like the Praetorian Guard of Imperial Rome, to sell their political support.

Such slave armies were not matched in European colonies. The large Indian forces raised by the French and, even more, British East India Companies were not slave armies. Service was conditional, an aspect of the European presence in South Asia as a whole; although that did not make it less effective.[6]

The effectiveness of the governments of Christian Europe varied greatly. Government was most successful in implementing policies in certain small states such as Savoy-Piedmont, and most obvious in capital cities: in 1784 there were 3,500 officials in Berlin. The ability of certain states to raise formidable armies and the world's leading navies, and to conduct aggressive foreign policies, reflected the strength of their system of administration, although it was also dependent on the consent, assistance and often initiative of local government and the socially powerful, particularly the aristocracy. Both processes were more apparent from the mid-seventeenth century than earlier, and this adds an important chronological dimension and dynamic. Societies that put a premium on continuity and order reacted against the political, religious and social turmoil of $c.1520$–$c.1660$[7] and searched for an order based on stability and consensus (albeit socially circumscribed). However much they were dependent on the landed élites and their urban counterparts,[8] these governments proved more successful in power-projection than those of states characterised by aristocratic federalism.

If there was nothing in Europe or the European world to compare with the scale and ethos of the Chinese governmental system, there was also nothing to match the overthrow of the Ming in the 1640s, a cataclysm that indicated that administrative scale and sophistication did not suffice for continuity, still less for success. The nearest comparisons took place on the frontiers of Europe, a reminder of a constant factor in the history of that continent: its frequently troubled relations with neighbours and the impact of their pressure. The invasions of central Muscovy by the Crimean Tatars brought serious devastation in the sixteenth century, with Moscow sacked in 1571, and helped force Tsar Mikhail's government to negotiate peace with the Poles in 1634. However, Russia was not overthrown, and, from the 1680s, the Russians made major efforts to project their strength south across the steppe in order to crush the Tatars. Unsuccessful in the 1680s, the Russians were victorious in 1696, when Azov fell, and again in 1736–39, in the war of 1768–74, and finally in 1783.

Further west, the Ottomans failed at Vienna in 1683, a spectacular instance of a more general tempering of Ottoman pressure that can be traced back to their failure to complete and move beyond the conquest of Hungary in the early sixteenth century. In the Mediterranean, the conquests of Cyprus and Crete proved sequels to the development of Ottoman naval strength and their dominance of neighbouring land masses, not preludes to a conquest of the western basin of the sea. There was nothing therefore to match the collapse of Ming China.

Nor were the states of Christian Europe after the loss of Hungary vulnerable to the degree of Christian states outside Europe. In the Caucasus, Georgia was subject to Ottoman and Persian attack, and in 1795 Persian cavalry overran Georgia and sacked its capital, Tbilisi.[9] Ethiopia was also subject to serious attacks, for example by Adal and the nomadic Galla in the sixteenth century, and by, in the eighteenth century, the Yeju, whose cavalry defeated the Ethiopians at Amed Ber in 1787. It was not only for that reason that neither Ethiopia nor Georgia proved the kernel of a process of development similar to that seen in Europe. Other factors were also important, including resources and distance from the ocean. Yet external challenge was a major factor.

As another instance of development, European states increasingly moved away from a dependence on the monarch, at least for government although not for politics. Administrative institutions developed a measure of autonomy and in some states, especially, though very differently, Britain and Russia, there was a considerable gain in governmental capability and sophistication. 'Capability' is not itself necessarily attractive. It included surveillance. In Florence, in 1788, Charles Abbot, a British tourist, noted, 'At the door of the theatre we saw a man masked observing everybody who entered. It is usual here, and at all the theatres in Italy, for government to station such a person there.' In Venice in 1755, George, Viscount Villiers, another British tourist, wrote, 'the gondoliers are in the secret of all the intrigues but are obliged to tell everything to the Inquisitors of State and are generally employed as spies by them'.[10]

Yet, if the modern world is to be understood in functional terms, at least in part, in terms of big government able to execute planned policies in a predictable fashion and to integrate feedback readily into decision-making and policy execution, then modernity was still absent. This definition, however, is less convincing in the 2000s than it would have been three decades earlier, because now there is far less certainty about the values of centralisation and state control.

On the global scale, there was a major shift. The unique European experience of creating a global network of empire and trade was based on a distinctive type of interaction between economy, technology and state formation, and led to a major development in relations between parts of the world, sufficiently important to encourage the view that a new period in world history had been ushered in.[11] Wide-ranging interaction was not new, but it increased in frequency, range and impact, both on economies and on demographics. China, Korea and Japan were, by the seventeenth century, relatively centralised states. They could build large ships and manufacture guns, and their economies and levels of culture were not clearly weaker than those of contemporary European states. However, there was hardly any interaction in these three states between economy, technology and state formation, aimed at creating maritime effectiveness. Instead their conception of power, like that of Mughal and Maratha India, was based on, and defined by, territorial control of land.

The Manchu did not attempt at sea anything equivalent to what they achieved on land: solving the logistical problems central to managing steppe warfare, which was considered the supreme strategic threat by all Chinese dynasties. In order to wage war with the Dzhungars in the 1750s, there was a massive transfer of resources from eastern to western China: the application to military purposes of the great demographic and agricultural expansion of China during the century. Similarly, Ottoman military efforts rested on an impressive administrative and supply system, and these continued to be impressive.[12]

Economic gain was a very important factor behind European maritime power projection, while applied science fostered both maritime projection and economic gain. In Britain, geography offered a new ideal of science as a tool for understanding and controlling the world, and this potential brought popularity. The service of the state encouraged interest in mathematical geography, and there was an important relationship between the study of geography, as well as other subjects, and the development of ideas about imperial expansion. Joseph Banks (1743–1820), a great explorer as well as director of the new Royal Botanic Gardens at Kew, for example, advised the East India Company, suggesting that India be made a source for as many raw materials as possible for the British market. More generally, the ideology and practice of a rational culture widely imbued with a belief in scientific progress was important to a conviction of the possibility of achieving beneficial change.[13]

In the seventeenth and eighteenth centuries, rulers and ministers eagerly supported trans-oceanic trading companies in an attempt to benefit from the developing global market economy. However, competition between European powers had an adverse affect, particularly on Portugal in the seventeenth century, France in the eighteenth, and Austria in the early eighteenth. Furthermore, state-directed systems were heavily dependent on government financial stability and were affected by shifts in ministerial support. The latter had a detrimental impact on French efforts in the Indian Ocean in the 1670s,[14] although the French joined with the British and Dutch in providing Europe with the products – coffee, tea, cocoa, tobacco, sugar and rum – that radically changed European diet and health.[15]

The liberal political systems of the United Provinces and Britain, in contrast to those of state-directed systems, were notably successful in eliciting the co-operation of their own and, also, other capitalists, producing a symbiosis of government and the private sector that proved both effective and, especially, valuable for developing naval strength. Profit encouraged compromise, although this was not without costs and did not encompass all. In Britain, in particular, the corporatist character of economic activity and regulation that remained so important in economic life across much of the continent, usually with the support of government, certainly local governments,[16] played a far smaller role. Guilds and local tariffs were at issue in Germany, but not Britain. More generally, the possibility of profit acted as a strong stimulus to technological development and improved organisation for war, trade and colonisation. These were to frame the nineteenth-century world.

Similarly, the market came to play an important role in the cultural centres of trading networks, with individual patronage playing a diminished, although still important, part. This was true, for example, of Antwerp in the sixteenth century and Amsterdam in the seventeenth.[17] The relationship between modes of patronage and style is a complex one, and it would be inappropriate to adopt a deterministic approach, but the character of culture was different in various parts of Europe and this can be related to their access to liberal politics and marketplace patronage. The role of the market, as constructed, mediated and serviced by print capitalism, can also be seen in the expansion of printed news, and thus of public politics.

As a consequence of the symbiosis of government and the private sector in parts of Atlantic Europe, the enhanced governmental effectiveness and state power of what became the leading states of Eastern and Central Europe did not have the consequences that some commentators anticipated. In 1778, Charles Jenkinson, an under-secretary of state, told the House of Commons that the great military powers in the interior parts of Europe, who have amassed together their great treasures, and have modelled their subjects into great armies, will in the next and succeeding period of time, become the predominant powers. France and Great Britain, which have been the first and second-rate powers of the European world, will perhaps for the future be but of the third and fourth rate.[18]

In fact, it required the strength of Austria, Prussia and Russia combined, with the crucial support of British finances and naval power (as well, more surprisingly, as the British army) to subjugate Napoleon in 1814–15. However powerful these states were on the Continent, the trans-oceanic European world was very much under British influence or control, while France, then also the second leading European oceanic power, indeed, under Napoleon III, made a powerful riposte against Russia and Austria in the 1850s.

An emphasis on continuities in European history can focus on society, economics, politics or culture. In each case there has been a stress in much of the literature on change, but long-term continuities are as readily apparent whether the issue is gender relations, Christianisation, the nature and role of agriculture, or most other topics, especially if the focus is on the typical rather than the exceptional. Thus an emphasis on the cultivation of nitrogenous plants, on convertible husbandry and on the greater capability for land management that stemmed from enclosure, which leads to the description 'Agricultural Revolution' is, in whole or part, pertinent for parts of England, the United Provinces and Catalonia in the eighteenth century but far less so for most of Europe.

Alongside continuity within Europe, it is possible to emphasise the extent of change in Europe's global position. This stemmed in part from territorial expansion, but the development of a maritime capability that enabled Europeans to direct much of the process of globalisation was more important. However, the impressive nature of this shift can lead to a misleading focus on change within Europe, with an understandable stress on linkages and interacting causes and consequences that, nevertheless, extrapolates from important sectors in Atlantic Europe in order to describe the entire continent, much of which did not see comparable developments. This matches similar comments about other facets of change, such as the Enlightenment, although there are no exact parallels.

The range of military capability developed by European powers was of great importance in helping to channel the products of nineteenth-century technological change and economic and demographic growth to European military and political advantage elsewhere in the world. From the perspective of the early twenty-first century, the resulting imperial hegemony, however, proved shortlived: less than seventy years across most of Africa and South-

East Asia. Instead, there was subsequently, in the late twentieth century, a reversion on the part of Western states to the economic and financial strength that was an essential prelude to this territorial stage. This was also seen in the case of American power, although in addition the Americans deployed unprecedented military strength.

This development in the European position in the world suggests a need to rethink the stages and nature of European capability and strength, and, again, to question the value of apparently strong state forms, especially powerful and authoritarian central governments. Instead, it is the versatility and durability of forms of association that were based on co-operation that deserve attention, and these should be seen not as a stage on the progress towards a stronger state, but as valuable and capable in their own right.

The last sentence might be an appropriate point to end the book, but, at the risk of being ahistorical and exposing myself to heavy criticism, I want to ask the question whether the thesis of this book matters in the sense of having any application today. This is a very unfashionable approach to the subject, but not therefore an invalid one. This study has emphasised a number of points that are pertinent today, not least the advisability of grounding political programmes and governmental systems on consent, or, at least, co-operation, whatever the formal constitutional and institutional structure of the state. By emphasising the limitations of government, this study has also opened the way to a revisionist perspective on the nineteenth and twentieth centuries, not least on the various projects for modernity offered during this period. It is possible to emphasise continuity in terms of the limited purchase of liberalism and the degree to which conservatism rested on popular support, not coercion.[19]

It may seem surprising to argue that the early modern period, which has been presented in this book in an essentially conservative light, should offer much for scholars working on the following two centuries which, particularly after 1850, were dominated by governments self-consciously committed to improvement through change. There were important continuities in the century 1750–1850, with reform impulses and ideas (whether radical or conservative in their goals) increasingly affecting states and impacting on society,[20] while socio-economic trends, such as the spread of European agrarian settlement in North America and North Asia, transformed environments and changed geopolitics.[21] In addition, the period 1850–2000 underlined a lesson from the entire sweep of 1550 to 1850: that political ideologies that encouraged authoritarian governments to neglect domestic opinion were, as a result, fragile and, therefore, vulnerable. This proved abundantly the case with communism in the Soviet Union and Eastern Europe. In both, terror could achieve only so much. In China, the use of terror was also abandoned as the communist government moved to embrace capitalism after the death of Mao Zedong in 1976. In the countries of the 'Third World', the attempt to resist capitalist globalisation by means of state socialism proved a dismal failure economically in the second half of the twentieth century, and, in many countries, the authoritarian politics that matched this policy similarly proved unsuccessful.

As in the early modern period, the pressures of globalisation as well as the political and economic equations of co-operation within states provided very different levels of benefit as well as much hardship. However, countries such as communist and authoritarian North Korea, which sought to avoid globalisation, seeing it as a pernicious way to spread capitalist influences and American power, and others, which were deemed too unstable or otherwise unattractive for investment, suffered from these exclusions and were unable to provide their citizens with the benefits of economic growth.

Global economic pressures thus helped define and sustain different levels of opportunity, as well as interacting with processes of change within states. Whereas the impact of such pressures had been restricted during the early modern period, by the twentieth century there was a more integrated system not only spanning the world but also affecting societies far more intensively than hitherto. As a consequence, financial and price movements in different parts of the world were closely linked. This was different from the situation in the early modern period, as were the urban location of most of the world's population, the far greater role of industry and services compared with agriculture, the size and growth rate of the world's population, and the nature of environmental pressures. For all these reasons, comments on early modern globalisation are of limited applicability today.

To conclude, however, on a different note, the twentieth century saw profound challenges to optimistic accounts of the scope of change and the perfectibility of man. The liberal, free-trading optimism of the nineteenth century was derailed by the First World War and its internationalist, democratic successor by the Depression; fascist solutions were discredited by the nature and fate of Hitler's Germany; and communism was discredited by political and economic failures in the last quarter of the twentieth century. Alongside powerful signs in the 1990s and 2000s of the resilience of religion and ethnicity as forms of identity and forces for action, all of these led to a querying of the parabolic, teleological account of change and renewed interest in more pessimistic theories, including cyclical ones.

Due to the continuous impact of technological innovation, this could hardly lead to a sense of continuity as a likely option, but the political agenda became more cautious, particularly about the domestic capability of states, although a conviction that international order could and should be created and enforced was expressed by liberal interventionists in the 1990s and, somewhat more surprisingly, American conservatives from late 2001. A more cautious assessment of the capability of states and the prospects for beneficial change encourages interest in past problems and solutions, and takes us back past ideologies of facile optimism to the compromises and complexities of power and authority in the early modern Europe. This is a subject worth studying and capable of offering much instruction.

Notes

1. For just one period of destruction and disruption, P. K. Grimsted, *Trophies of War and Empire. The Archival Heritage of Ukraine, World War II, and the International Politics of Restitution* (Cambridge, MA, 2001), pp. 177–207.

2. Pelham journal, BL Add. 33125 fol. 30.

3. D. Headrick, *When Information Came of Age. Technologies of Knowledge in the Age of Reason and Revolution, 1700–1850* (New York, 2000).

4. Ex. inf. David Sturdy.

5. BL Bowood Mss. vol. 104 fol. 11.

6. D. H. A. Kolff, *Naukar, Rajput and Sepoy. The Ethnohistory of the Military Labour Market in Hindustan, 1450–1850* (Cambridge, 1990).

7. T. Robisheaux, *Rural Society and the Search for Order in Early Modern Germany* (Cambridge, 1989), re county of Hohenlohe.

8. C. Tilly and W. P. Blockmans (eds), *Cities and the Rise of States in Europe, 1000–1800* (Boulder, CO, 1994).

9. N. K. Gvosdev, *Imperial Policies and Perspectives Towards Georgia, 1760–1819* (Basingstoke, 2000).

10. London, Public Record Office. 30/9/40 p. 169; Greater London Record Office. Acc. 510/255, p. 47.

11. J. Abu-Lughod, *Before European Hegemony: The World System A.D. 1250–1350* (New York, 1989); W. Green, 'Periodizing world history', *History and Theory*, 34 (1995), pp. 99–111; J. H. Bentley, 'Cross-cultural interaction and periodization in world history', P. Manning, 'The problem of interactions in world history', *American Historical Review*, 101 (1996), pp. 749–70, 771–82; Bentley, 'Hemispheric integration, 500–1500 C.E.', *Journal of World History*, 9 (1998), pp. 237–54.

12. R. Murphy, *Ottoman Warfare, 1500–1700* (1999); V. Aksan, 'The one-eyed fighting the blind: mobilization, supply, and command in the Russo-Turkish War of 1768–1774', *International History Review*, 15 (1993), p. 238.

13. L. B. Cormack, *Charting an Empire. Geography at the English Universities, 1580–1620* (Chicago, IL, 1997); J. Gascoigne, *Joseph Banks and the English Enlightenment* (Cambridge, 1994) and *Science in the Service of Empire. Joseph Banks, the British State and the Uses of Science in the Age of Revolution* (Cambridge, 1998); L. Stewart, *The Rise of Public Science. Rhetoric, Technology and Natural Philosophy in Newtonian Britain 1660–1750* (Cambridge, 1992); M. Jacob, *Scientific Culture and the Making of the Industrial West* (Oxford, 1997).

14. G. J. Ames, *Colbert, Mercantilism and the French Quest for Asian Trade* (Dekalb, IL, 1996).

15. R. Matthee, 'Exotic substances: the introduction and global spread of tobacco, coffee, cocoa, tea, and distilled liquor, sixteenth to eighteenth centuries', in R. Porter and M. Teich (eds), *Drugs and Narcotics in History* (Cambridge, 1995), pp. 38–46.

16. G. S. Ogilvie, *State Corporatism and Proto-Industry. The Württemberg Black Forest, 1580–1797* (Cambridge, 1997).

17. M. J. Bok, 'The rise of Amsterdam as a cultural centre: the market for paintings,

1580–1680', in P. O'Brien, M. 't Hart and H. van der Wee (eds), *Urban Achievement in Early Modern Europe. Golden Ages in Antwerp, Amsterdam and London* (Cambridge, 2001), p. 202.

18. W. Cobbett (ed.), *The Parliamentary History of England from the Earliest Period to the Year 1803* (36 vols, 1806–20), vol. 19, col. 948.

19. D. Laven, *Venice and Venetia under the Habsburgs 1815–1835* (Oxford, 2002).

20. T. C. W. Blanning and P. Wende (eds), *Reform in Great Britain and Germany 1750–1850* (Oxford, 1999); R. Blaufarb, 'The *ancien régime* origins of Napoleonic social reconstruction', *French History*, 14 (2000), p. 423, and *The French Army 1750–1820. Careers, Talent, Merit* (Manchester, 2002), pp. 194–5; F. Kramer, 'Bavaria: reform and *Staats-integration*', *German History*, 20 (2002), pp. 371–2.

21. David Moon takes this process forward into the 1950s in 'Peasant migration and the settlement of Russia's frontiers, 1550–1897', *Historical Journal*, 40 (1997), p. 892.

Select Bibliography

Adamson, J. (ed.), *The Princely Courts of Europe. Ritual, Politics and Culture under the Ancien Régime 1500–1750* (1999).

Anderson, P., *Lineages of the Absolutist State* (1974).

Asch, R. G., *The Thirty Years War: The Holy Roman Empire and Europe, 1618–1648* (1997).

Asch, R. G., and H. Duchhardt (eds), *Der Absolutismus – ein Mythos?* (Cologne, 1996).

Aymard, M. (ed.), *Dutch Capitalism and World Capitalism* (Cambridge, 1982).

Beales, D., *Joseph II. I. In the Shadow of Maria Theresa* (Cambridge, 1987).

Behrens, C. B. A., 'Enlightened absolutism', *Historical Journal*, 18 (1975).

— *Society, Government and the Enlightenment. The Experiences of Eighteenth-Century France and Prussia* (1985).

Beik, W., *Absolutism and Society in Seventeenth-Century France* (Cambridge, 1985).

Bell, D. A., *The Cult of the Nation in France. Inventing Nationalism, 1680–1800* (Cambridge, MA, 2001).

Bercé, Y. M., *Revolt and Revolution in Early Modern Europe* (Manchester, 1987).

Black, J., *Europe in the Eighteenth Century* (2nd edn, Basingstoke, 2000).

— *Europe and the World, 1650–1830* (2002).

Blanning, T. C. W., *Joseph II* (Harlow, 1994).

Blickle, P. (ed.), *Resistance, Representation and Community* (Oxford, 1997).

Blussé, L., and F. Gaastra (eds), *On the Eighteenth Century as a Category of Asian History: Van Leur in Retrospect* (Aldershot, 1998).

Bonney, R., *The European Dynastic States, 1494–1660* (Oxford, 1991).

— (ed.), *Economic Systems and State Finance* (Oxford, 1995).

— (ed.), *The Rise of the Fiscal State in Europe, c. 1200–1815* (Oxford, 1999).

Boxer, C. R., *The Dutch Seaborne Empire, 1600–1800* (1965).

Brackett, J. K., *Criminal Justice and Crime in Late Renaissance Florence, 1537–1609* (Cambridge, 1992).

Brewer, J., and E. Hellmuth (eds), *Rethinking Leviathan. The Eighteenth-Century State in Britain and Germany* (Oxford, 1999).

Brockliss, L. W. B., and J. H. Elliott (eds), *The World of the Favourite* (New Haven, CT, 1999).

Buelow, G. L. (ed.), *The Late Baroque Era from the 1680s to 1740* (Basingstoke, 1993).

Burgess, G., *Absolute Monarchy and the Stuart Constitution* (New Haven, CT, 1996).

Burke, P., *The Fabrication of Louis XIV* (New Haven, CT, 1992).

Butterwick, R. (ed.), *The Polish-Lithuanian Monarchy in European Context, c. 1500–1795* (Basingstoke, 2001).

Casey, J., *The Kingdom of Valencia in the Seventeenth Century* (Cambridge, 1979).

Chambers, D., B. Pullan and J. Fletcher (eds), *Venice: A Documentary History, 1450–1630* (Oxford, 1992).

Collins, J. B., *Fiscal Limits of Absolutism: Direct Taxation in Seventeenth-Century France* (Berkeley, CA, 1988).

— *The State in Early Modern France* (Cambridge, 1995).

Contamine, P. (ed.), *War and Competition between States* (Oxford, 2000).

Cowan, A. F., *The Urban Patriciate: Lübeck and Venice, 1580–1700* (Cologne, 1986).

Dandelet, T. J., *Spanish Rome 1500–1700* (New Haven, CT, 2001).

Davids, K., and J. Lucassen, *A Miracle Mirrored: The Dutch Republic in European Perspective* (Cambridge, 1995).

Dewald, J., *The European Nobility, 1400–1800* (Cambridge, 1996).

Dickson, P. G. M., *Finance and Government under Maria Theresa 1740–1780* (Oxford, 1987).

Downing, B. M., *The Military Revolution and Political Change: Origins of Democracy and Autocracy in Early Modern Europe* (Princeton, NJ, 1991).

Doyle, W., *Venality. The Sale of Offices in Eighteenth-Century France* (Oxford, 1996).

Elliott, J. H., *The Revolt of the Catalans: A Study in the Decline of Spain, 1598–1640* (Cambridge, 1963).

— *The Count-Duke of Olivares: The Statesman in an Age of Decline* (New Haven, CT, 1986).

Ertman, T., *Birth of the Leviathan. Building States and Regimes in Medieval and Early Modern Europe* (Cambridge, 1997).

Evans, R. J. W., *The Making of the Habsburg Monarchy, 1550–1700* (Oxford, 1979).

Evans, R. J. W. and T. V. Thomas (eds), *Crown, Church and Estates. Central European Politics in the Sixteenth and Seventeenth Centuries* (1991).

Friedrichs, C. R., *Urban Politics in Early Modern Europe* (2000).

Frost, R. I., *The Northern Wars: War, State and Society in Northeastern Europe, 1558–1721* (Harlow, 2000).

Fulbrook, M., *Piety and Politics. Religion and the Rise of Absolutism in England, Württemberg and Prussia* (Cambridge, 1983).

Gawthrop, R. L., *Pietism and the Making of Eighteenth-Century Prussia* (Cambridge, 1993).

Glete, J., *Warfare at Sea, 1500–1650: Maritime Conflicts and the Transformation of Europe* (2000).

— *War and the State in Early Modern Europe. Spain, the Dutch Republic and Sweden as Fiscal-Military States, 1500–1660* (2002).

Gordon, S., *The Marathas 1600–1818* (Cambridge, 1993).

Graves, M. A. R., *The Parliaments of Early Modern Europe* (Harlow, 2001).

Gutmann, M. P., *War and Rural Life in the Early Modern Low Countries* (Princeton, NJ, 1980).

Hanlon, G., *The Twilight of a Military Tradition: Italian Aristocrats and European Conflicts, 1560–1800* (1998).

Henshall, N., *The Myth of Absolutism. Change and Continuity in Early Modern European Monarchy* (1992).

Hess, A. C., *The Forgotten Frontier: A History of the Sixteenth-Century Ibero-African Frontier* (Chicago, IL, 1978).

Hoffman, P. T. and K. Norberg (eds), *Fiscal Crises, Liberty and Representative Government* (Stanford, CA, 1994).

Hughes, L., *Peter the Great* (New Haven, CT, 2002).

Hughes, M., *Early Modern Germany 1479–1806* (1992).

Hurt, J., *Louis XIV and the Parlements. The Assertion of Royal Authority* (Manchester, 2002).

Imber, C., *The Ottoman Empire, 1300–1650. The Structure of Power* (Basingstoke, 2002).

Ingrao, C. (ed.), *The State and Society in Early Modern Austria* (West Lafayette, IN, 1994).

Israel, J. I., *The Dutch Republic and the Hispanic World, 1606–1661* (Oxford, 1982).

— *Dutch Primacy in World Trade, 1585–1740* (Oxford, 1989).

— *The Dutch Republic: Its Rise, Greatness, and Fall, 1477–1806* (Oxford, 1995).

Kamen, H., *Spain 1469–1714: A Society in Conflict* (1991).

— *Spain's Road to Empire. The Making of a World Power* (2002).

Kimmel, M. S., *Absolutism and Its Discontents. State and Society in Seventeenth-Century France and England* (New Brunswick, NJ, 1988).

Kirby, D., *Northern Europe in the Early Modern Period: The Baltic World, 1492–1772* (1990).

Klingensmith, S. J., *The Utility of Splendor. Ceremony, Social Life, and Architecture at the Court of Bavaria 1600–1800* (Chicago, IL, 1993).

Knecht, R. J., *The Rise and Fall of Renaissance France 1483–1601* (1996).

Koenigsberger, R. G., *Estates and Revolutions: Essays in Early Modern European History* (Ithaca, NY, 1971).

Lockhart, P. D., *Denmark in the Thirty Years' War: King Christian IV and the Decline of the Oldenburg State* (Selinsgrove, 1996).

Lovett, A. W., *Early Habsburg Spain, 1517–1598* (Oxford, 1986).

Lukowski, J., *Liberty's Folly. The Polish-Lithuanian Commonwealth in the Eighteenth Century, 1697–1795* (1991).

McKay, D., *The Great Elector* (Harlow, 2001).

Marino, J. A. (ed.), *Early Modern History and the Social Sciences. Testing the Limits of Braudel's Mediterranean* (Kirksville, MO, 2002).

Mettam, R., *Power and Faction in Louis XIV's France* (Oxford, 1988).

Miller, J. (ed.), *Absolutism in Seventeenth-Century Europe* (Basingstoke, 1990).

Monod, P. K., *The Power of Kings. Monarchy and Religion in Europe, 1589–1715* (New Haven, CT, 1999).

Mooers, C., *The Making of Bourgeois Europe. Absolutism, Revolution and the Rise of Capitalism in England, France and Germany* (1991).

Mullett, M. A., *The Catholic Reformation* (1999).

Oresko, R. et al. (eds), *Royal and Republican Sovereignty in Early Modern Europe* (Cambridge, 1997).

Parker, D., *Class and State in Ancien Régime France. The Road to Modernity?* (1996).

Parker, G., *The Thirty Years' War* (1984).

— *The Dutch Revolt* (1985).

— *The Grand Strategy of Philip II* (New Haven, CT, 1998).

Pomeranz, K., *The Great Divergence: China, Europe and the Making of the Modern World Economy* (Berkeley, CA, 1999).

Porter, R. and M. Teich (eds), *The Scientific Revolution in National Context* (Cambridge, 1992).

Price, J. L., *Holland and the Dutch Republic in the Seventeenth Century. The Politics of Particularism* (Oxford, 1994).

Raeff, M., *The Well-Ordered Police State. Social and Institutional Change through Law in the Germanies and Russia 1600–1800* (New Haven, CT, 1983).

Robisheaux, T., *Rural Society and the Search for Order in Early Modern Germany* (Cambridge, 1989).

Rowen, H. H., *The King's State. Proprietary Dynasticism in Early Modern France* (New Brunswick, NJ, 1980).

Scott, H. M. (ed.), *Enlightened Absolutism. Reform and Reformers in Later Eighteenth-Century Europe* (1990).

— (ed.), *The European Nobilities in the Seventeenth and Eighteenth Centuries* (Harlow, 1995).

Scott, T. (ed.), *The Peasantries of Europe from the Fourteenth to the Eighteenth Century* (Harlow, 1998).

Sturdy, D. J., *Louis XIV* (Basingstoke, 2000).

Subetlny, O., *Domination of Eastern Europe. Native Nobilities and Foreign Absolutism 1500–1715* (Gloucester, 1986).

Szabo, F., *Kaunitz and Enlightened Absolutism 1753–1780* (Cambridge, 1994).

Thompson, J. E., *Mercenaries, Pirates and Sovereigns. State-building and Extra-territorial Violence in Early Modern Europe* (Princeton, NJ, 1994).

Thornton, J., *Africa and Africans in the Making of the Atlantic World, 1400–1800* (2nd edn, Cambridge, 1998).

Tilly, C., *Coercion, Capital and European States* AD *990–1992* (Oxford, 1992).

Tilly, C. and W. P. Blockmans (eds), *Cities and the Rise of States in Europe, 1000–1800* (Boulder, CO, 1994).

Tracy, J. (ed.), *The Political Economy of Merchant Empires. State Power and World Trade 1350–1750* (Cambridge, 1992).

Waquet, J. C., *Corruption. Ethics and Power in Florence 1600–1770* (Oxford, 1991).

Wilson, P. H., *War, State and Society in Württemberg, 1677–1793* (Cambridge, 1995).

— *German Armies. War and German Politics 1648–1806* (1998).

— *The Holy Roman Empire 1495–1806* (1999).

— *Absolutism in Central Europe* (2000).

Index